Geoffrey Bawa
Drawing from the Archives

GEOFFREY BAWA TRUST

Geoffrey Bawa

Drawing from the Archives

Edited by Shayari de Silva

LARS MÜLLER PUBLISHERS

Geoffrey Bawa at Lunuganga, chromogenic color print, Christoph Bon, ca. 1986

Geoffrey Bawa

Suhanya Raffel and Michael Snelling

To mark the birth centenary of Geoffrey Bawa in 2019, the Geoffrey Bawa Trust embarked on a raft of projects bookended by *The Gift* (involving artists Lee Mingwei and Chandraguptha Thenuwara; photographers Dayanita Singh and Dominic Sansoni; and architect Kengo Kuma) and *It Is Essential to Be There*, the first exhibition in Sri Lanka of works from the Collections and Archives of the Geoffrey Bawa Trust, curated by Shayari de Silva. *The Gift* used the centenary celebration to invite audiences to consider the contributions made by Bawa across many disciplines, including architecture. Siting this project at Lunuganga, Bawa's country estate, was vital.

Lunuganga provides a living space that performs Bawa's biography in the most lyrical, poetic and immediate fashion. Along with his home in Colombo, it is a critical place in which Bawa's practice was formed, where his language as an architect and a maker of gardens is expressed, while always being a place of hospitality and a site for artist friends to make work. It brings into focus his thinking about the relations between the external and internal worlds and his propositions about the choice of materials, arrangement of space and how life itself could ideally be conducted. Lunuganga is a site of expansive thinking, where large spaces offered freedom to explore buildings and gardens together and to devise broad vistas.

Bawa's home in Colombo, at 11, 33rd Lane, was a different proposition: an internally focused, constrained and urbanized space, where he could

Geoffrey Bawa, gelatin silver print

Geoffrey Bawa on site, Tangalle, color film slide

push the boundaries of the site to open up courtyards and play with light and tight vistas while shutting out the pressures of the city.

Bawa purchased 25 acres of abandoned rubber estate, which he named Lunuganga, in 1948 on his return to Sri Lanka after a two-year grand tour of Europe, the United States and parts of Asia. Prior to that he read English at St. Catharine's College at Cambridge University (1938–41), followed by successfully completing his studies to be a lawyer in London (1944). These early years of study and travel were formative, and travel was always an important aspect of Bawa's life. However, the choice to become an architect was arrived at almost by accident. Over the first years, his steps toward shaping the garden and the bungalow led to friends' and colleagues' persuading him to formally study architecture. He returned to London in 1952 and enrolled at the Architecture Association in 1954, passing his degree in 1957, at which time he became an associate member of the Royal Institute of British Architects.

From his earliest architectural commissions, Bawa's approach to his work was driven by being there. His was a practice that was shaped by an account of each site. The trees, boulders, watercourses and views were

Geoffrey Bawa on site at Ruhuna University, Matara, chromogenic color print, ca. 1988

Geoffrey Bawa on site at House for Mr. Bashir Currimjee, Mauritius, chromogenic color print, ca. 1988

integral to the forming of his architecture, and his interventions were as much amplifications of, as they were making of, places. The experience of arrival, the narrative gestures of moving through spaces, revealing hidden vistas, the controlled encounters were all part of developing the experience that is Bawa's architecture.

The exhibition *It Is Essential to Be There* was structured with this idea as the central principle. It is built around Bawa's own words and, although the exhibition was much delayed by the misfortunes of the global pandemic, it was finally realized in 2022 as the culmination of the centenary celebration. In this volume of essays and illustrations, the magnificent breadth of Bawa's career is now made available in a form that none of the many previous publications set out to achieve. By mining the Geoffrey Bawa Collections and Archives, we can now see the working of Bawa's architecture, through the many collaborations, partnerships, professional relationships and sustaining friendships that formed the basis of a brilliant career.

Photographs from travels in Europe, contact prints, Geoffrey Bawa, ca. 1944–48

This text first appeared in the book *Geoffrey Bawa: Architect of Sri Lanka* by Brian Brace Taylor, published by Concept Media, Singapore in 1986.

Statement by the Architect

Geoffrey Bawa

In my personal search I have been aware of the past – many periods of the past: Medieval Italian hill towns with their splendid instinctive massing of buildings which although varied in purpose and age make a magnificent total picture; great English country houses and their essential complement of park and garden; Greek, Roman, Mexican and Buddhist ruins, the Alhambra in Granada, the chapel in Ronchamps, the Mogul forts in Rajasthan and the marvelous palace of Padmanabapuram. There are so many instances when my eye was caught by a landscape, a small, unimportant but beautiful building, or a large and splendid one, sometimes seen for a moment from a swiftly moving car or train, for a day or two, or something lived amongst, like the buildings in Cambridge and Rome. The beauty of some of these buildings, gardens and landscapes leaves a considerable residue of subconscious understanding in the mind – a help to solve some present need; for the right placement of a building on the site; for the need to frame and emphasize a view or to open or construct a space; a wish to get a definite degree of light or shadow in a room. Good building in Sri Lanka has always taken these into account from the temples, monasteries and places of Anuradhapura, Polonnaruwa, Sigiriya and its water garden and the other buildings that followed through the ages to the present day. I like to regard all the past and present good architecture in Sri Lanka as just that – good Sri Lankan architecture – for this is what it is, not narrowly classified as Indian, Portuguese or Dutch, early Sinhalese or Kandyan or British Colonial, for all the good examples of these periods have taken the country itself into first account.

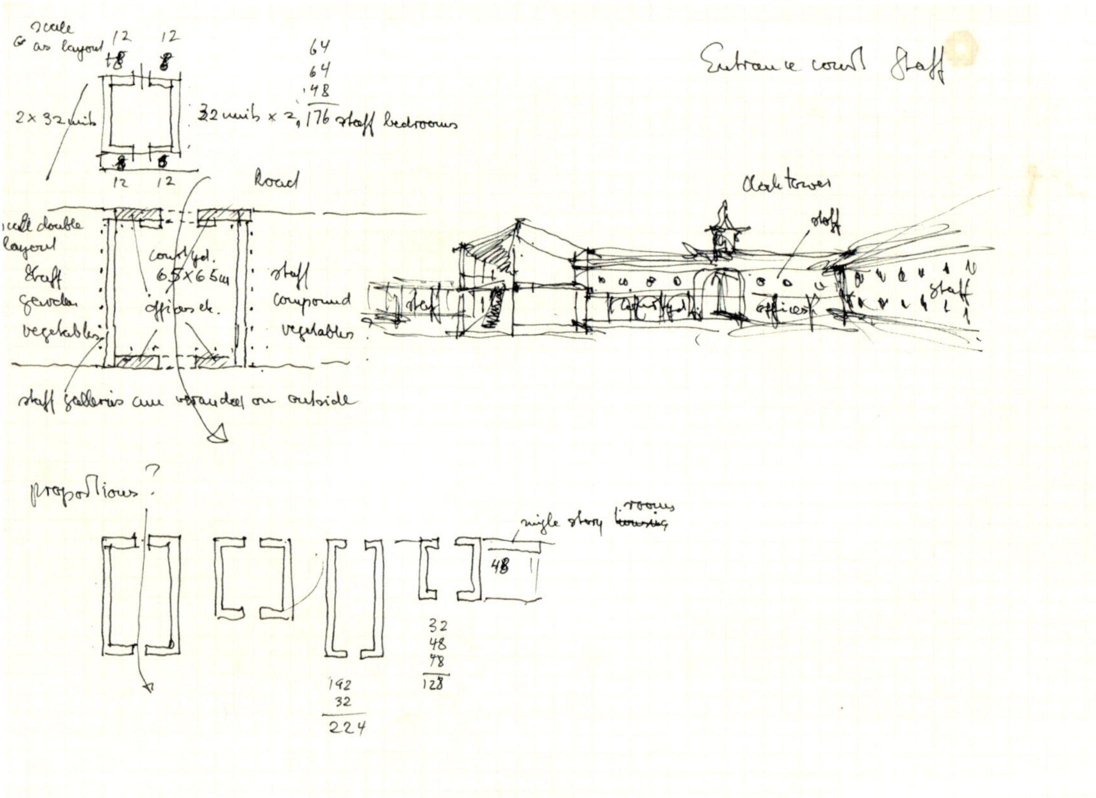

Mangapwani Beach Hotel, Zanzibar, preliminary sketches, ink on square-ruled paper, Geoffrey Bawa, 1987

Building detail, Kandy, gelatin silver print, Geoffrey Bawa (attributed)

Temple of the Tooth, Kandy, gelatin silver print, Geoffrey Bawa (attributed)

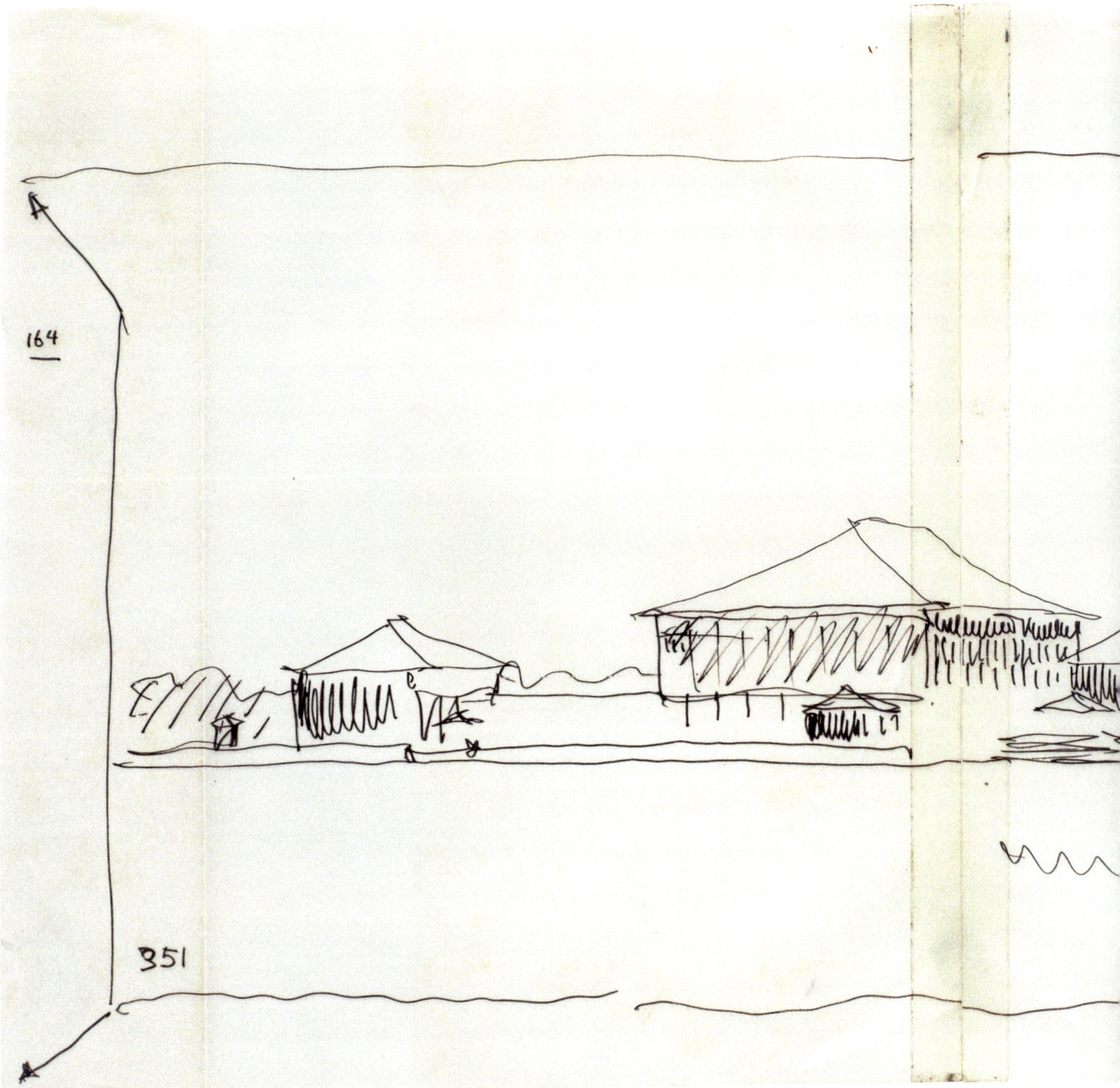

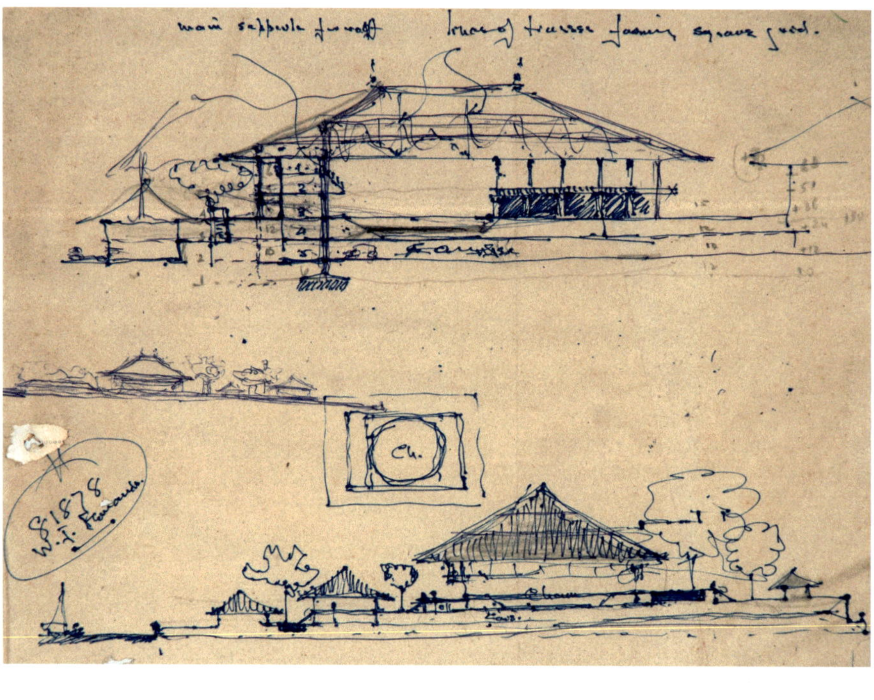

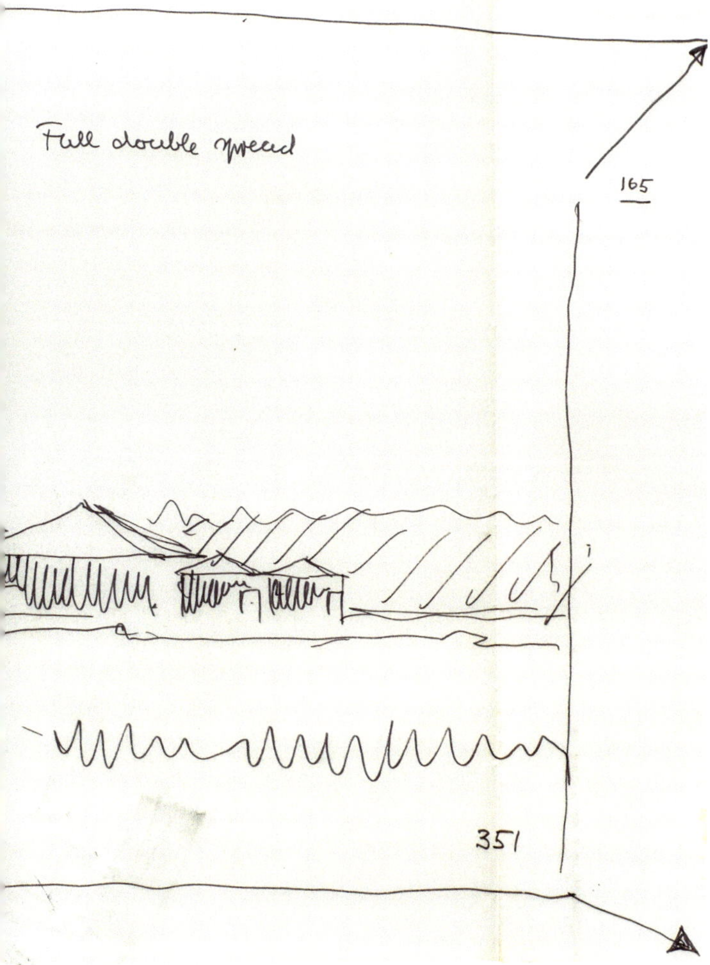

New Sri Lankan Parliament,
Sri Jayawardenepura Kotte
Sketches, ink on vellum, Christoph Bon (top) and ink on paper, Geoffrey Bawa (bottom)

When you look at the better examples of what remains of these earlier buildings you find they all have met the essentials of life in Sri Lanka, but although the past gives lessons it does not give the whole answer to what must be done now. It is true that many of the materials available to us are the same as in the past, and their use – if sensible and right – very alike except where new techniques have added to or changed their qualities. With these and other new materials we must now design for a society living in a framework of a difficult economy, a much faster life – sometimes a freer one – new conventions and a greater liberality of belief to all the dictates of ever-changing needs. But there is, against this background of life, the great constant of the climate.

One unchanging element of all buildings is the roof – protective, emphatic and all important – governing the aesthetic whatever the period, wherever the place. Often a building is only a roof, columns and floors – the roof dominant, shielding, giving the contentment of shelter. Ubiquitous, pervasively present, the scale or pattern shaped by the building beneath. The roof, its shape, texture and proportion is the strongest visual factor.

At random I take an isolated item, the – what now is called – Sinhala tile. The Arab traders introduced to Sri Lanka many centuries ago the half-round clay roofing tile of the Mediterranean world, but the roofs built in Sri Lanka with them were more steeply pitched to shed the huge rainfall of our country. The Portuguese and the Dutch used the same tile and the roof pitch but the latter raised roofs higher for coolness, with wide eaves and verandahs to shade the walls. In the hill country the Kandyans used a flat clay tile like shingle on their double-pitched roofs in meeting halls which had only columns, no walls – an answer to a way of life – a great roof to give shade and shelter, open to the drift of air and the encompassing view. More than functional building it is first rational building, for it is rational to give presence to both function and form, to admit beauty and pleasure as well as purpose.

These are my basic thoughts but there are many more: thoughts on details; the proportions of rooms, doors and windows; the heights, the sweeps and pitches of roofs; where one looks from a room, at what, and through what, at what is to be seen; how open or closed a view from a room should be. In these considerations no rules can guide, or if they could, would not always give exactly the right answer. It is in this realm of part emotion part thought, that the rest of the way must run, and it is at this stage that the architect steps, from the relative security of known and learnt things, into the world of intuition, inspiration, talent, gift – call it what you will, a world inside his head and far outside it at the same time – almost sub- or super-conscious. This may seem extravagant when written down but it is the unknown factor. I suppose it is here that each one of us has a separate and

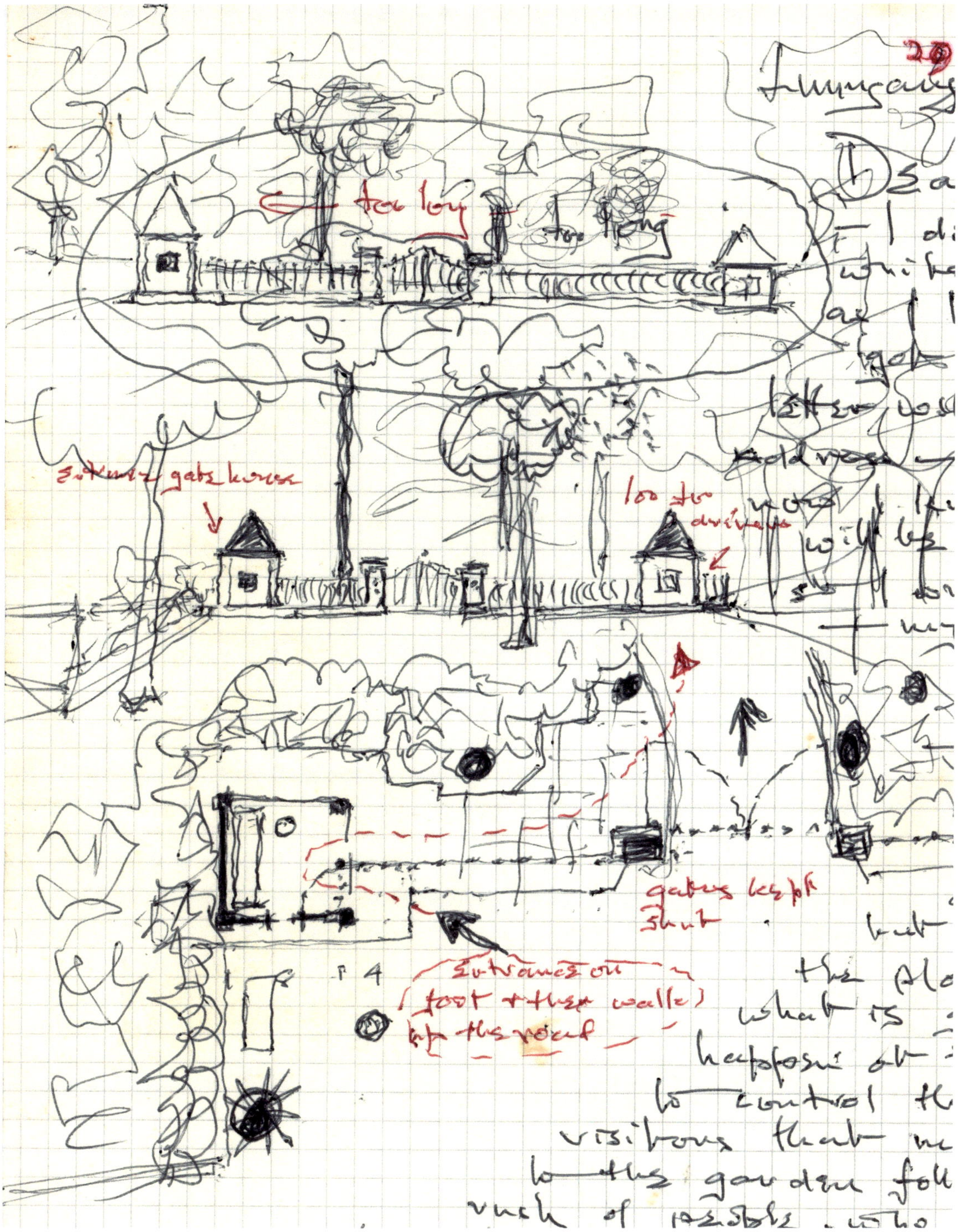

Letter to Jean Chamberlin, describing addition of gatehouse at Lunuganga, ink on square-ruled paper, Geoffrey Bawa, ca. 1986

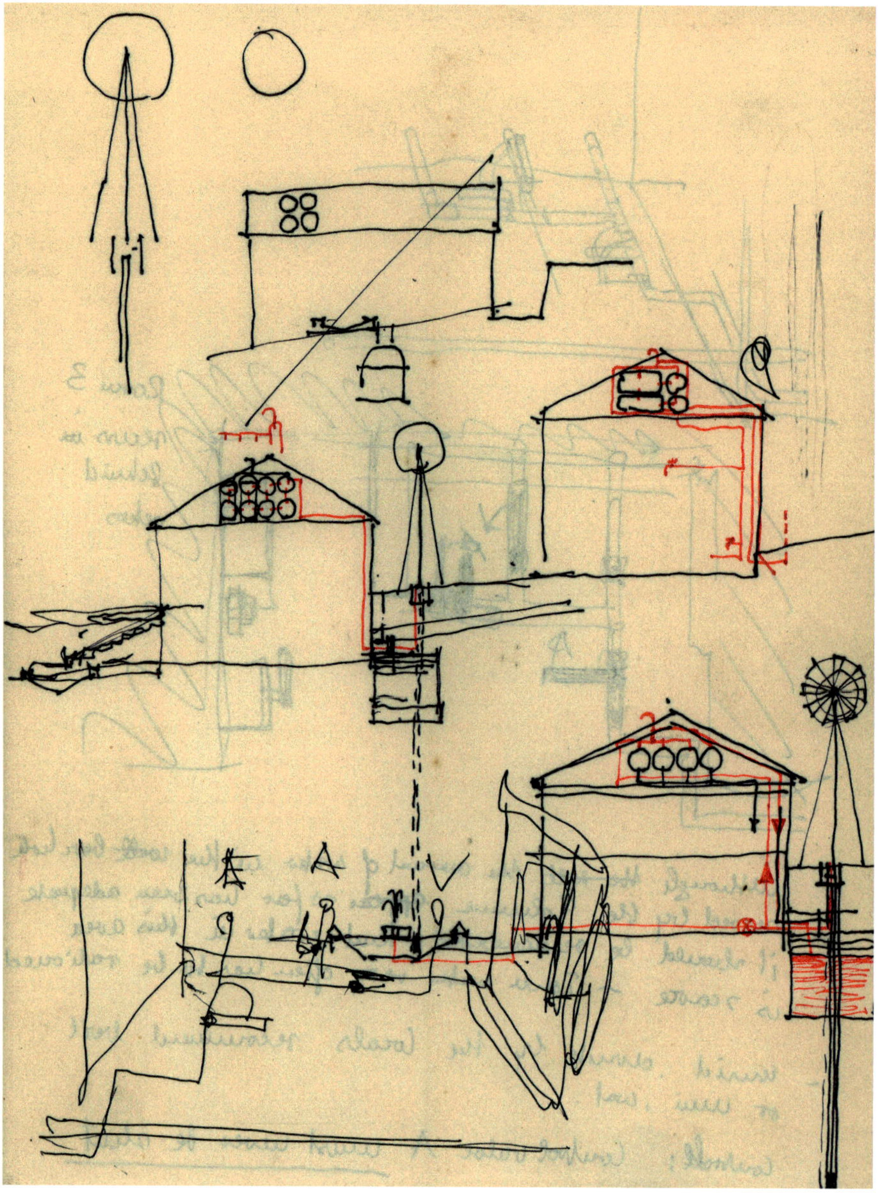

Lunuganga, Bentota, sketch of windmill and turbine (left) and of section through lower gallery (right) at Lunuganga, ink on paper, Geoffrey Bawa

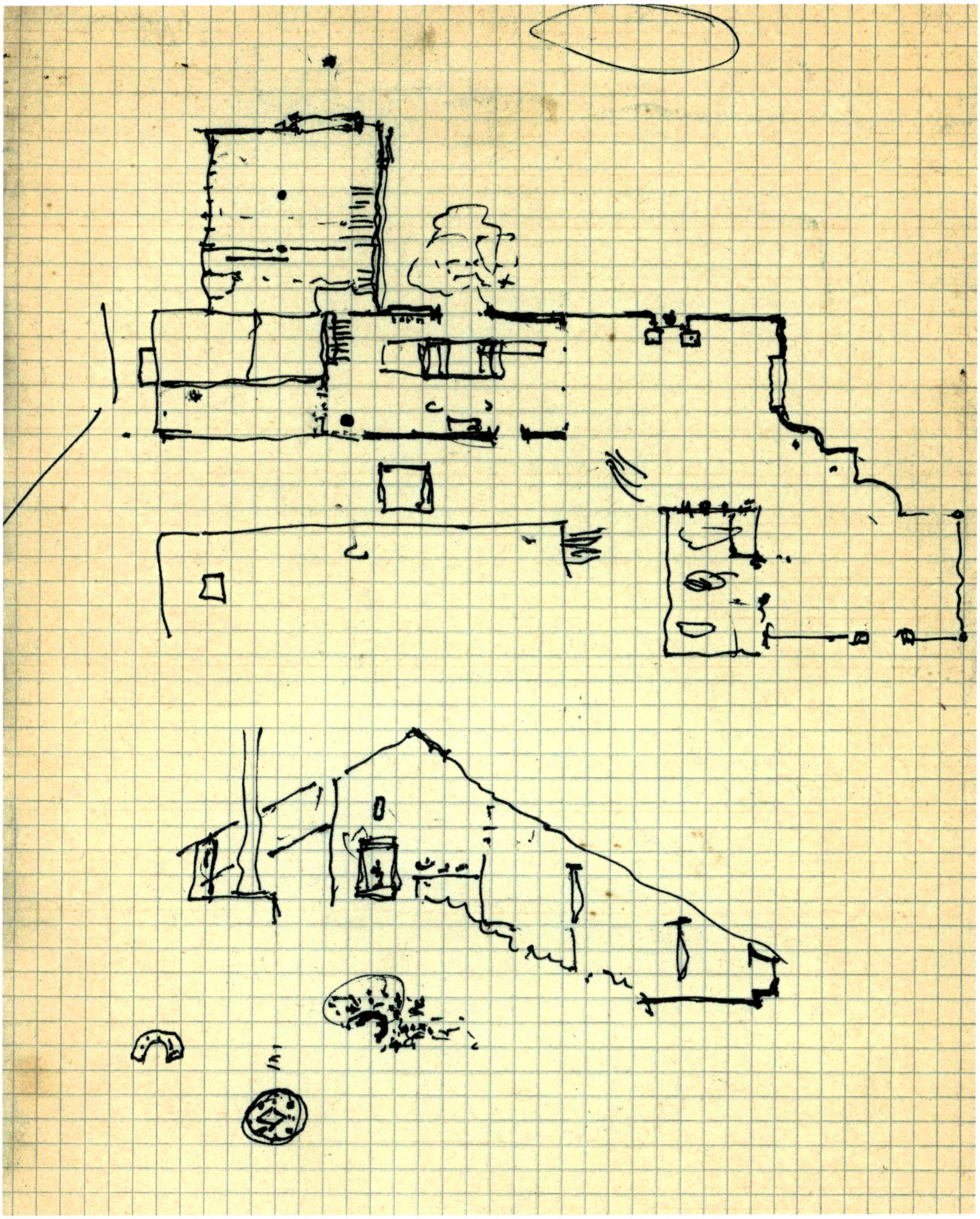

personal impulse – the point at which, although surrounded by the fact and reality of a project, one is alone and must make a decision to do this and not that, to do what seems at the moment inevitable.

The buildings shown on the following pages illustrate, as far as drawings and photographs can, the architectural answers I have found to a variety of needs. For myself a building can only be understood by moving around and through it and by experiencing the modulation and feel of the spaces one moves through – from the outside into verandahs, then rooms, passages, courtyards – the view from these spaces into others, views through to the landscapes beyond and from outside the building, views back through rooms into inner rooms and courts. Equally important, the play of light in both garden and inner rooms and courts. Equally important, the play of light in both garden and inner room – from a shaded inner space to the celebration of light in a courtyard. To achieve the possibility of enjoyment and pleasure is so necessary, in addition to comfort and functional use. When one delights as much as I do in planning a building and having it built I find it impossible to describe the exact steps in an analytical or dogmatic way. Every project is different, and each approach, each individual design based on the differing backgrounds of site and purpose, requires a separate and total involvement and a care that must extend from the foundations of the structures to the smallest detail of the ultimate furnishing of rooms.

I have touched on a variety of points that have occurred to me which might be useful in helping to understand my buildings but I have a very strong conviction that it is impossible to explain architecture in words – I have always enjoyed seeing buildings but seldom enjoyed reading explanations about them – as I feel, with others, that architecture cannot be totally explained but must be experienced.

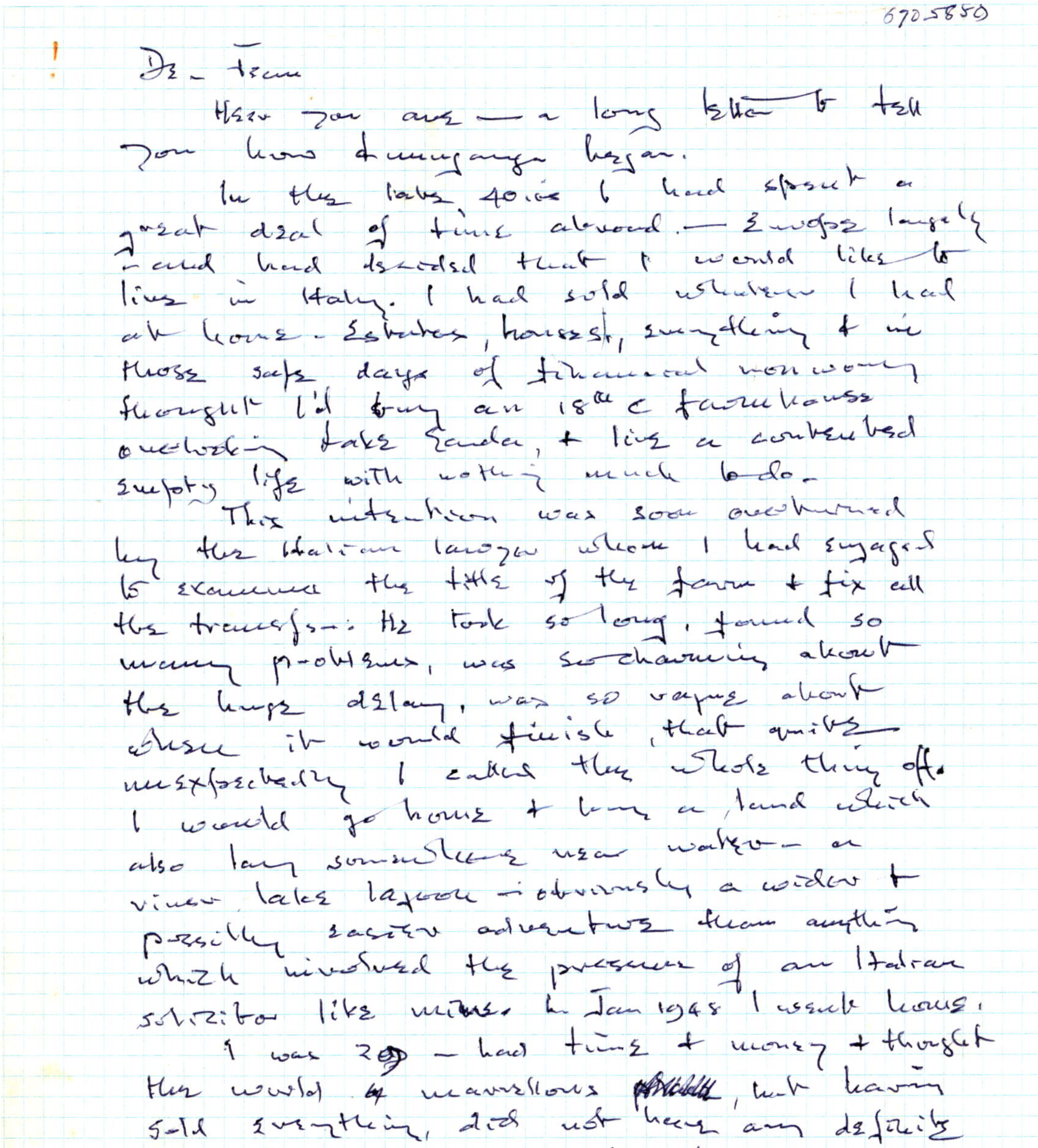
6705850

Dear Jean

Here you are — a long letter to tell you how Lunuganga began.

In the late 40's I had spent a great deal of time abroad — Europe largely — and had decided that I would like to live in Italy. I had sold whatever I had at home - estates, houses, everything & in those safe days of financial non-worry thought I'd buy an 18th c farmhouse overlooking Lake Garda, & live a contented empty life with nothing much to do.

This intention was soon overturned by the Italian lawyer whom I had engaged to examine the title of the farm & fix all the transfers. He took so long, found so many problems, was so charming about the huge delay, was so vague about when it would finish, that quite unexpectedly I called the whole thing off. I would go home & buy a land which also lay somewhere near water — a river, lake lagoon — obviously a wider & possibly easier adventure than anything which involved the presence of an Italian solicitor like mine. In Jan 1948 I went home.

I was 29 — had time & money & thought the world marvellous, but having sold everything, did not have any definite place to make my headquarters for this search.

My brother has an estate in Bentota & he let me have a small separate wing of his house — stay as long as you like — do as you will! — & he would help in looking for what I wanted. It was a long search — the news of my quest

Letter to Jean Chamberlin describing the process of creating Lunuganga, ink on square-ruled paper, Geoffrey Bawa, ca. 1986 spread quickly in the neighbourhood and beyond, and very soon I had a wide circle of village friends who made my cause their immediate interest. At that time I had a huge open tourer, a Silver Ghost RR which contributed hugely to the enjoyment of travelling — so whatever land had been put forward as a possibility I was driven to at speed, with picnic baskets & hopes held high — and even if the site proved not agreeable enough, the search turned into a celebration with the disappointment almost disappearing.

I must have seen at least 30 sites — flat land on the banks of the Bentota River, an early 19th C house on the Balapitiya Lagoon — well built houses — huts with splendid views — we visited them all but all had some hopeless drawback. — until at last I found Lunuganga.

An inspector of Excise at Bentota, one late evening when we were all sitting on the terrace of the Old Bentota Resthouse & I had finished a short grumble on how difficult life was when one searched for an inexact dream said — There is a small rubber estate nearby, at the moment lived in and partially used by the local District Revenue Officer — its a promontory, a small hill, ~~[illegible]~~ which is owned by a woman who lives in Britain — why not look at it but I expect the DRO will never leave.

We drove over the next morning & after the first two moments I knew the search was ended.

The owner of the land, a spirited & splendid lady — in the village called Nella fifty thousand — agreed at once that

the land should be mine — she named her
price & I accepted it. She said it had been
part of her marriage dowry which had been
fifty thousand gold sovereigns & this small
plantation of rubber & cinnamon. Her father
had left no will, but had on his deathbed
made it clear to his relatives that the land
was certainly Nellas. 'Dont worry' she said,
the land is mine, & you can have it.

I did worry. I pictured another bout
with lawyers & a bout it was. I hired an
excellent solicitor renowned for his cunning
and patience – (he later became a Buddhist
monk) who came to Bentota, lived in the
resthouse & with cunning and patience
and a great capacity to encourage village
gossip discovered thirty two who were in
one way or another kin to Nella [struck] &
who consequently could claim some part
of her inheritance — the gold sovereigns
were safely hidden or spent, but the
land was vulnerable. Shades of Lake Garda.
— I am eternally grateful to him. Cadet
Jayawardena (his brother later became
President), for he — with a background of
stormy impatience from me — managed
to persuade, threaten, charm and bribe
thirty one people, who had not the slightest
[struck] moral rite to a penny, to sign
the deed of transfer..—

There were more problems ahead.
Lunuganga was now mine, but it had
the wretched DRO & his wife living there.
They reluctantly agreed to shift, but the
only alternative house they would shift

It was occupied by the Excise communications office. So they had to move & then only when the house occupied by the village schoolmaster was available — so the schoolmaster had to move, & he would only do so if I built him a sizable addition to his brothers house nearby. All this was agreed to, promises made & kept, except by the initial mover of these moves — the villainous DRO, who on the promised day of his departure said that he would move but only when he came back from his annual leave which he had now decided to take before the trauma of housemoving. We said yes, yes do, by all means, but when the dim tail light of his Hillman Minx vanished down the road we summoned an already arranged prepared gang of masons carpenters & a large number of villagers, & broke down the outer walls of the veranda. Patience no more we enjoyed the evening — we built a shed on a cleared patch of land between the rubber trees, moved all the furniture into it & locked the door. The house was empty — a free wind swept through it. It had been won in battle — a rather unfair warlike move, but exciting & wholly pleasurable. Nothing had been broken except the DROs promise & the walls of his erstwhile house, & the land of Lunuganga was mine so I could begin to mould it into something that could be shaped by my present and future dreams & imaginings.

When I had first seen Lunuganga I had known that with a first few clearings of trees and opening up of obvious vistas an inevitable basic pattern would emerge. It was enormously exciting, and the morning after the dramatic breaking of walls and the feel of possession the adventure began — and adventure that has lasted 40 years + the pleasure of which has never palled.

One entered the house from the west — driving through a cutting then doubling back up the hill to arrive under a portico. The lake was not seen from there, the rows of rubber trees, carefully planted 20 feet apart on the contours down to lake level formed a dense screen surrounding the house. The first need was to cut through this. It was soon done — by evening the lake lay in view from the top of the hill, the view North, clear + lovely, to the distant shore. While the trees were being felled — so was the the outer wall of the North verandah broken to leave only the columns intact but looking a bit beaten about. The next day saw more clearing — more distant views across the lake. I had decided by them that it would be best to enter the house from the South — walk through an entrance hall, then through the main livingrooms, on to the verandah + then to a terrace which ~~[illegible]~~ overlooks the wide long view, ~~[illegible]~~ now established, with the last of the rubber plantation to the North + west now gone. A lot of flesh had been cut away and the bones began to show — good strong shapes that would soon ~~[illegible]~~ be made well + much improved by the savagery of the last week. Most of the labour, at this moment a vast number, thought the new owner mad. — he had bought a house which he then proceeded to demolish, + a rubber plantation where the grafted high yielding trees were to be felled + given away as firewood, — doors + windows moved from one place to another, what next?

Next is next time — more

love

[signature]

Introduction: Drawing from the Geoffrey Bawa Archives

Shayari de Silva

Geoffrey Bawa's architectural and landscape work is renowned for its experiential richness; spaces that engage the senses and enchant the imagination as much as they capture one's corporeal presence. The qualities of *being there*, in all the multivalent aspects of *place* evoked by Bawa's architecture, are a central component of the work. Bawa cared deeply about the places made through buildings and gardens. The interplay between time and space was key to how he envisioned them: movement through spaces, melding interiors and exteriors and the effect time would have on a place are woven into his conception of a place. He is known to have said "Give me twenty minutes on the site and I'll know what to do" and this ability has been recounted by countless colleagues and clients.[1] In a practice so attuned to the generative aspects of place, drawings play a complex role. Part process, part record, the drawings were often a vehicle for the ideas about a place. In retrospect, the drawings offer clues to these ideas and suggest additional readings of the ways in which the practice grappled with its spatial and temporal context.

"The site gives the most powerful push to a design along with the brief. Without seeing the site I cannot work. It is essential to be there. After two hours on the site, I have a mental picture of what will be there and how the site will change and the picture does not change."

Bawa did not expound on his work or on architecture in general and chose his words carefully when they were required. For this reason, I pay great attention in this essay to the words which Bawa did choose to publish. The text by Bawa which is reproduced in this book – the statement from the architect included in the 1986 Mimar publication, now widely referred to as "The White Book" – is notably a version of a text previously published in *The Architect's Journal* in 1969 – which itself was initially published in the *Times of Ceylon Annual* in 1968. While there are many possible readings that could be ascribed to the ethos expressed repeatedly by Bawa in these texts, my own is that his focus in establishing a practice in the newly independent island was a long-standing commitment to an idea of place, underlined by an understanding of that place as multilayered, nuanced and heterogeneous. Consequentially, the site – in the most immediate, technical terms in which an architect might frame an idea of site,

1 Author interview with Philip Fowler, June 28, 2019, transcript, GBT/AUD/OH/003/000, Oral Histories, Geoffrey Bawa Archives, Colombo, Sri Lanka.

Lunuganga, Bentota
View to Dedduwa Lake (left), view of rear terrace (top right), view of frangipani tree from rear terrace with Festival of Britain chair in foreground (middle right) and view over upper terrace with Dedduwa Lake in background (bottom right), gelatin silver print, Geoffrey Bawa with Ulrik Plesner, ca. 1958–60

as well as the broader sociopolitical notions embedded within – was integral to his work.

In Bawa's words, "The site gives the most powerful push to a design along with the brief. Without seeing the site I cannot work. It is essential to be there. After two hours on the site, I have a mental picture of what will be there and how the site will change and the picture does not change."[2]

When he says it is essential to be *there*, I read the phrase as an insistence to understand the context of the place, to recognize what it takes to build there, to live there. Bawa inadvertently began his career as an architect while still practicing professionally as a lawyer – with the purchase of Lunuganga, an abandoned rubber estate, in 1948. The decision to buy land on the brink of the island's independence from the British Empire was a key step in determining the drive behind an architecture practice that was deeply embedded in exploring notions of place.[3] During his lifetime, several significant events in Sri Lanka's history shaped the island's identity from colony to independent nation.

Bawa understood Sri Lanka to be a layered, multifaceted country. "I like to regard all past and present good architecture in Sri Lanka as just that – good Sri Lankan architecture – for this is what it is, not narrowly classified as Indian, Portuguese or Dutch, early Sinhalese or Kandyan or British Colonial, for all the good examples of these periods have taken the country itself into first account."[4] The colonial rulers, particularly the British, relied on a divide-and-conquer approach that widened demographic factions. A consequent emphasis on ethnic and religious identities as driving forces, impeding a united national identity, drove the independence movement in Sri Lanka, which ultimately gained independent rule in 1948. The mounting ethnic tensions that resulted from this process ultimately drove a civil war which lasted twenty-six years, from 1983 to 2009. Many of the intellectual and artistic endeavors in the twentieth century aligned with these ethnic affinities, yet Bawa, himself of mixed ancestry, consistently emphasized the country over any narrower classification. His essay in 1969 used the same sentence quoted above, substituting Sri Lanka for Ceylon,[5] in recognition of the country's official name change in 1972. This insistence on taking "the country itself into first account" is radical, especially given that when he reuses the words fourteen years after *The Architect's Journal* text in the "Statement by the Architect" in Taylor's monograph in 1986, racial tensions were surging in Sri Lanka and the civil war was ongoing.

When Bawa formally began his architecture career as a partner at Edwards, Reid and Begg (ER&B) in 1957, the practice was inspired by the possibilities for building innovation unlocked by technological advancements of the previous decades. However, these options were soon cut short when Sri Lanka's economy

"I like to regard all past and present good architecture in Sri Lanka as just that – good Sri Lankan architecture – for this is what it is, not narrowly classified as Indian, Portuguese or Dutch, early Sinhalese or Kandyan or British Colonial, for all the good examples of these periods have taken the country itself into first account."

2 Channa Daswatte, "Bawa on Bawa," in *Geoffrey Bawa: 1919–2003*, ed. David Robson and Channa Daswatte (Colombo: Geoffrey Bawa Trust, 2011), 43.

3 He wrote to Jean Chamberlin: "I would go home and buy a land somewhere near home [...]. In Jan 1948 I went home." Correspondence from Geoffrey Bawa to Jean Chamberlin, undated, GB/DOC/012/09, Box 01, Folder 012, Geoffrey Bawa Archives, Colombo, Sri Lanka.

4 Geoffrey Bawa, "Statement by the Architect," in *Geoffrey Bawa: Architect in Sri Lanka*, ed. Brian Brace Taylor (Singapore: Mimar with Concept Media, 1986), 16.

5 Geoffrey Bawa, "Ceylon a Philosophy for Building," *The Architect's Journal* (October 15, 1969).

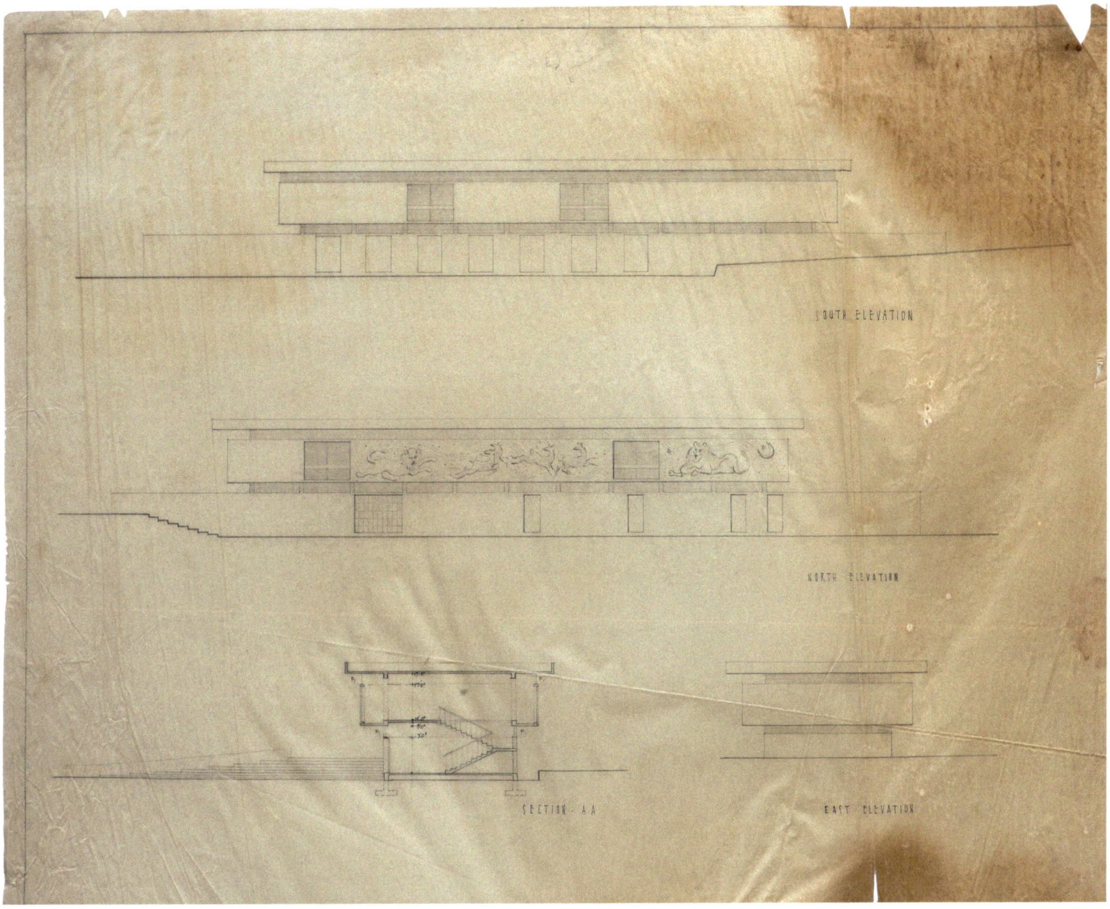

St. Thomas' Preparatory School, Colombo
Ink on tracing paper, section drawing, 1958

Detail of bas-relief by Anil Gamini Jayasuriya on north elevation, gelatin silver print, Geoffrey Bawa, ca. 1962

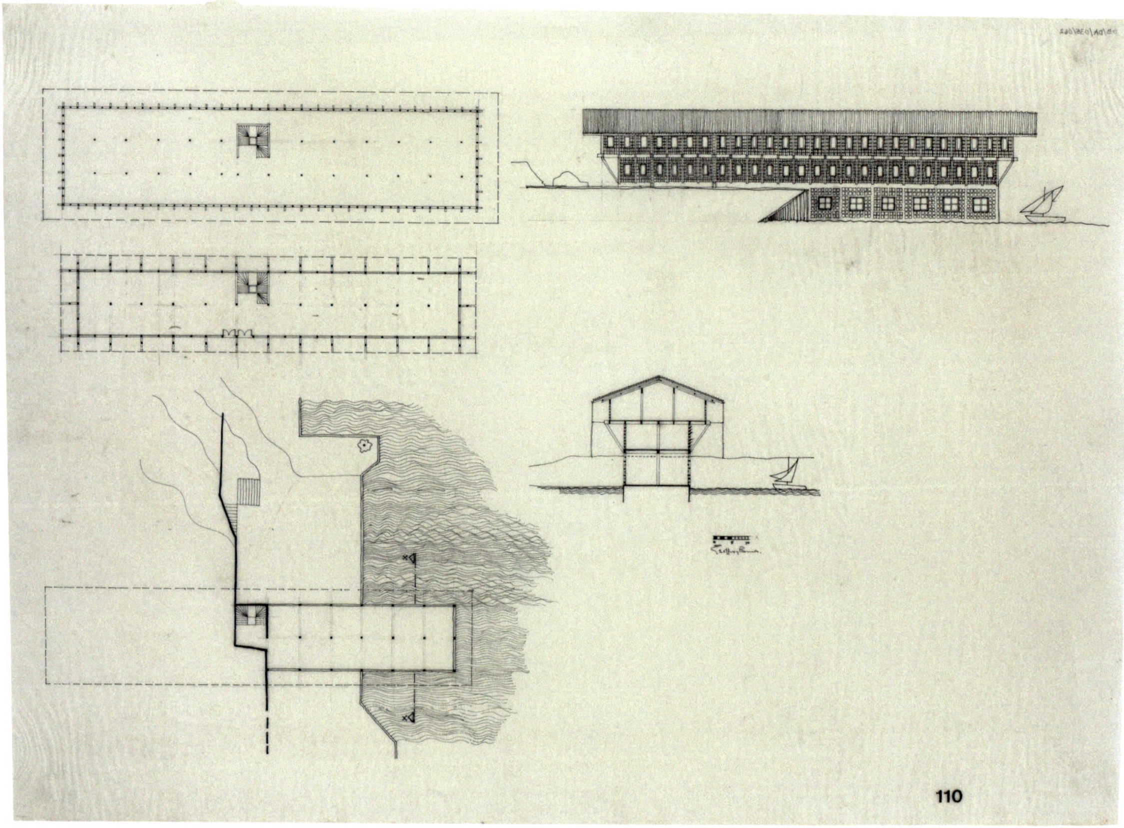

Steel Corporation Offices and Staff Housing, Oruwela, Administrative Building
Plans, section and elevation, ink on tracing paper, ca. 1986

Color film slides, Geoffrey Bawa (attributed)

Bentota Beach Hotel, Bentota
West elevation with Dr. Poologasundram's shadow visible, gelatin silver print, Dr. K. Poologasundram, ca. 1973

Section, ink on tracing paper, ca. 1969 (redrawn 1986)

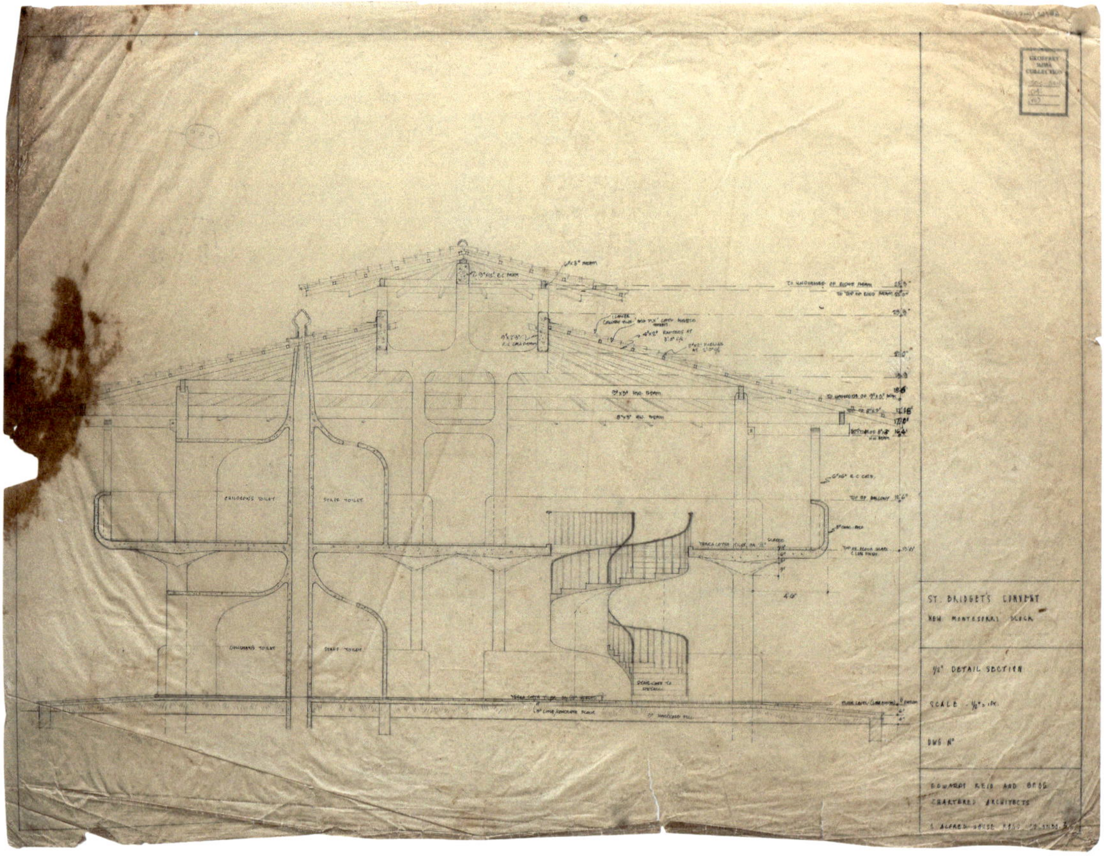

St. Bridget's Montessori, Colombo
Section, graphite and ink on tracing paper, ca. 1963

Exposed concrete stair with murals by Barbara Sansoni, chromogenic color print, Geoffrey Bawa, ca. 1963 closed with ensuing austerity measures in the 1960s, which continued until 1977, as part of the island's association with the Non-Aligned Movement and the drive toward self-sufficiency. Steel and glass, the two materials which enabled much of the architectonics which define modern architecture, were in short supply in Sri Lanka. Bawa and his associates were left to find alternative means to express the forms and spaces they were conceiving of, using materials at hand. At the same time, they began to explore the materials and methods of building from a pragmatic standpoint: the steel reinforcements that held up St. Thomas' Preparatory School (1957–63) corroded, and while the building – replete with murals and a work in relief by Anil Gamini Jayasuriya – was magnificent when it first opened, its unsuitability to the island's climate and the building's coastal location soon became apparent. While St. Bridget's Montessori School (1963–64) is ostensibly still made of exposed concrete, a monitor roof was explored through drawing, although unbuilt, in the design of a building that could better serve the Sri Lankan climate. This evolving exploration is continued in the concrete fins on the floor plate supporting a double-cantilevered roof at the Simon Block (1965) at Ladies' College; the buttressed supports at the Steel Corporation; and the remarkable innovation of the roof-hung suspended balcony floor plates at the Bentota Beach Hotel.[6] Bawa's partnership with Dr. K. Poologasundram, a brilliant structural engineer whom Bawa initially worked with as a consultant starting in 1961, and whom Bawa persuaded to join the ER&B partnership in 1966, was instrumental in these innovations. As Dr. Poologasundram stated, "textbook designs wouldn't work [...] there was no standard design."[7] His research in concrete and his academic background were key to realizing the firm's projects.[8] The work, marked by multiplicities rather than categorization, evolved to respond to the local climate while also serving as reflections of the zeitgeist, with their emphasis on functionality and the innovative use of available resources and materials during a period of scarcity.

In Bawa's own words, "At random I take an isolated item, the – what is now called – Sinhala tile. The Arab traders introduced to Sri Lanka many centuries ago the half-round clay roofing tile of the Mediterranean world, but the roofs built in Sri Lanka with them were more steeply pitched to shed the huge rainfall of our country. The Portuguese and the Dutch used the same tile and roof pitch but the latter raised the roofs higher for coolness, with wide eaves and verandahs to shade the walls. In the hill country the Kandyans used a flat clay tile like a shingle on their double-pitched roofs in meeting halls which had only columns, no walls – an answer to a way of life – a great roof to give shade and shelter, open to the drift of air and the encompassing view. More than functional building it is first rational building, for it is rational to give presence to both function and form, to admit beauty and

"At random I take an isolated item, the – what is now called – Sinhala tile. The Arab traders introduced to Sri Lanka many centuries ago the half-round clay roofing tile of the Mediterranean world, but the roofs built in Sri Lanka with them were more steeply pitched to shed the huge rainfall of our country. The Portuguese and the Dutch used the same tile and roof pitch but the latter raised the roofs higher for coolness, with wide eaves and verandahs to shade the walls. In the hill country the Kandyans used a flat clay tile like a shingle on their double-pitched roofs in meeting halls."

6 Author interview with Channa Daswatte, September 2, 2019, transcript, GBT/AUD/OH/002/000, Oral Histories, Geoffrey Bawa Trust Archives, Colombo, Sri Lanka.
7 Author interview with Dr. Kandasamy Poologasundram, September 15, 2020, transcript, GBT/AUD/OH/005/000, Oral Histories, Geoffrey Bawa Trust Archives, Colombo, Sri Lanka.
8 Dr. Poologasundram was also a pragmatist and handled the management and finances of the firm while engineering not just the structures but the process of delivering buildings amid varied challenges.

Ena de Silva House, Colombo, interior view of central courtyard, gelatin silver print, Geoffrey Bawa, ca. 1962

Yahapath Endera Farm School, Hanwella, exterior view of Mother Superior's house with thatched roof, gelatin silver print, Geoffrey Bawa, ca. 1965–71

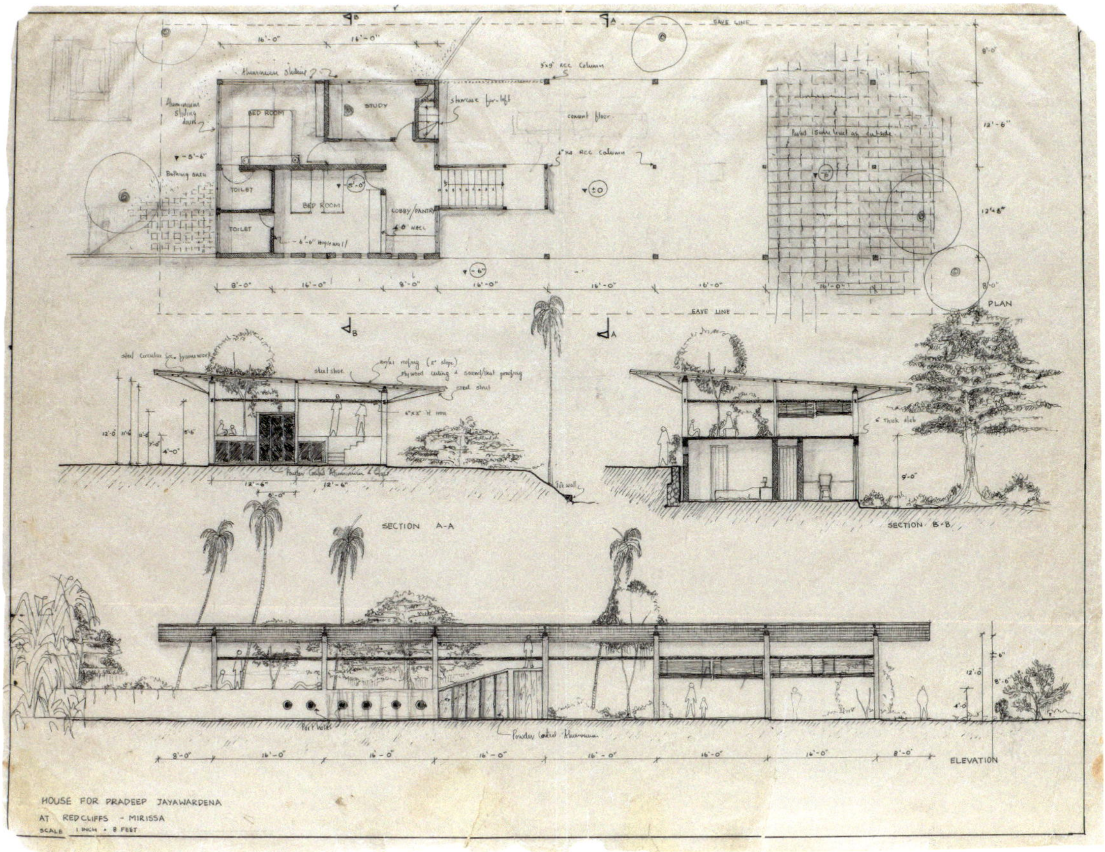

Jayawardena House, Mirissa, plan, section and elevations, ink on vellum, Murad Ismail, 1997

Polontalawa Estate Bungalow, Nikaweratiya, gelatin silver print, Geoffrey Bawa, ca. 1965–67

Jayawardena House, Mirissa, site plan, ink on vellum, Waruna Gomis, 1997

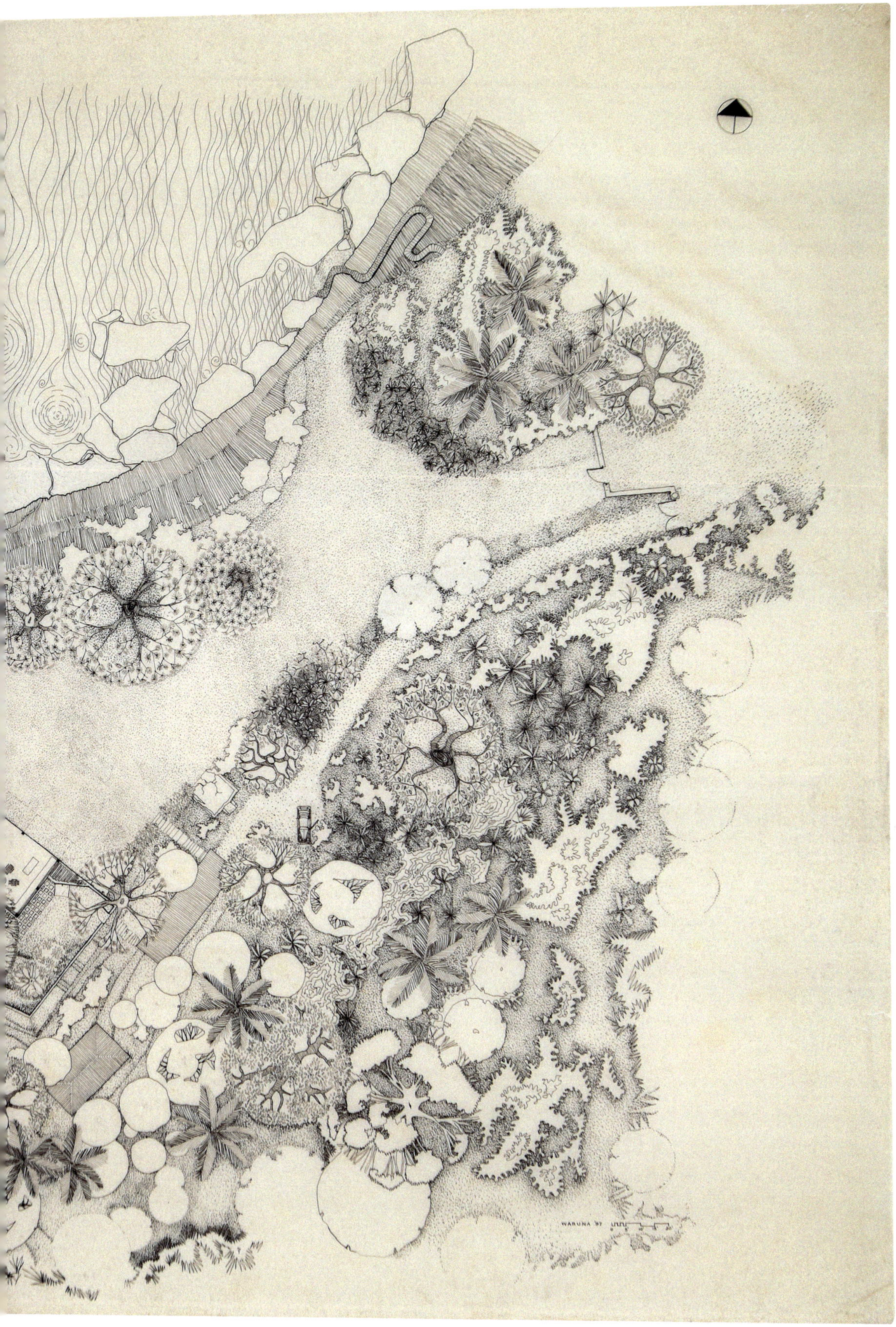

pleasure as well as purpose."[9] Let us pause on this notion of building for function and form against the varied terrains of the island by turning to four projects: Ena de Silva's urban house; the Polontalawa Estate Bungalow in the dry zone; hilly Hanwella farm school in the Western Province; and the Jayawardena house on the southern coast.

The Ena de Silva House (1962) responded to Colombo's increasing density through an inward-looking courtyard and became a crucial exploration of the contemporary urban dwelling in Sri Lanka. The common approach of positioning a house at the center of a plot, surrounded by garden on all sides was challenged as densification began to sweep through Sri Lanka's cities. Ena's site, 750 square meters in area, was unusually small for a house in Colombo at the time and here, the courtyard is used along with high boundary walls to enclose the property, creating an expansive sense of space within tight confines. The courtyard is a trope that traditionally appears in vernacular Sri Lankan homes across ethnicities, geographies and epochs. However, Bawa draws on the vernacular here in the manner of a Modernist architect looking back at the past while looking to the future, much like Le Corbusier[10] had done with the Maisons Jaoul (1954–56), Notre-Dame du Haut (1951–55) and Chandigarh (1950–65), and as Frank Lloyd Wright had done with the Prairie Style houses (1900–10) and Willey House (1934).[11] In Sri Lanka, a traditional domestic courtyard would be slightly sunken and offer a sacrosanct space for the household deities or the women of the house.[12] The courtyard would carve out separation from the floor, which is raised on a plinth above the ground plane. In the Ena de Silva House, the ground continues from floor to garden; the courtyard serves to bring the inside out in what was at the time a very small site. The courtyard is not a shelter but a stage and would become the site of Ena's avant-garde batik practice. The communal spaces of the home are not merely adjacent to the courtyard, they rely on the extension of space afforded by the central void.

The Jayawardena House in Mirissa (1997–98), Bawa's penultimate project, a partly belowground structure with a ground-level living space defined by columns rather than walls, allows residents to engage with the stunning cliff-top site unimpeded by buildings. This house, designed four decades after the Ena de Silva House, is in some ways an expression of how little building is required in the face of a captivating site "where even in darkness/there is no horizon without a tree," as described by Michael Ondaatje.[13] Intended to be used as the client's holiday home, Bawa's design is an exercise in restraint against a richly captivating setting, at one time a tea estate owned by the Ferranti family. The estate bungalow was burned to the ground during the JVP insurrections of 1989, and when former president J. R. Jayawardena's grandson Pradeep approached Bawa to rebuild at the premises, he remarked that

9 Geoffrey Bawa, "Statement by the Architect," in *Geoffrey Bawa: Architect in Sri Lanka*, ed. Brian Brace Taylor (Singapore: Mimar with Concept Media, 1986), 16–17.

10 Jean-Louis Cohen, introduction to *Le Corbusier: The Lyricism of Architecture in the Machine Age* (Cologne: Taschen, 2006), 12.

11 See Steve Sikora, "Willey House Stories Part 2: Influencing Vernacular Architecture," *Frank Lloyd Wright Foundation*, December 14, 2017, franklloydwright.org/willey-house-stories-part-2-influencing-vernacular-architecture (accessed June 30, 2022).

12 Ronald Lewcock, Barbara Sansoni and Laki Senanayake, *The Architecture of an Island: The Living Heritage of Sri Lanka*, 4th ed. (Colombo: Barefoot (Pvt.) Ltd., 2010), 19, 53 and 67. This publication is an excellent resource on traditional secular and religious building types. For more on architecture of antiquity in Sri Lanka, see *The Art and Archaeology of Sri Lanka I: Archaeology, Architecture and Sculpture*, ed. Leelananda Prematilleke, Bandaranayake, Deraniyagala and Silva (Colombo: Central Cultural Fund, Ministry of Cultural Affairs, 2007).

13 Quote from Michael Ondaatje, "House on a Red Cliff," in *Handwriting* (Toronto: Knopf, 1999). Accessed via a print dedicated by hand by Ondaatje to Geoffrey Bawa, Lunuganga Guest Book, GB/DOC/148/001, Geoffrey Bawa Archives, Colombo, Sri Lanka.

Ceylon Pavilion at Expo '70, Osaka,
exterior and interior view, gelatin silver print,
Geoffrey Bawa (attributed), 1970

It is dressed to be unique

The Hotel at Kandalama – an architect's dream turns into a phantasmic nightmare

by Old Timer

It is only in a place like Sri Lanka that a commonplace occurrence like the building of a tourist hotel can be blown up beyond all normal proportions to almost constitute a national issue.

In a situation where big money is at stake or, at a lower key, self interest is involved, make even a mere suggestion to touch Buddhist, Hindu, Catholic or Muslim religious sensitiveness; add the notion that there will be cultural damage and environmental pollution; make available some sort of political ammunition to an opposition ready to use any weapon against the government; sprinkle some communal pepper for good measure, and we have the perfect ingredients for the concoction of a witches' brew which will froth and bubble to create national pandemonium. This is what happened at Iranavila, and this is what is happening at Kandalama.

Kandalama is reachable by a road newly built by the developers, about two and a half kilometres long which branches off from a secondary road, itself branching off from Dambulla town, and about five and a half kilometres to the turn off to Kandalama tank.

The site selected for the hotel is on the eastern perimeter of Kandalama tank which was naturally fed by waters from the Dambulu Oya valley catchment area, but not so important as to find mention in R. L. Brohier's classic "The Irrigation Works of Ancient Ceylon".

It is a comparatively small village tank capable of feeding at full spill level some hundreds of acres of paddy lands.

On first thought, it is beyond the perception of a non–partisan observer's objectivity, why in the first place a tourist hotel which purports to service mostly transients visiting Cultural Triangle projects in the area, should be built there, and more relevantly, how such a hotel could be socially, culturally and environmentally unacceptable.

A visit to the site makes it clear that the choice of the site has primarily been for aesthetic reasons. As for the rest, the pros and cons have had full public exposure in the written media in recent weeks. There is no need to add to the confusion.

As in most matters of this nature, rub hard enough, and the dirt will show; delve deep enough and the truth will surface. Even from the beginning, the reason for the opposition to the Iranavila project was being whispered in knowledgeable quarters. Among the several smuggling points on the north–western coast, Iranavila area was a predominant one.

Tucked away inconspicuously on the coast off Mahaweva, it was a safe refuge for large scale smuggling. Had the Iranavila project been permitted, the first persons to be affected would have been the mafia type millionaire smugglers. Their fate would have been sealed.

The innocent fisherfolk were led to believe that the present benefits they received from the smuggler overlords would not be available to them, if the Complex materialised. Perhaps with some arm twisting, and other inducements too, for the counter propaganda had already commenced, the case for the fisherfolk, economic deprivation, social evils, damage to religion and culture was put with full force to the Church by locals who swung power in the area.

The Church naturally espoused the cause of their flock, for reasons it honestly felt to be valid, and a public outcry arose, some Buddhist interests in the region also joininh the Church, or so the story goes. Unlike at Kandalama there were no grey areas in the reasons for the Iranavila protest.

The point however is, that had smuggling interests not been involved, the protest may not have got under way, in the manner it did.

The origins of the opposition to the Kandalama hotel, according to cognoscenti, are not dissimilar. The absentee and local landlords of paddy lands, (they do exist in some areas, despite the Paddy Lands and Land Reforms Acts), under the Kandalama tank who were powerful dayakayas of the Rangiri Dambulu Temple smelled danger to their feudal hold on the cultivators, and feared that they would be deprived of the already expensive and scarce agricultural labour, if the hotel came up in the area, however groundless their fears actually were.

Just as the Church was made to get involved at Iranavila, the Chief Incumbent of the Dambulla Temple and other Buddhist clergy in the area were readily roped in. This was easy because temple lands and fields were part of the scenario. If the opposition to the site became a success, temple land of which there was plenty in the area could be offered to resite it.

The notions of damage to culture and the local mores and the environment which have been exposed to public discussion fully, the Minister for Tourism forming the communal pepper component were added to the witches' brew. Trade rivalry would also have played its part.

To the opposition politicians and others opposed to the government, any public outcry was grist to the mill; this was a heaven sent opportunity, and now the witches' brew has come to full boil.

These matters apart, there is another aspect of this matter, which is the main purpose of this article, an aspect which may have rather distressing consequences personally, to one who has been acclaimed as the country's leading architect, and also be a loss to the world of art in general.

It is in a way ironic that aesthetic compulsions rather than the ordinary needs of the travel trade, played a predominant part in the selection of the site. Helicopter borne in his search for a suitable site in the area, which the government had expressed its willingness to allocate for the purpose, his artist's eye spotted the shimmering waters of Kandalama tank with the massif of rock outcrop in the background, the Sigiriya Rock colourfully silhouetted six direct vision miles away and an amphitheatre of low hills green and rock bespattered in various hues, surrounding the entire complex.

There could be no better place. Who would think of environmental pollution and the damaging impact of tourism on culture in this secluded wilderness of scrub jungle? The developers went along with the proposal of their team of architects, although they could have with more success financially, sited the hotel elsewhere at much less expense.

For them apparently, a mere hotel would not suffice; it had to be something outstanding despite the cost. It is evident that to the entrepreneur developers, making profits was not the only consideration; enhancing the tourist image of the country by erecting a unique hotel edifice, was equally important. And so the die was cast, and they are today facing fearful odds which they never anticipated.

This artistic aspect of course, is on a different plane and of a different dimension to the reasons adduced for and against the site. It is of limited interest to the general public, although it would mean a deprivation to the world of art and architecture. This aspect cannot reasonably be expected to be given consideration in the prevailing heat of contention.

If the hotel comes up on the site presently selected, the country could be proud of an artistic achievement comparable with the best in architecture anywhere else.

The man who planned the Triton at Ahungalla, where, as one enters the foyer, one gets the impression that the sea is perpetually flowing into the hotel and receding, is leading the team of architects at Kandalama, where, to judge by present trends, the viewer from the shores of the tank would get the impression of a terraced hotel hanging in mid air from the face of the rock, merging with the natural surroundings; the vision is hard to match.

It is in the nature of things that in the area where the ancient architectural marvel of Sigiriya stands, there should emerge a modern edifice which, although of quite a different genre, would be unique by any present day standard, the brain child of a leading Sri Lankan aesthete.

The doyen of Lankan architects would indeed be a very sad man if in the twilight of his career, his artistic conception of the hotel at Kandalama were not to materialise due to the collision of forces beyond his control, and the country would be poorer by a work of art.

Cartoon in *The Island* newspaper about the Kandalama Hotel, ink on paper, Sudeepa Purnajith, 1992

Daily News, "It is Dressed to be Unique: The Hotel at Kandalama – an architect's dream turns into a phantasmic nightmare," newsprint, Old Timer, 1994 "there should be no house there" and the site should be left as is.[14] A thin, almost flat roof over the footprint of the old bungalow establishes the house, emphasizing the views and the magnificence of the site.

In Hanwella, the Yahapath Endera Farm School (1965–71), an ambitious project for orphaned girls to learn agricultural and craft skills, negotiated a complex terrain to manage a diverse set of agricultural and fabrication goals while retaining a connection to the rural landscape. As described by David Robson, the project used the existing landscape and incorporated buildings on the site in an orthogonally organized plan "to 'run with the contours' in section. Individual buildings were positioned carefully to define open spaces and axes and to regulate the vistas between them."[15] The project is described in Bawa's own words as follows: "It was important to end up with a building that related to buildings in the countryside with which the girls were familiar. This was achieved, and formed the visual framework within which this particular education, technical, practical and spiritual, could blossom."[16] Using local materials and simple techniques, the buildings were made in conjunction with craftsmen from the neighboring villages. The success of the project provided a model for the government for rural development projects in the 1980s.[17]

By contrast, the Polontalawa Estate Bungalow (1963–67) in the rocky terrain of dry-zone Nikaweratiya recasts a colonial building typology into a new form, in which the existing boulders and features of the land are used to define the spaces of the bungalow. While the colonial practice would be to create a tabula rasa at the site and then to erect a building that would shut out the landscape, Bawa worked with the existing conditions, much like the *kuti* (monks's huts) of antiquity. He would take this same approach on a much larger scale three decades later with the Kandalama Hotel.

Architecture inevitably takes on a symbolic role – and buildings can often be deployed to signify meanings and convey ideas. Although Bawa eschewed writing and theorizing on his work, he was unable to avoid this aspect of the discipline completely. At the Expo '70 in Osaka, a forum where the avant-garde Metabolists (from Japan) and Archigram (from the UK) also exhibited, Ceylon's pavilion was an occasion to demonstrate an evolving national identity.[18] ER&B's design for the nation's pavilion displayed an array of archaeological objects in a modern structure: once more looking to the future while looking back. The pavilion was conceived and constructed in a mere six weeks, with a minimal budget and with much of the design detailed by Anura Rathnavibushana.[19] Yet it received wide acclaim, described by Jim Richards, then editor of *The Architectural Review*, in a personal letter to Bawa as "one of the very best [...] elegant and without the fuss most of them only confuse the visitor by making"[20] and in *The Hindu* as "notable for economy, austerity and elegance."[21] The pavilion

14 Author interview with Murad Ismail, project architect for the Jayawardena House, October 2, 2021.
15 David Robson, *Geoffrey Bawa: The Complete Works* (London: Thames & Hudson, 2002), 89–91.
16 Gallery Guide, *Geoffrey Bawa: An Exhibition of the Work of a Leading Sri Lankan Architect*, Royal Institute of British Architects, March 6–April 3, 1986, GB/DOC/036/00, Archival Documents, Box 02, Geoffrey Bawa Archives, Colombo, Sri Lanka.
17 Robson, *Geoffrey Bawa*, 89–91.
18 In 1972 Ceylon became a republic within the Commonwealth, and its name was changed to Sri Lanka.
19 Author interview with Dr. Kandasamy Poologasundram, September 15, 2020.
20 Photo album with press clippings for Expo '70, Osaka, 1970, Geoffrey Bawa Archives, Colombo, Sri Lanka.
21 "India Puts Up Good Show at Expo '70," *The Hindu*, May 4, 1970.

consisted of two glass-walled, steel-framed cubes set at an obtuse angle, connected by a balcony. Light fittings were ceiling-hung paper *atapattam* (cuboctahedron) lanterns and the triangular lamp niches of temples from antiquity and the famous cloud walls from the Kandyan Kingdom were flattened to form a rice-paper screen that modulated light coming through the glass walls. Minnette de Silva and Bawa had already modernized these wall niches for adapted use in houses.[22] Archaeological artifacts were placed alongside contemporary batiks by Ena de Silva in this modern structure, emphasizing an image of Ceylon looking to its past as it looked ahead.

The Kandalama Hotel (1991–95) located in Dambulla, the heart of Sri Lanka's cluster of ancient kingdoms, impelled a new environmental and cultural consciousness in relation to building on the island. On the part of the environmentalists, there was great concern that a large-scale hospitality project would emerge on this hitherto undeveloped land. Much was done on Bawa's part to ensure the design and function of the hotel would remain sensitive to its environmental and cultural context; trees were treated as sacrosanct, and only endemic species were used for planting. The difficulties in getting the project approved and built, amid protests from the public and threats to terminate it from the State, meant all those involved were deeply passionate about the project, which was turning out to be much more than a mere hotel.[23] Bawa himself emphasized the need for controlled development in this environment and remarked that in his view the project would be complete when it had turned to ruin, with its corridors roamed by leopards once more.[24]

What do a series of drawings and documents add to our readings of Bawa's architectural practice, which was so deeply embedded in its actual context? How do materials that disengage the idea of place by being separate from the place itself influence our readings of that place? It is important to note that the Geoffrey Bawa Archives as it exists today is by no means comprehensive or even cohesive. Bawa's view toward his legacy is a topic that merits scholarship in its own right and is a subject that space precludes us from going into here. He was certainly apprehensive of the archival afterlife of his work, and when he moved offices from Number 2, Alfred House Road to his home at Number 11, 33rd Lane, he set up a bonfire through which several drawings were destroyed.[25] Those who knew him repeatedly emphasize that he was a "deeply private person"[26] and for reasons we can now only speculate upon, he did not retain correspondence nor for the most part the contracts, drawing sets, revisions and maquettes that often constitute the greater part of an architectural archive. What we are left with are fragments that piece together to create a portrait of a design practice. Tariq Jazeel's text in this volume adopts a comparative approach between Bawa's and Minnette de Silva's archives,

22 Minnette de Silva used them in square form at the Peiris House in Colombo as lamp niches (completed 1956), and Bawa would use them in later in the gateposts at Lunuganga.

23 Author interview with Amila de Mel, Channa Daswatte, Jaime de la Pena and Sumangala Jayatillaka, November 15, 2019, transcript, GBT/AUD/OH/004/000, Oral Histories, Geoffrey Bawa Archives, Colombo, Sri Lanka.

24 Author interview with Channa Daswatte, September 2, 2019.

25 Author interview with Channa Daswatte, September 2, 2019. See also author interview with David Robson, November 10, 2019, transcript, GBT/AUD/OH/012/000, Oral Histories, Geoffrey Bawa Archives, Colombo, Sri Lanka.

26 Author interview with Sunethra Bandaranaike, March 21, 2019, transcript, GBT/AUD/OH/006/000, Oral Histories, Geoffrey Bawa Archives, Colombo, Sri Lanka.

Yala Bungalows, Yala, Sand Dune House perspectival drawing, ink on tracing paper, Nihal Amarasinghe (attributed), 1968

Hotel at Candolim, Goa, Sand Dune scheme perspectival drawing, graphite on tracing paper, 1977 fragmentary though they may be, to explore the value of these types of repositories in this particular geography. When it comes to parsing the documents, insights from those who worked in the practice are invaluable, and the epilogue to this volume by Channa Daswatte, the last partner at the practice, offers a personal and unique insight into this experience.

In their recent discussion presented in a text titled "The Appeal of Tedious Folders," Kieran Long and Mark Wigley state "an archive is determined not so much by the objects inside it but by what it means to enter that space and what it means to bring an object out."[27] Having previously encountered the works in the archives through the mediated pages and electronic screens of reproductions of the drawing, physically working in the archives over the last five years offered new insights into this repository. I approached the archive looking for clues on architectural intent and process, but the sheets of paper began to read as illustrative drawings at times in addition to working architectural documents. Some drawings were clearly tools: coded instructions for the builders on-site while at other times, drawings were generated after the buildings were completed, a seductive portrayal of building and landscape intertwined.[28] Very few of these sheets bear the folds and crimps that result from being taken to a construction site and worked over in situ, as architecture drawings so often are. The opportunity to look at the drawings up close presents careful draftsmanship coupled with flights of fancy and moments of ennui by their authors; margins of some sheets are filled with doodles, cigarette burns and ink blots, suggesting the type of labor to which the drawing contributed. Based on the descriptions of those who did work on the drawings, it is easy to imagine these kinds of sheets of paper on Geoffrey Bawa's desk over an extended period of time and the conversations and endeavor of envisioning the places that the drawing was charting.

There are certain overall attributes to the drawings from the 1960s onward, especially in those which are redrawings made for publications or exhibitions, where textures of surfaces, objects and plants are rendered with extensive detail and accuracy. The personalities of the various makers of the drawings also comes through; Laki Senanayake and Sumangala Jayatillaka's drawings, for example, show trees as central components of the architecture, with great accuracy given to their shapes and species. Others, like Nihal Amarasinghe, pay much attention to the people depicted in the elevations and perspectival drawings; while Ismeth Raheem inserts cartographic touches with birds and beasts bearing the compass rose. Each drawing with its specificity of a place, gives us clues to the connected influences, ideas and materials which were embedded in the conceptualization of the project. In this book, Jyoti Dhar's text on Lunuganga, which uses a map to explore the relationship of the garden to stories and metanarratives embedded in

27 Ed. Borasi et al., *The Museum Is Not Enough* (Montreal: CCA, 2019), 97.

28 Author interview with Suhanya Raffel and Michael Snelling, May 21, 2019, transcript, GBT/AUD/OH/001/000, Oral Histories, Geoffrey Bawa Archives, Colombo, Sri Lanka. Suhanya quotes Geoffrey Bawa's response to a question at the Asia Pacific Triennial in Brisbane on how the drawings were so pristine, as "Oh we always do our drawings after the building has been built."

Yala Bungalows, Yala, sketch of Tree House, ink on tracing paper, Nihal Amarasinghe (attributed), 1968

these two formats, is an example of the expressly nonarchitectural formats the practice at times adopted. To examine Bawa's practice through the lens of the archive is therefore an occasion to present an analysis that is derived from an indexical series of drawings viewed in conjunction with other materials, primarily the photograph. Sean Anderson's text, "Vanishing Points," reflects further on this relationship between the drawings and the genesis of space.

Both the drawings and the photographs present a view of what Bawa's buildings could be – moments, moods and open-ended scenarios that are key to accessing the essence of an architecture that defied categorization and definitive readings. The backdrop to Bawa's career was a time in which the discipline of architecture in Sri Lanka itself was established as a profession. This was also a period in which construction by highly skilled makers in traditional building techniques were replaced by mechanized fabrication and less-skilled labor, alongside urbanization of a country that had predominantly subsisted through agriculture until the twentieth century. Naturally, the demands of the drawing as a medium of instruction and a tool for planning also evolved during this time, alongside the course of Bawa's practice. Meghal Perera's essay on the Galle Face Report is one example of the granular attention paid by Bawa to places, even vast public spaces such as the Galle Face Green in Colombo, and offers a tantalizing glimpse into early efforts by the State in urban design and planning, a time in contrast to the present urbanization efforts in Sri Lanka, in which the rift between architecture and urbanization seems insurmountable.

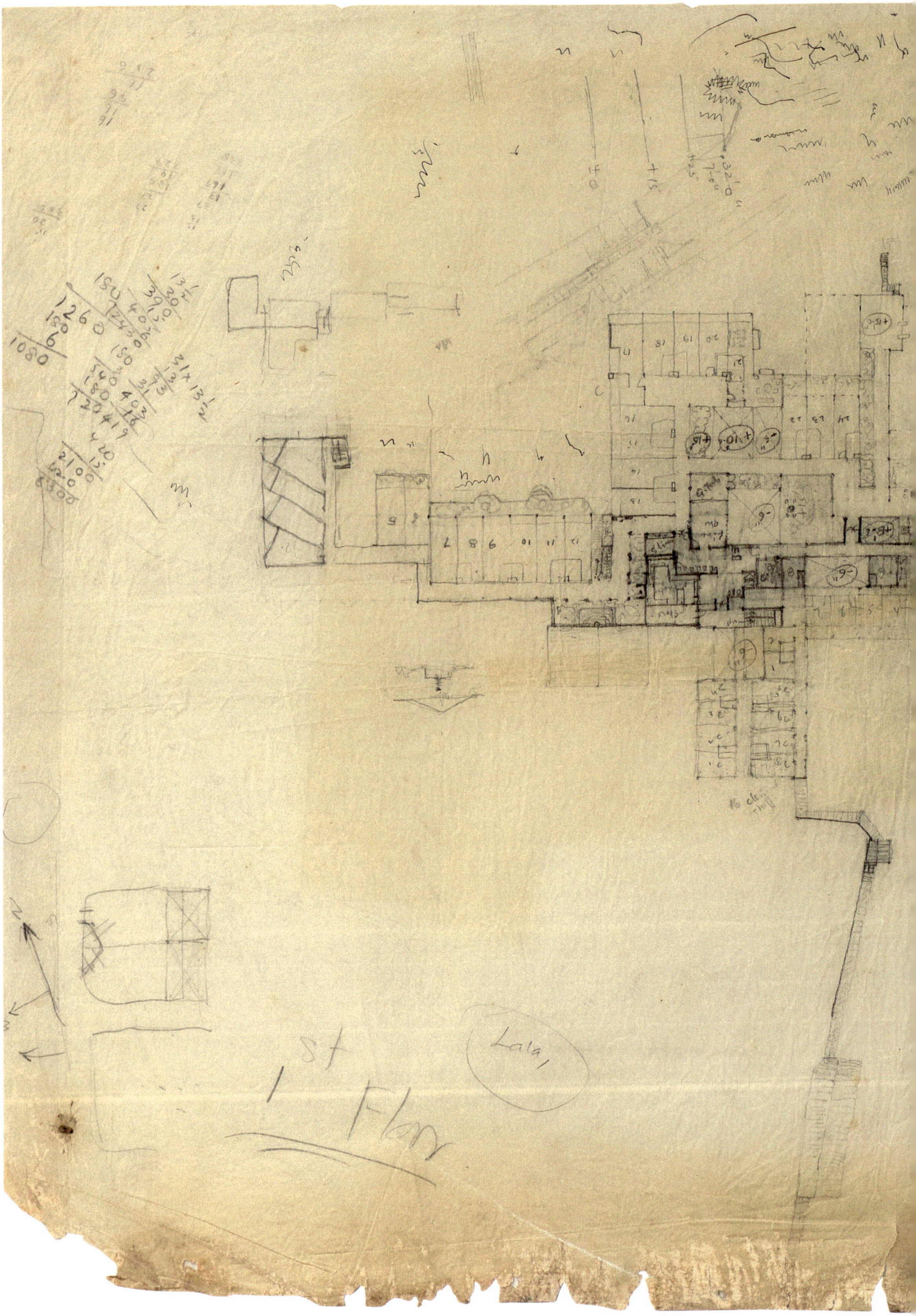

Triton Hotel, Bentota, sketch plan, graphite and ink on tracing paper, Geoffrey Bawa (attributed), ca. 1978

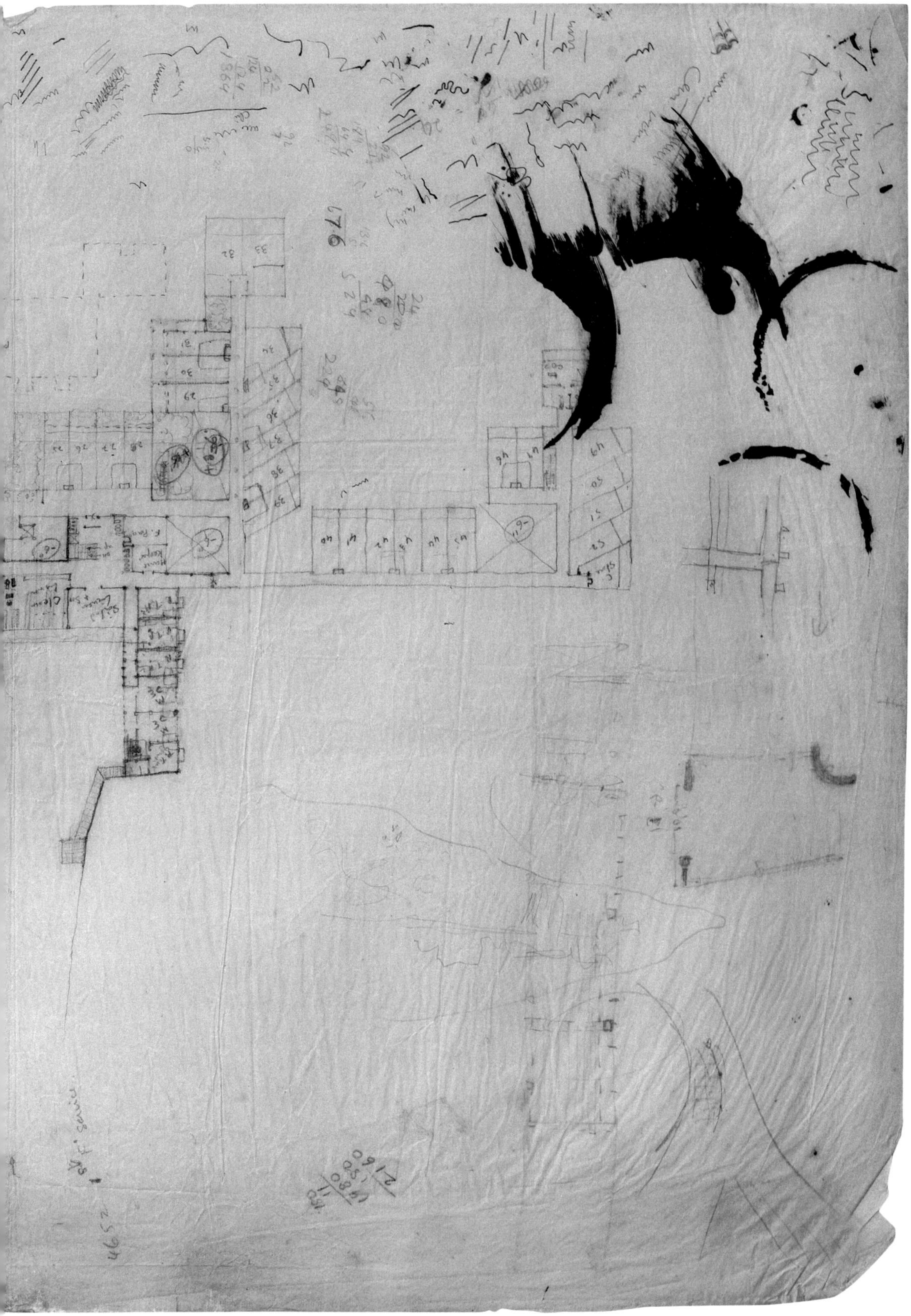

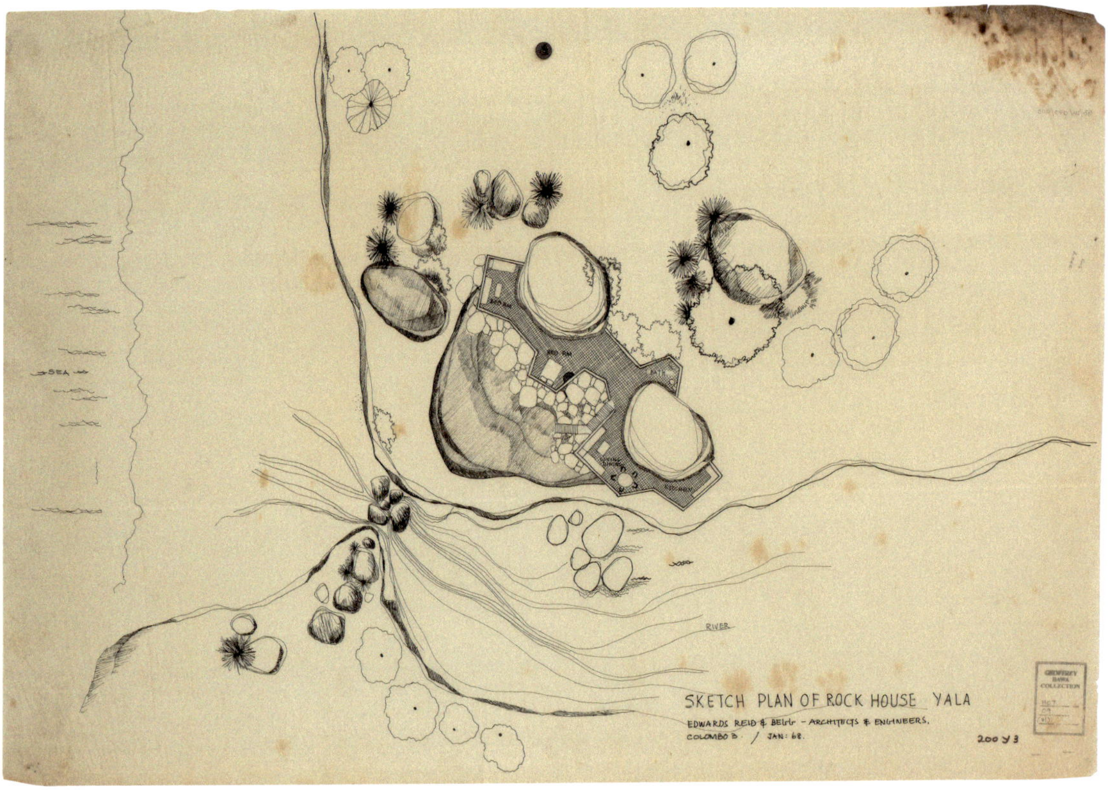

Yala Bungalows, Yala, sketch plan (top) and perspectival sketch (bottom) of Rock House scheme, ink on tracing paper, Nihal Amarasinghe (attributed), 1968

The archive is also a repository of places that extend much further than the built landscape Bawa's practice left behind. We can use it to investigate the reflexive and recursive tendencies of the practice. For example, the three bungalow schemes laid out for Yala (1968), thought to be drawn by Nihal Amarasinghe, are exceptional in their inventiveness and the three distinct approaches taken by each.[29] Consisting of a rock village, a sand dune and tree house, the schemes provide approaches which are additive and subtractive; stereotomic and tectonic. And yet they combine to form a cohesive project apt for Yala, one of the island's most vital wildlife parks, defined by its distinctive landscape of coastal dry-zone forests and rangelands. The Dune House scheme then emerges again in 1977 for the Hotel at Candolim in Goa. While this idea never saw fruition as a built work, Channa Daswatte recounts in his essay the translation of an unbuilt idea from the Mahakanda Hotel (1967) that was realized at the Kandalama Hotel (1991–95). Shirley Surya's essay in this book, on the Batujimbar development in Bali, further examines the relationship between the built and unbuilt through one of the few projects in which much of the process material and publicity documents have been preserved in the archive.

The architectural archive encompasses a Sisyphean task at best; buildings themselves rarely submit to the archiving processes in their built form and no architectural archive is ever exhaustive.[30] The project of such an archive is then to record the ideas, materials and techniques and the many collaborators that go into making buildings. Of the activities I was entrusted with at the Geoffrey Bawa Archives, it was the process of digitization that most clearly highlighted all that was lost in presenting the drawings devoid of their material support: their *opus operatum*, the work done. As Walter Benjamin stated, "Even the most perfect reproduction of a work of art is lacking in one element: its presence in time and space, its unique existence at the place where it happens to be."[31] Looking at the drawings in person, next to other drawings, allows us to make connections that are a vital part of archival study. They chart a rich network of places that consistently ask, What is this place? The unrealized ideas increase our understanding of the depth and breadth of approaches taken by the practice, although they now reside only in the form of sheets of yellowing paper and the onus is on us to glean the information embedded within. But this is the thing about places – in the end they mostly exist in our minds.

29 Author interview with Anura Rathnavibushana, May 24, 2019, transcript, GBT/AUD/OH/007/000, Oral Histories, Geoffrey Bawa Archives, Colombo, Sri Lanka.
30 The Ena de Silva House, which was dismantled from its Colombo site and reassembled exactly as it was at Lunuganga by the Lunuganga Trust for preservation, is a notable exception to this general inability to archive buildings. See comment by Sean Anderson in Smriti Daniel, "Sri Lanka: Ena de Silva's Moving House," *Al Jazeera*, September 20, 2016, www.aljazeera.com/features/2016/9/20/sri-lanka-ena-de-silvas-moving-house.
31 Benjamin, "The Work of Art in the Age of Mechanical Reproduction," in *Illuminations* (New York: Schocken Books, 1968), 220.

St. Thomas' Preparatory School, Colombo

1957–63

Gelatin silver print, Geoffrey Bawa, ca. 1962
GB/DOC/106/006

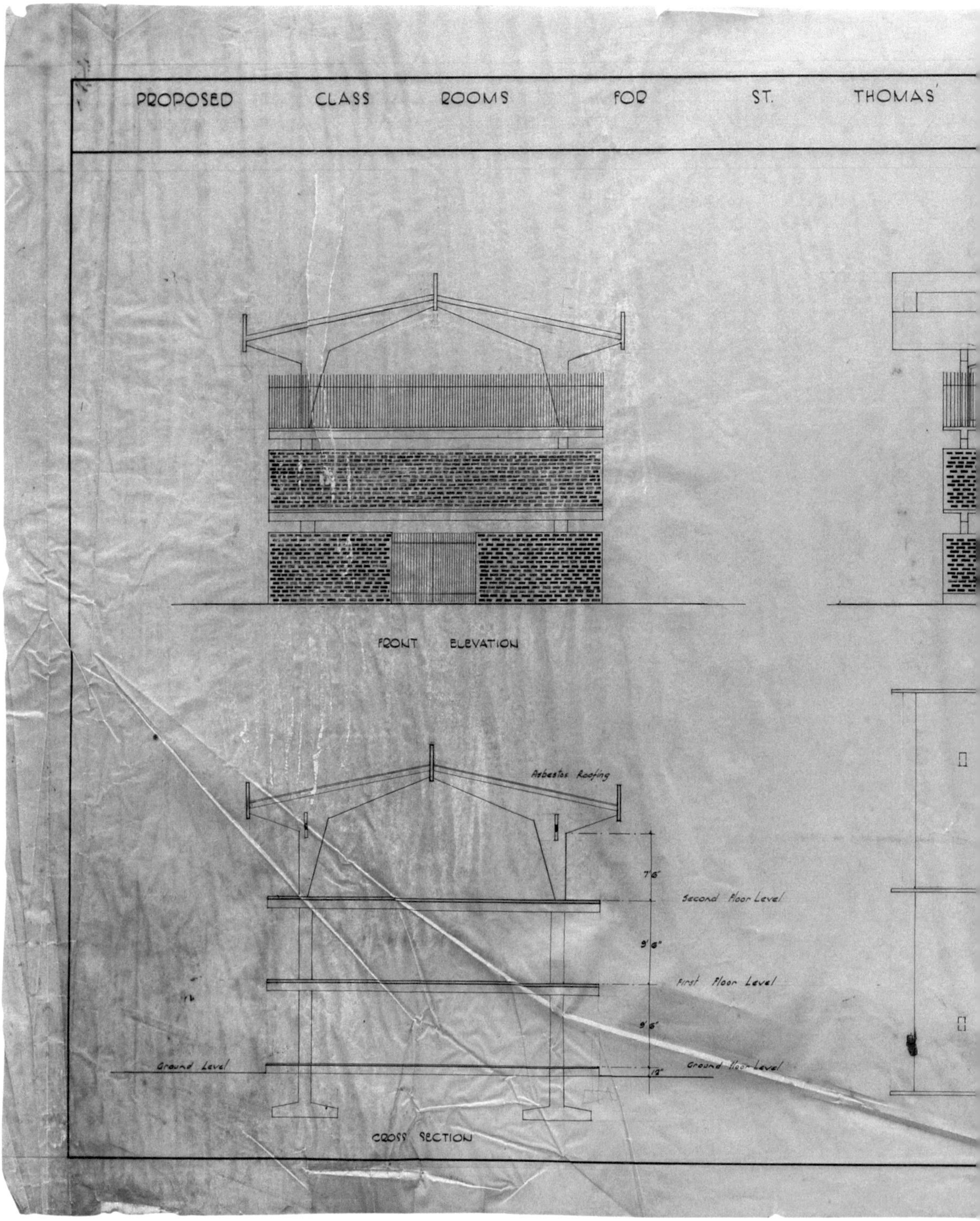

Proposed classrooms; plan, section and elevations, ink on tracing paper, ca. 1958
GB/DOC/106/004

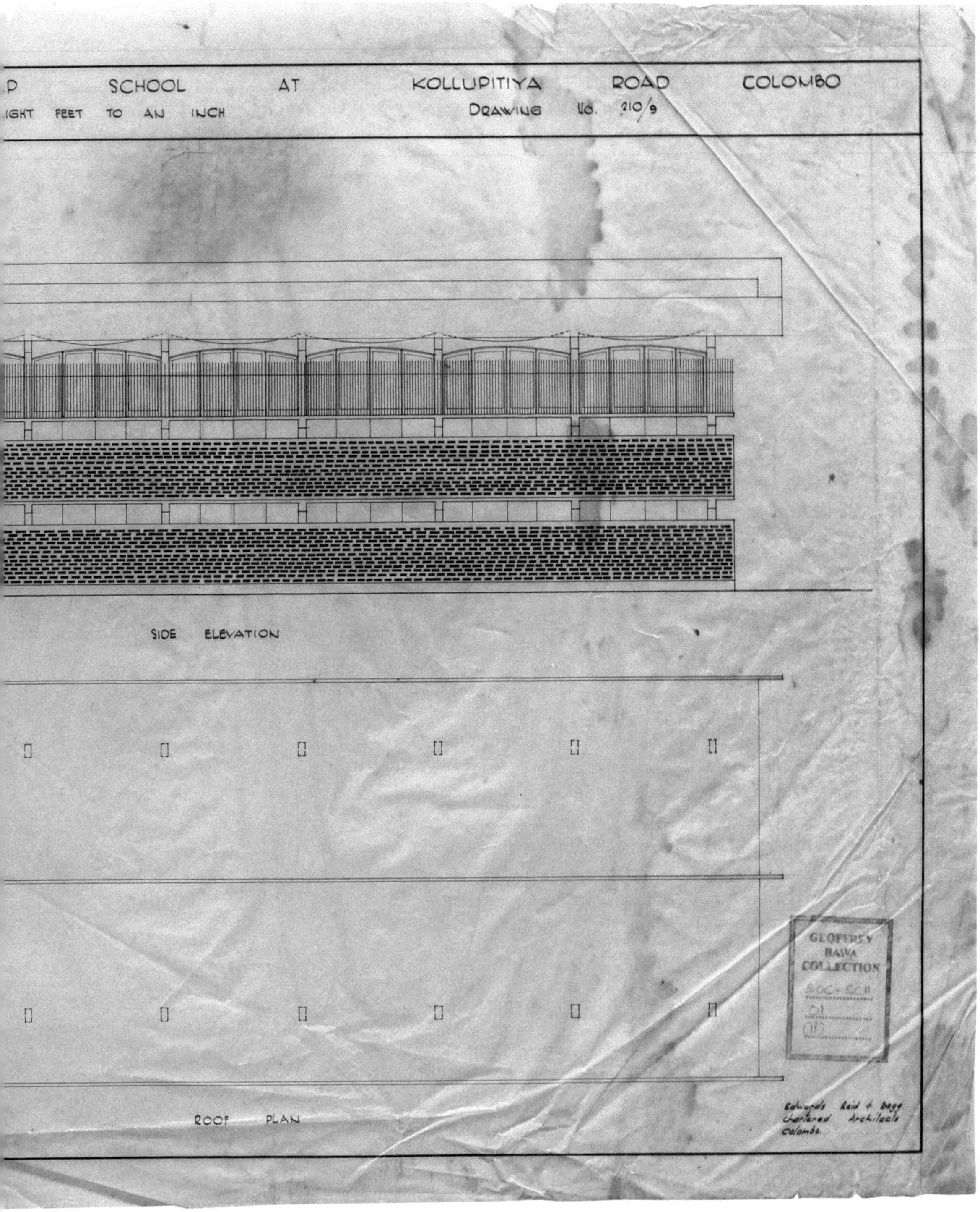
P SCHOOL AT KOLLUPITIYA ROAD COLOMBO
IGHT FEET TO AN INCH
DRAWING NO. 210/9
SIDE ELEVATION
ROOF PLAN
GEOFFREY BAWA COLLECTION
Edwards Reid & Begg
Chartered Architects
Colombo

Gelatin silver print, Geoffrey Bawa.
Ulrik Plesner, pictured here holding the branch, worked closely with Bawa from 1959 to 1966.
GB/DOC/106/006

Exterior view, gelatin silver print, Geoffrey Bawa GB/DOC/106/008

Interior view showing murals by Anil Gamini Jayasuriya, gelatin silver print, Geoffrey Bawa GB/DOC/106/009

The school is situated on the coast of the Indian Ocean, which is visible beyond the east elevation. Gelatin silver print, Geoffrey Bawa GB/DOC/106/008

Detail of cement hollow blocks set at 90 degrees to the north/east, south/west monsoon winds, gelatin silver print, Geoffrey Bawa GB/DOC/106/005

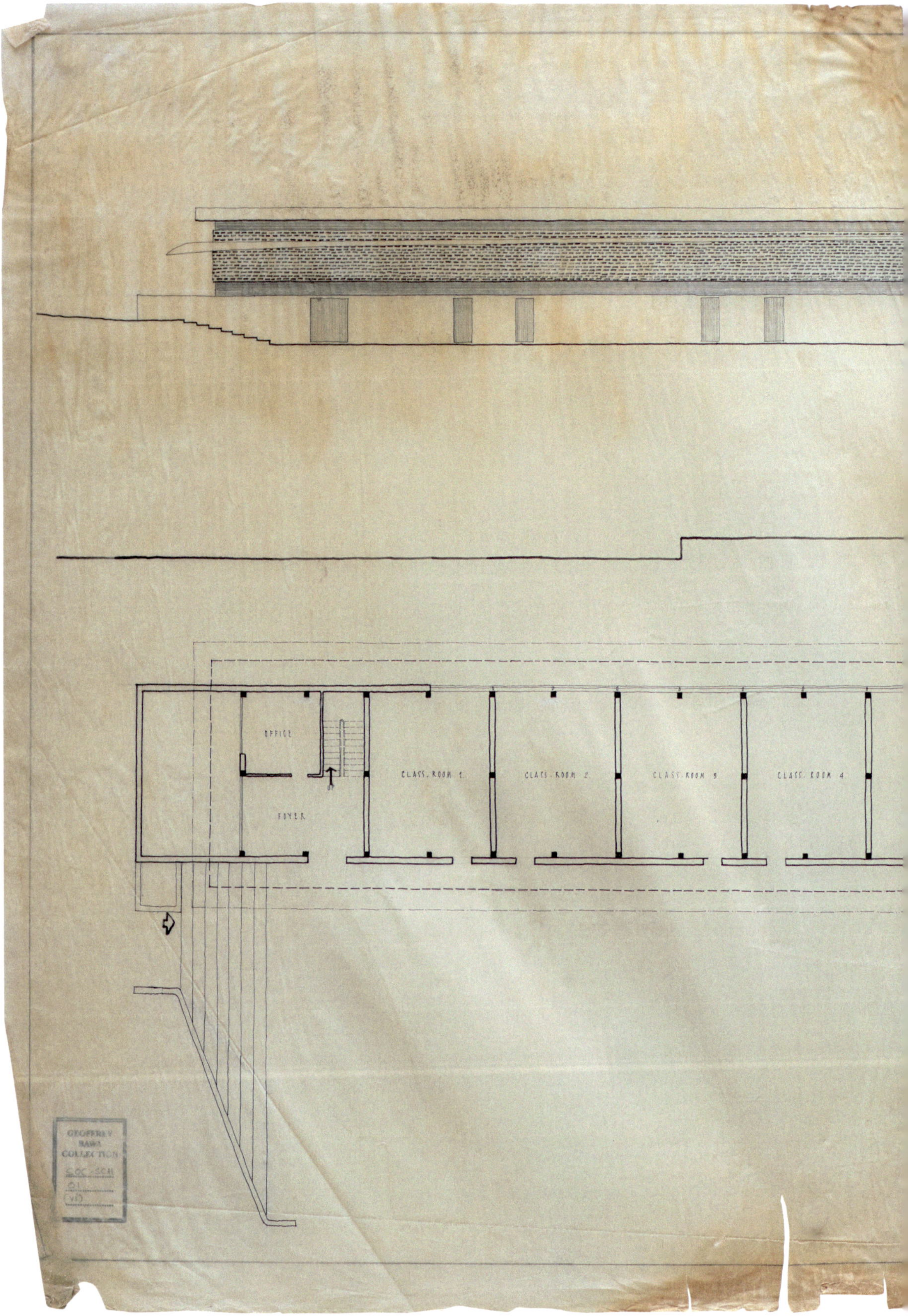

Plan and elevation, ink on tracing paper, 1958
GB/DA/077/004

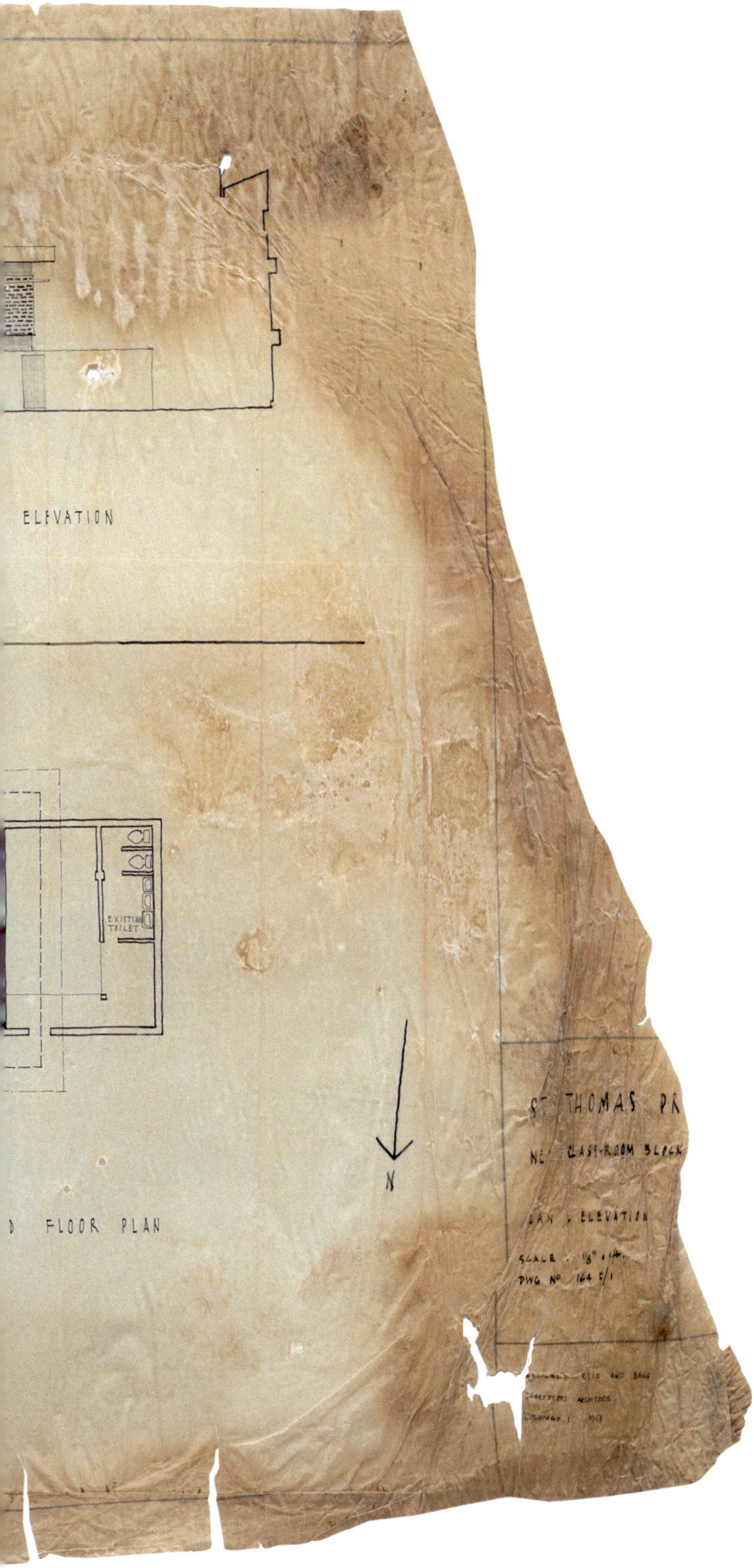
ELEVATION
EXISTING TOILET
N
FLOOR PLAN
ST THOMAS PR
SCALE
DWG No 164 E/1

Exterior view showing bas-reliefs by Anil Gamini Jayasuriya. The design is non-repetitive and shows a variety of Sri Lankan birds. Smaller children can look out of the holes left in the panels for that purpose. Gelatin silver print, Geoffrey Bawa GB/DOC/106/010

North elevation with bas-relief by Anil Gamini Jayasuriya, gelatin silver print, Geoffrey Bawa GB/DOC/106/011

View of both classroom blocks, gelatin silver print, Geoffrey Bawa GB/DOC/106/012

Ena de Silva House, Colombo

1960–62

Exterior view of the house from the street, gelatin silver print, Geoffrey Bawa
GB/DOC/104/003

Interior view of central courtyard, gelatin silver print, **Geoffrey Bawa** GB/DOC/104/009, 006

Interior view (top) and view across living room (bottom), gelatin silver print, Geoffrey Bawa
GB/DOC/104/001/D, 005

Section, ink on tracing paper, Laki Senanayake, 1963 GB/DA/034/001

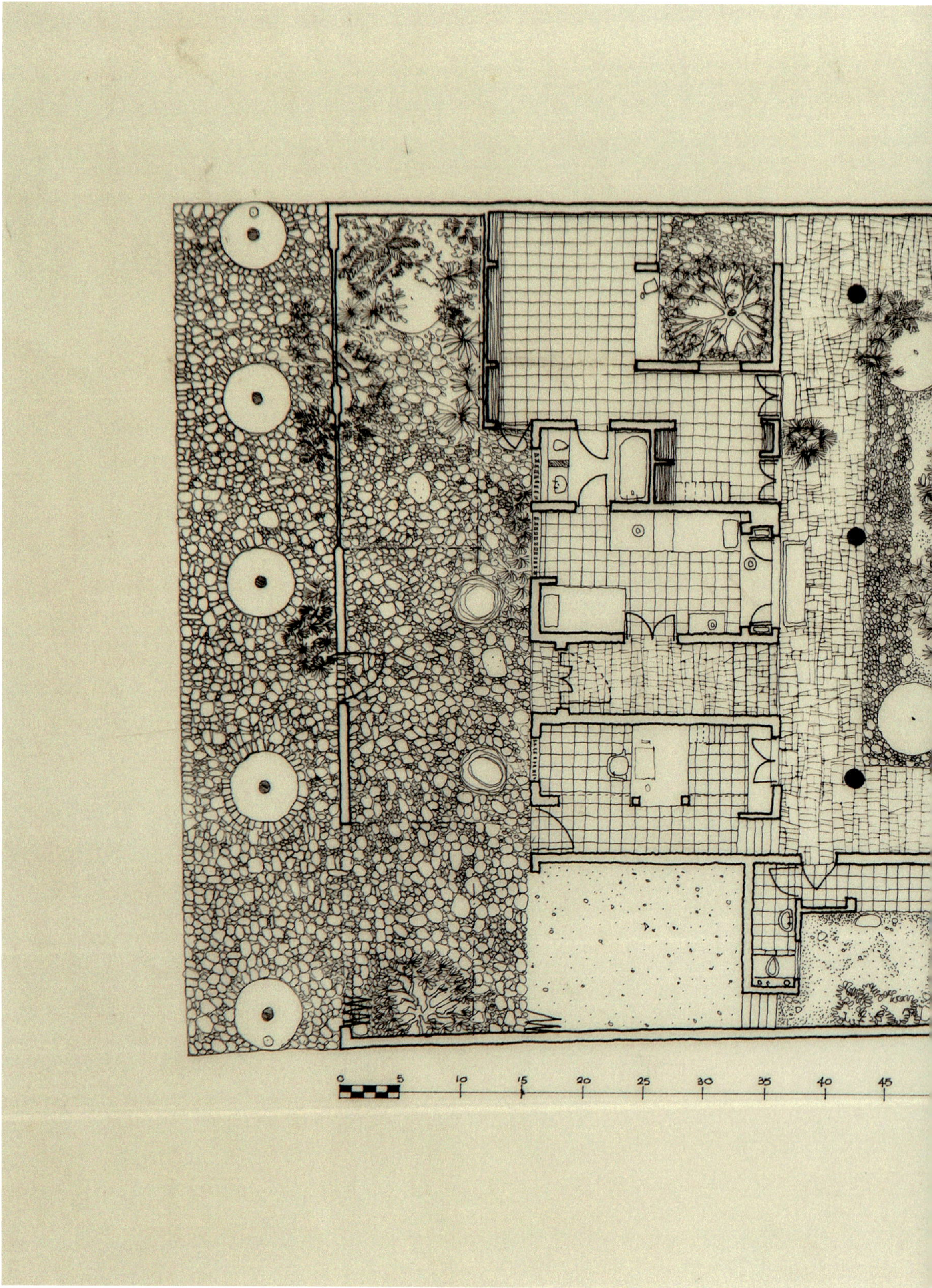

Ground-floor plan, ink on vellum, redrawn by Vernon Nonis (original author unknown; possibly Laki Senanayake), 1962 (redrawn ca. 1986) GB/DA/034/002

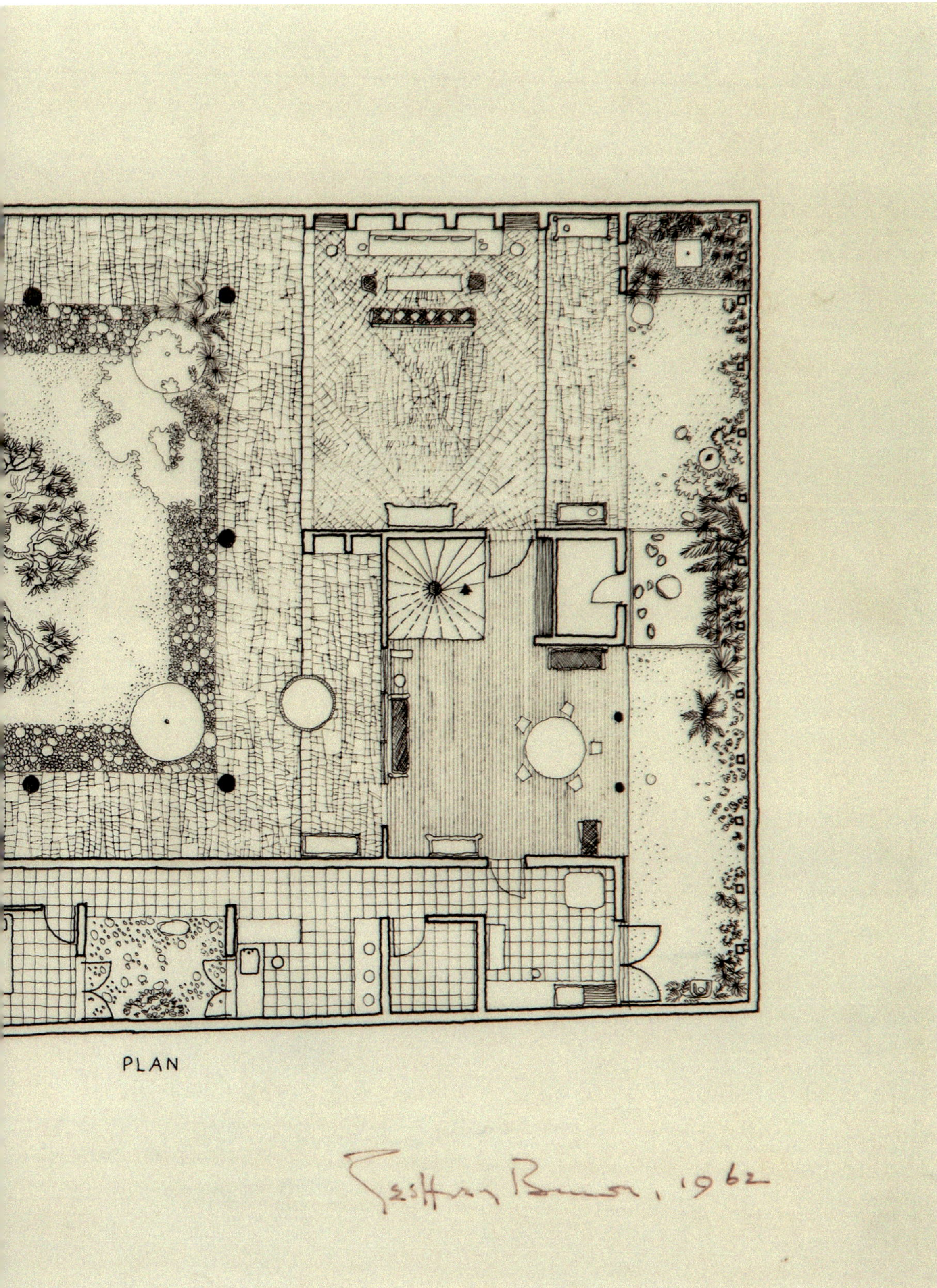
PLAN

Ground-floor bedroom, gelatin silver print, Hélène Binet, 2001 GB/DOC/104/008

View through to courtyard from ground-floor bedroom, gelatin silver print, Hélène Binet, 2001 GB/DOC/104/007

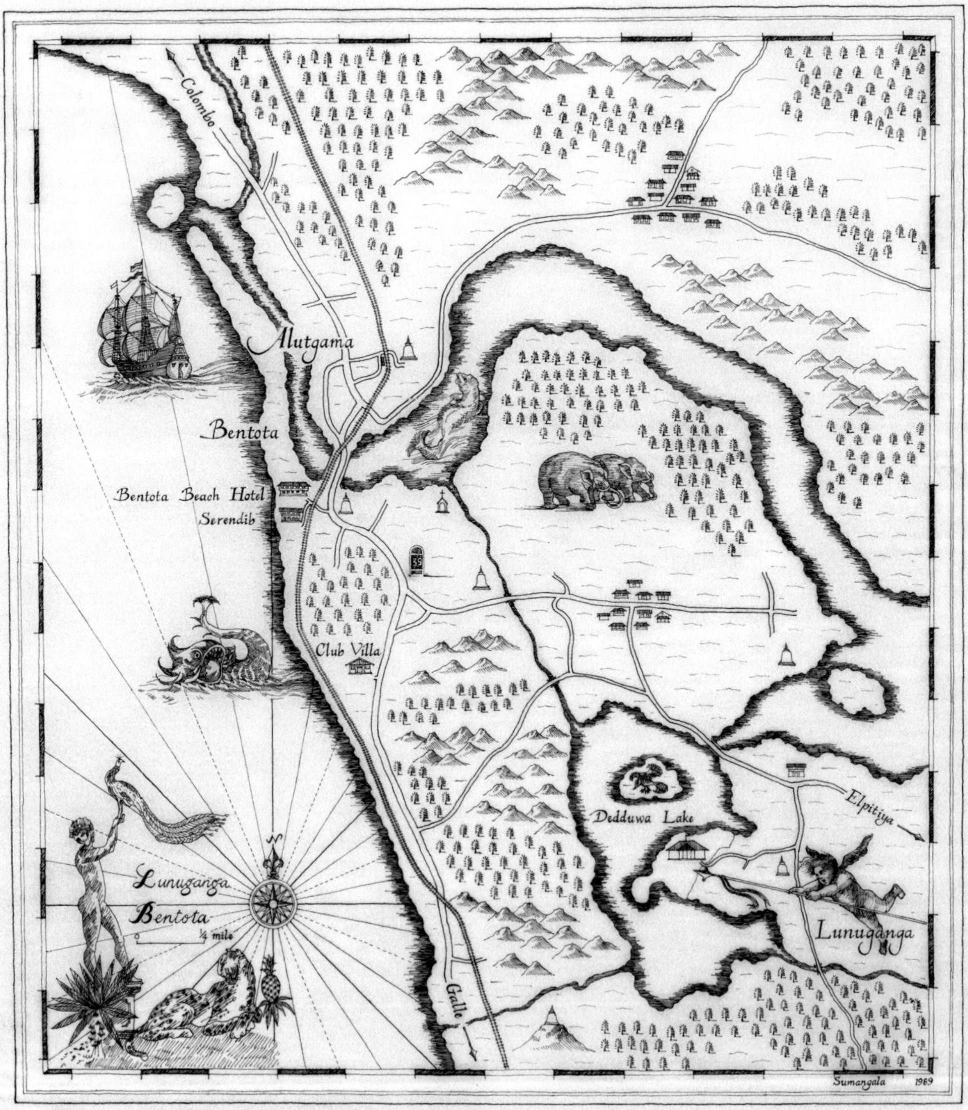

Map to Lunuganga, ink on vellum,
Sumangala Jayatillaka, 1989

The Lore of Lunuganga

Jyoti Dhar

Seen in its original scale, the monstrous creature in the middle of the map appears to have the face of a fish baring its jagged teeth at us, as it matches our gaze head-on. Shrunk down within the page of a book, for which the image was always intended, the monster's face becomes more ambiguous and starts to resemble that of an elephant's with multiple tusks, sitting on the body of a spiky, scaly tail.[1] The hybrid beast, along with other aspects reminding us of seafarers' maps of ancient Lanka – such as a sea serpent in the river, an island in the shape of a giant bird and a majestic ship off the coast of the country – all distract us from the destination of the map.

In the bottom right-hand corner of the drawing, a cherub holding a spear points to a patch of land with a house in the middle of it. Across the cherub's foot reads the lone word: Lunuganga. The word is repeated once more on the drawing, in the opposite corner, next to a cartouche: Lunuganga Bentota, it says. However, it is still not evident from the map as to what Lunuganga is, where exactly it is or how to get to it. A small signature underneath, "Sumangala 1989," helps to orient us and directs us to the fact that the map was drawn more than thirty years ago by the then twenty-nine-year-old artist-turned-architect Sumangala Jayatillaka, upon the suggestion of his mentor Geoffrey Bawa.[2]

A year earlier, Bawa had come across Jayatillaka's architectural drawings and asked him to create various mappings of his own living, growing, evolving home and garden – a place that had been his labor of love for four decades at that point: Lunuganga.[3] Interestingly, the name Lunu-ganga is also a hybrid. *Lunu* means "salt," and *ganga* denotes "river."[4] Bawa named it so after the brackish body of water it rests upon: Dedduwa Lake. We see the lake as one of the few places to be named on the map, along with Alutgama [*sic*] and Bentota, marked on the road from Colombo to Galle. Aside from this, the only other structures to be labeled are Bentota Beach Hotel and Serendib.

Serendib here marks the spot of an eponymous hotel built by Bawa. However, in tandem with its other mythical symbols, this

1 Geoffrey Bawa, Christoph Bon and Dominic Sansoni, *Lunuganga* (Singapore: Times Editions PTE LTD, 1990).
2 "He would never tell you what to do, he would simply drop a seed," Sumangala Jayatillaka said in reference to Geoffrey Bawa. Interview with the author, Colombo, January 2020.
3 The drawings he liked of Jayatillaka's were made around the time Lewcock et al.'s *The Architecture of an Island: The Living Legacy of Sri Lanka* was being prepared. (Colombo: Barefoot (Pvt) Ltd, 1998).
4 This naming of Lunuganga is in keeping with Sinhala place names, where many are compound nouns, with the first half of the name being an adjective and the second referring to a topographical feature of the place.

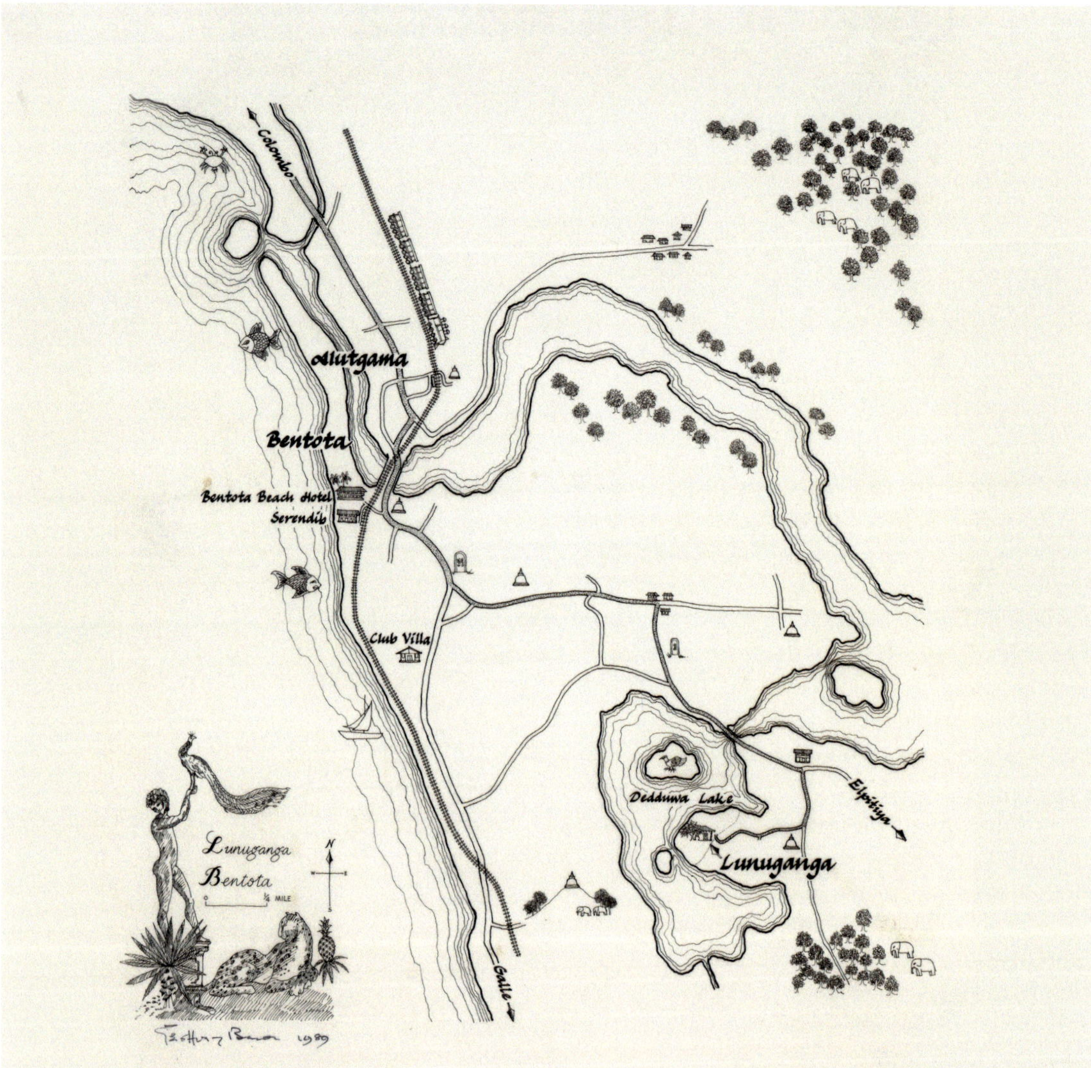

Map to Lunuganga, ink on vellum,
Sumangala Jayatillaka, 1989

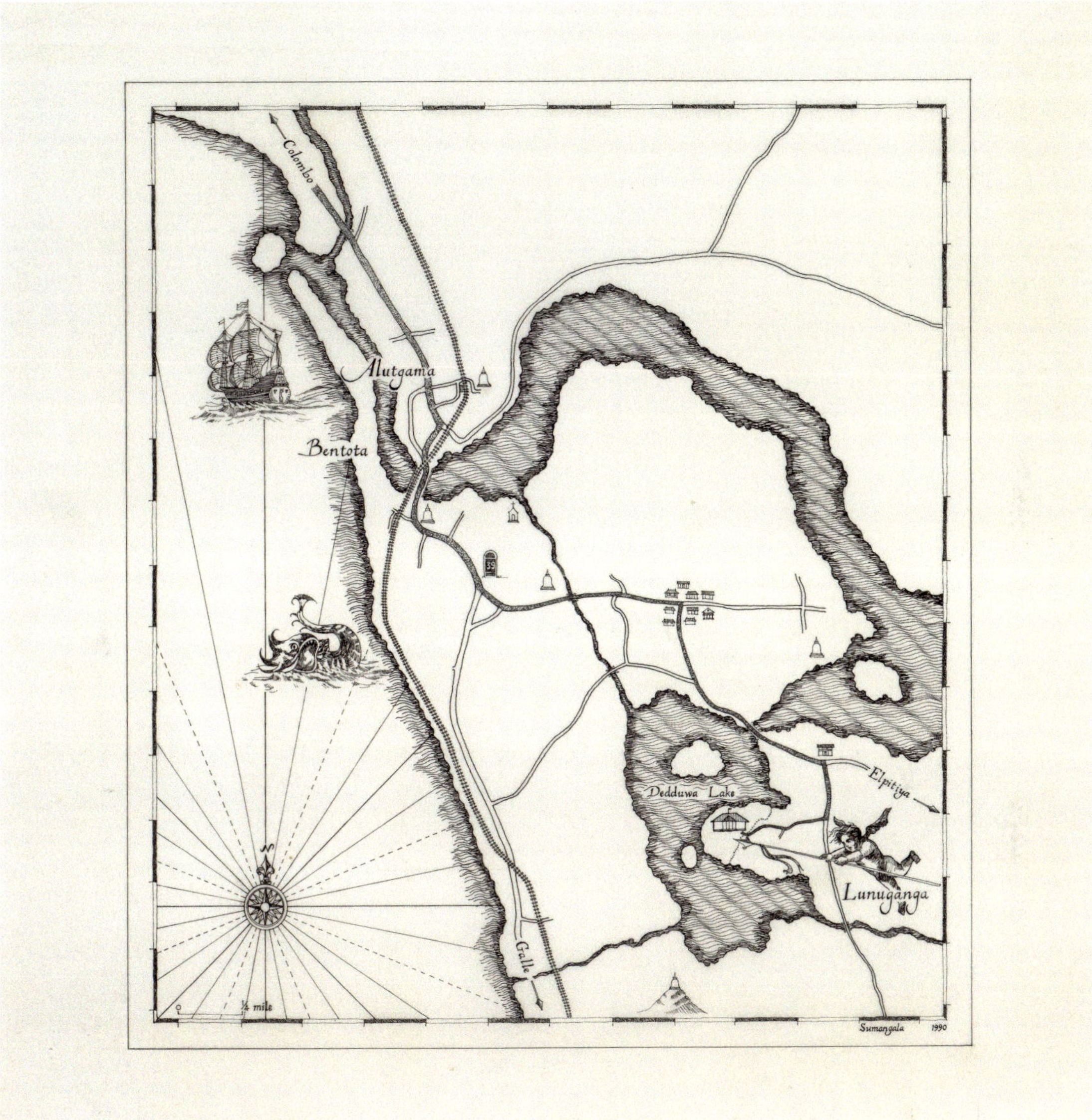

Map to Lunuganga, ink on vellum,
Sumangala Jayatillaka, 1990

olden name of Sri Lanka, conjured up by Arab sailors, adds to the evoking of stories and histories we see throughout the map. For example, historical writer Richard Boyle refers to "giant serpents and strange fish,"[5] like the ones depicted here, in his discussion of Sinbad's voyages to Serendib as chronicled in *One Thousand and One Nights*. Boyle explains that the fish were probably based on Dugong, the marine mammals mistaken for mermaids and known as the "sea equivalent of elephants," which can be found off the coast of Kudremalai.[6]

It becomes clear that the map, much like Lunuganga itself, is a landscape borne from imagination. It takes the real world as a starting point and fills it with otherworldly elements – from fantasy and folklore to myth and magic. We know that Bawa had an avid fascination for ancient maps, and it is not a mistake that the book made to capture the essence of Lunuganga begins with one.[7] However, the more we look at this playful, fantastical map, the more it reiterates the underlying idea that it was not really made for anyone to follow. Instead, just as some of the earliest maps were travel itineraries, this one can be seen as Bawa marking out his own journey to Lunuganga.

Just before Ceylon gained independence from the British in 1948, twenty-nine-year-old lawyer-turned-architect Geoffrey Bawa set off in search of a place he could make his own. In a letter he wrote in the 1980s, Bawa described his initial "quest" to find land with a lake view in Sri Lanka, which had "shades of Lake Guarda" in Italy. Spurred on by his brother, Bevis, who had his own garden estate, he saw more than thirty sites along the Bentota River and in Balapitiya before finding a site with a rubber estate, cinnamon plantation and small hill by the water. "I could begin to mould it into something that would be shaped by my present and future dreams and imaginary," Bawa writes.[8]

From the very beginning, Bawa envisaged Lunuganga as a space for reverie and dreaming – a theatrical setting in which a cast of fictive characters could come and play. We are told that he was inspired by his love of gardens in Europe, which were often filled with mythological sculptures.[9] Critically, Bawa did not transplant this European imagination into a Sri Lankan context; rather, he sculpted a space guided by the local landscape. This approach ties into another idea evoked by the map: that it subverts the colonial notion of discovery or quest. The map's aesthetic mimics those first made of Tabrobane by and for foreigners, yet this one is made by a Sri Lankan.[10]

Another key reversal is that Jayatillaka's drawings, including the map and a number of architectural plans, are made to record the place rather than to plan it.[11] Most architects would do the latter first. In fact, the very first plan of Lunuganga was drawn in 1962 by artist Laki Senanayake – twelve years after it was initially created. One intriguing aspect of Senanayake's plan is the cartouche in the corner, which combines actual and artistic elements

5 Richard Boyle, *Sinbad in Serendib: Strange Tales and Curious Aspects of Sri Lanka* (Colombo: Visidunu Publication, 2008).

6 Kudremalai Point is off the northwestern coast of Sri Lanka.

7 "Bawa was fascinated by old drawings. At one point when he couldn't buy old Ceylon maps, he commissioned an artist in the Rijksmuseum in Amsterdam to copy some of them. Many contained the most extraordinary mythical moments." Channa Daswatte, interview with the author over Zoom, February 2020.

8 Correspondence from Geoffrey Bawa to Jean Chamberlin, undated, GB/DOC/012/09, Box 01, Folder 012, Geoffrey Bawa Archives, Colombo, Sri Lanka.

9 This included the gardens of Villa Caprarola north of Rome to the gardens of Villa Lante in Bagnaia – both filled with myriad examples of Greek and Roman mythology.

10 Claudius Ptolemy, the Greek Egyptian cosmographer, is cited with making some of the first maps of Sri Lanka in 150 AD, known then as Tabrobane, from the Greek Taprobana, adopted from the Sanskrit Tamraparni.

11 "Geoffrey often said that when he went onto a site, he knew the potential it had for life to be lived in it. The drawing was only a way of making others understand. In a way he knew what he was looking for when he found Lunuganga, then he carved it out. The drawing becomes a record of a myth that was in his mind." Channa Daswatte, interview with the author over Zoom, February 2020.

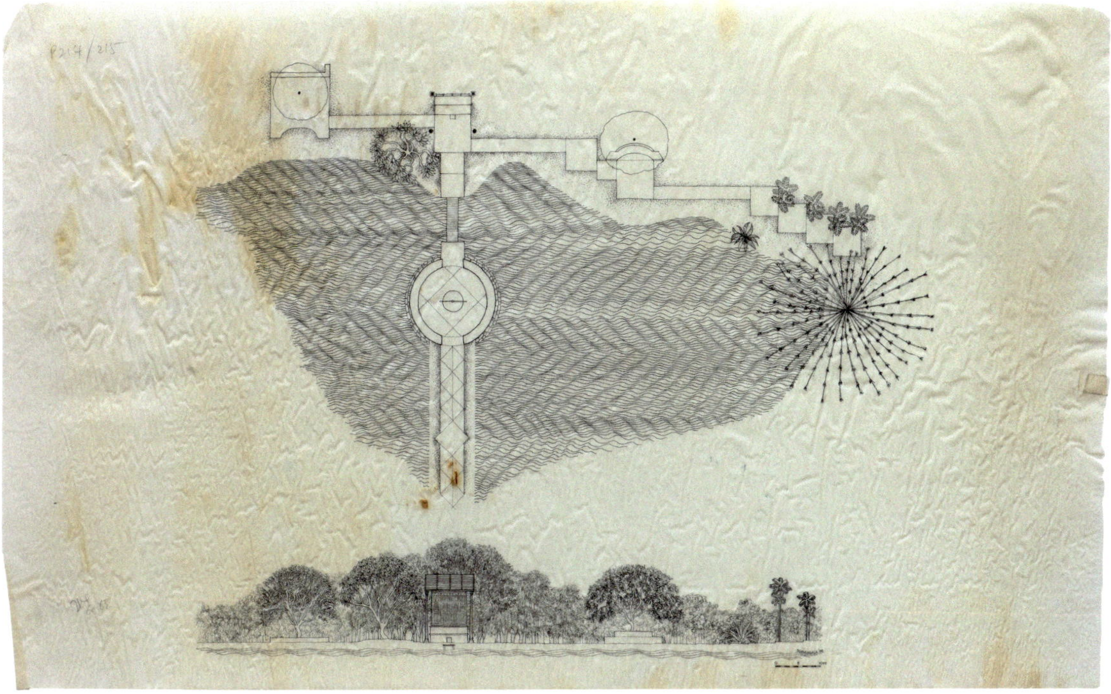

Lunuganga, Bentota, plan and elevation of the "Black Pavilion," ink on tracing paper, Sumangala Jayatillaka, 1990

Leopard by Lidia Duchini, Lunuganga, gelatin silver print, Christoph Bon (attributed), ca. 1988

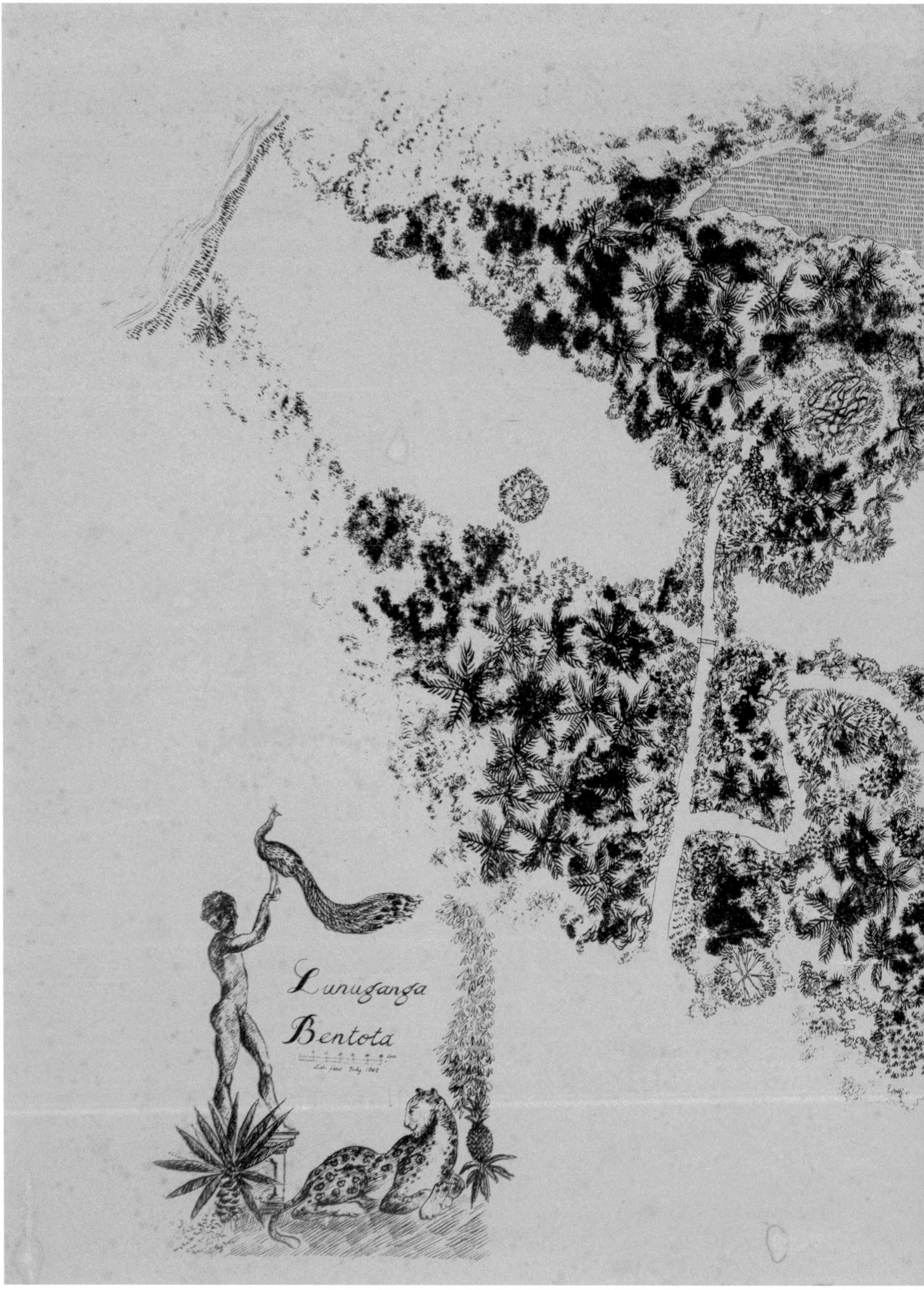

Lunuganga, Bentota, Lunuganga plan,
ink on tracing paper, Laki Senanayake, 1962

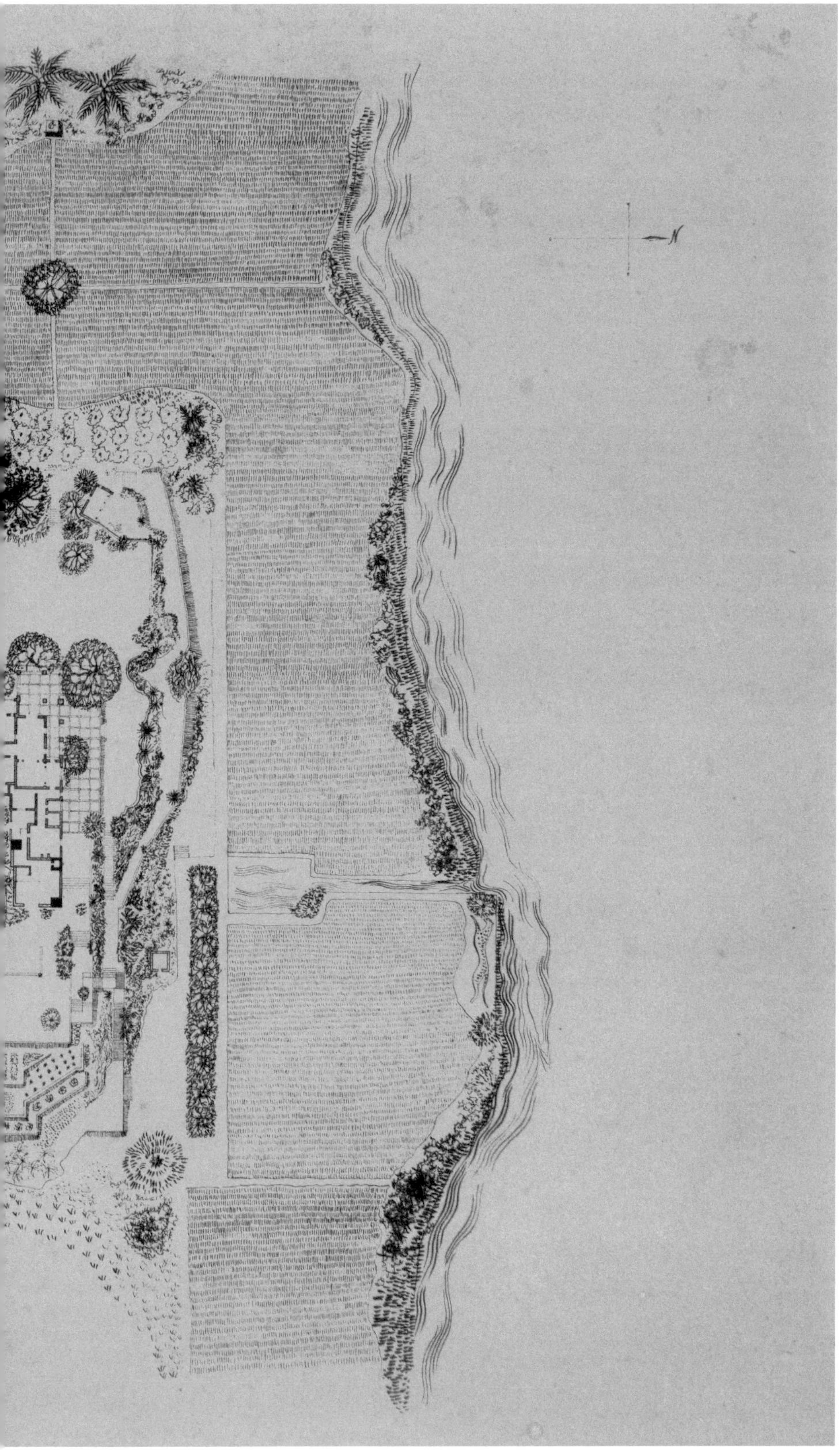
N

Lunuganga, Bentota, panorama of eastern terraces, ink on vellum, Sumangala Jayatillaka, 1988

SUMANGALA '88
141

reflected in the garden: the nude male figure is mirrored in the Roman statues seen around the estate, the sideways-seated leopard has a sculptural equivalent guarding the lake and the pineapple nods to the garden's pineapple fields.[12]

It is not so surprising that Bawa chose those with both an artistic and architectural sensibility to provide mappings and impressions for his book on Lunuganga. What is less discussed, though, is the mythology from a multitude of cultures which prevails throughout the drawings, book and garden. In the book, we see representations of centaurs, nagas and fauns (all hybrid, all half-human, half-animal) sitting side-by-side with Bawa's descriptions of a restless spirit of a dead monk who lives in a tree and the view of a place with buried treasure belonging to "Prince Doravana."[13] In the garden too are sculptures of "Horned Pan" and Janus as well as a "Serpentine Wall."[14]

One of the most symbolic drawings to be found in the Garden Room at Lunuganga, which is replicated in the book, is that of an imaginary scene depicting a person being carried in a palanquin in the "Field of Jars" – a space in the garden so called for its Chinese jars, said to have been brought to Sri Lanka by Portuguese traders in the sixteenth century.[15] Viewed together, such elements can be seen as evidence of how Lunuganga is viewed as a place full of stories, real and imagined, told and untold, by Bawa and those he invites into it. Again, this can be seen as an extension of a concept with local roots; that of *itihasaya*, the Sinhala word derived from the Sanskrit *itihas*, which means both "story" and "history."[16]

This adds to what those close to Bawa say, that he understood Lunuganga as an extension of its local surroundings, as a microcosm of Sri Lanka itself.[17] Apparently, he even saw the Buddhist stupa five kilometers away and the small island in Dedduwa Lake – both of which can be seen on Jayatillaka's map – as part of his extended garden. While Bawa's anecdotes and artifacts gesture toward multiple narratives, it is the garden that ultimately animates them. It was this realization that Jayatillaka had when spending time in Lunuganga, walking around and experiencing it while he was drawing his plans and map, that "living in Lunuganga is like living inside a book."[18]

Jayatillaka's notion is made manifest in "The Middle Walk," a path which connects down to the "Butterfly Lake," "Black Pavilion," "Field of Jars" and "Blue Pavilion," as well as up to Bawa's house.[19] With each possibility, one could indeed be in a fictional tale – perhaps that of "The Garden of Forking Paths,"[20] which, much like *One Thousand and One Nights* is also known as "a story within a story."[21] Is it possible that Bawa not only saw Lunuganga as a "garden within a garden,"[22] but also as a story within a story? It seems that Lunuganga offers us the space for such musings and new interpretations, continuing the legacy of those of old, from Lanka, Tabrobane, Serendib and Ceylon.

12 This cartouche later became the Bawa Trust's logo. Senanayake is credited with being the first one in the practice to incorporate elements of allegory and fantasy, such as leopards and centaurs, into these architectural drawings. These elements would add layers and, according to those close to him, brought the drawing closer to the building that was in Geoffrey's imagination.

13 Bawa, Bon and Sansoni, *Lunuganga,* 11 and 85.

14 Bawa, Bon and Sansoni, *Lunuganga,* 39 and 75.

15 Untitled work by artist and architect Gopinath Amarasinghe, 1986.

16 The *Mahavamsa* and *Mahabharata* are examples of epics that told history and were also filled with fables.

17 "People have been living in Sri Lanka for thousands of years, so Geoffrey saw it as a manicured landscape. He would look out at the hills, paddy fields and waterfalls, and see it all as part of a larger garden, as much as his own finely tuned one." Channa Daswatte, interview with the author over Zoom, February 2020.

18 Sumangala Jayatillaka, interview with the author, Colombo, January 2020.

19 Bawa, Bon and Sansoni, *Lunuganga,* 101–19.

20 Jorge Luis Borges, "The Garden of Forking Paths," in *Collected Fictions*, trans. Andrew Hurley (New York: Penguin, 1999) 119–28.

21 Numerous scholars have discussed how Borges's writing was influenced by *One Thousand and One Nights*.

22 Bawa, Bon and Sansoni, *Lunuganga,* 11.

Imagined scene in the Field of Jars,
ink on paper, Gopinath Amarasinghe, 1986

Lunuganga, Bentota, view of the pond
in the Field of Jars, gelatin silver print

Lunuganga, Bentota, view from the paved upper terrace down to the horned Hindu Pan sculpture, flooded rice fields and the northern lake, gelatin silver print

"It was under English trees that I meditated on that lost labyrinth: I pictured it perfect and inviolate on the secret summit of a mountain; I pictured its outlines blurred by rice paddies, or underwater; I pictured it as infinite – a labyrinth not of octagonal pavilions and paths that turn back on themselves, but of rivers and provinces and kingdoms.... I imagined a labyrinth of labyrinths, a maze of mazes, a twisting, turning, ever-widening labyrinth that contained both past and future and somehow implied the stars. Absorbed in those illusory imaginings, I forgot that I was a pursued man; I felt myself, for an indefinite while, the abstract perceiver of the world. The vague, living countryside, the moon, the remains of the day did their work in me; so did the gently downward road, which forestalled all possibility of weariness. The evening was near, yet infinite.

The road dropped and forked as it cut through the now-formless meadows. A keen and vaguely syllabic song, blurred by leaves and distance, came and went on the gentle gusts of breeze."

Jorge Luis Borges, "The Garden of Forking Paths," 1941

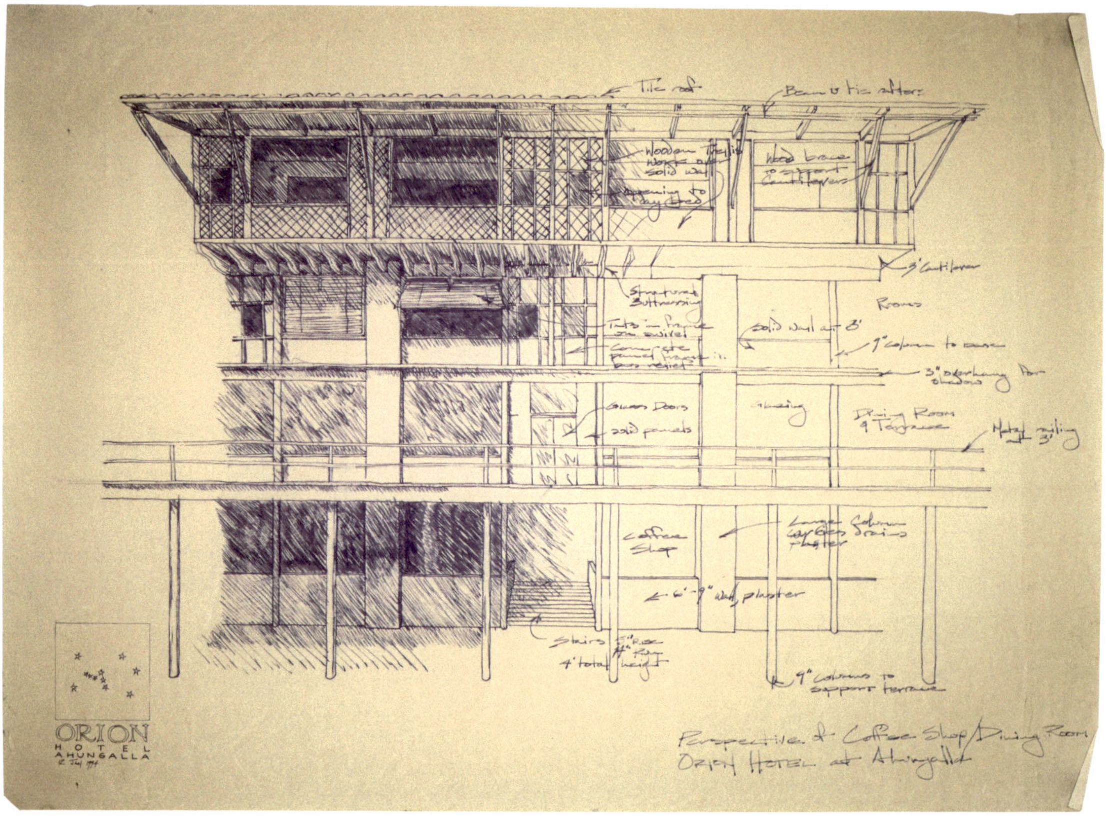

Orion Hotel, Ahungalla, partial building elevation of coffee shop, ink on paper, Erik Tellender, 1992

Rendering Place: On the Importance of Archives

Tariq Jazeel

What Does a Drawing Do?

Some years ago, I was lucky enough to be able to shadow two exceptional young architects who were interning at a Colombo-based firm known for its work in the "tropical style." I was conducting research for what would become a book on this kind of architecture: a book that attempted to situate the style within its wider social and cultural terrain.[1] One afternoon, the interns showed me some architectural drawings of an estate on which they were working. The drawings looked fairly typical to my architecturally untrained eye. Straight, clean and fine pen lines marked with precision, confidence and apparent scalar accuracy an overhead view of a plot that could have been any location in the world. The whole plan was scored with marks of measurement that authoritatively denoted metered architectural modernity. "It's dead," said one of the interns. She elaborated on what she meant, stressing that she did not like the clean, geometric, ruled-line method of architectural drawing, because it purges plans of the spatial fluidity and sense of place that architects in the tropics work hard to produce. The clean, straight line, she told me, does not lend itself to the interplay of inside and outside that is her practice's preferred aesthetic register. She went on to explain how, as a matter of course, she and her colleagues overscore the clinical exactitude of technical drawings with a free hand and impressionistic pen, lending to them what she referred to as "a kind of shaky effect" that gives the drawings "life." Drawing like this, she and her companion explained, aims for a detailed yet simultaneously poetic depiction of spatial design. What became clear to me was that for these architects, drawing was not simply representational in any direct or mimetic manner vis-à-vis the plots or buildings on which they worked. Instead, for architects in this region, drawing performs ideas and geographical imaginations, and as such it acts as a kind of interface between viewing subjects. And insofar as it does this kind of relational work, the practice of drawing cannot be pinned down by the clinical instrumentality

1 Tariq Jazeel, *Sacred Modernity: Nature, Environment and the Postcolonial Geographies of Sri Lankan Nationhood* (Liverpool: Liverpool University Press, 2013).

of technical plans. Rather, it articulates ideas, attitudes, poetics and a sense of place.

That this young architect's predilection for what she referred to as the "shaky effect" was no idiosyncratic quirk is a point that the texts in this anthology make very clear. She and her companion told me how, at their architectural school, their instructors look and give credit for this kind of "eye" and aesthetic disposition in their drawings. They referred to the technique as *rendering*, a process that merges technical and artistic processes, one which has a genealogy that is associated with the Bawa office. It was Laki Senanayake and Ismeth Raheem who first began to render architectural drawings this way in the early 1960s.[2] They in turn were influenced by Donald Friend, the now disgraced Australian artist and friend of Geoffrey Bawa's brother, Bevis. Their attempt to render grew out of a dissatisfaction with architectural modernism's uneasy relationship with site, where trees, shrubs and other unique features were represented by abstract geometric symbols whose sole purpose was to locate them on a plot.[3] For Senanayake and Raheem, this kind of abstraction was entirely at odds with the concerted attempt at opening houses and structures out, allowing inside and outside to merge, and building with and through trees, shrubs and other site-specific environmental features and indeed the landscape itself, all of which tactics were emerging as the hallmarks of the style of building practice in postindependence Sri Lanka. To render was, for Senanayake and Raheem, a completely different way of attuning viewers with site, intention and the particular kind of spatial experience that the architecture engendered.

2 David Robson, *Beyond Bawa: Modern Masterworks of Monsoon Asia* (London: Thames & Hudson, 2007), 49–60.

3 Jazeel, *Sacred Modernity*, 154.

Rajamaha Viharaya, Kelaniya, elevation, ink on tracing paper, Turner Wickramasinghe (attributed), 1968

Ena de Silva House, Colombo, section, ink on tracing paper, Laki Senanayake, 1963

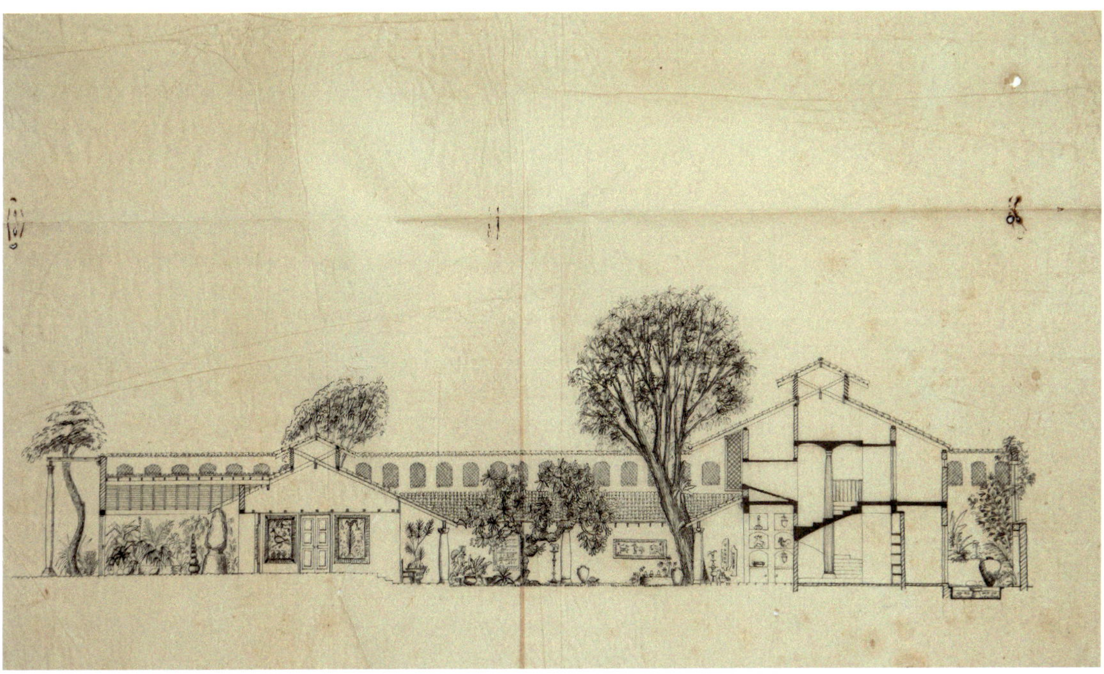

As David Robson puts it, "Senanayake's section of the Ena de Silva House, drawn in 1962, using an old fashioned dip-pen, is a phenomenological representation which tries to reproduce the emotional experience of inhabiting the space. The drawing blurs the distinction between the inside and outside and represents trees with botanical authenticity."[4]

Rendering is a word that usefully conveys much more than just a style of architectural drawing. To render is also to make, to cause to be or become. And as I have been suggesting, the drawings associated with the Bawa office do much more than the instrumentalist drawings traditionally associated with architectural modernism; they are drawings that play a constitutive role in causing this architecture to be or become what its architects intend it to mean. They are devices that help an architect convey spatial meaning and experience to those who might view the drawing. They are therefore representations that are a constitutive part of built space's meaning and should be seen as such by historians of the style and beyond.[5] This, in part, is why the Bawa Archives are such a valuable resource for anyone interested not just in the history of Sri Lanka's architecture, but also how we might begin to situate this form of cultural production in its wider social, cultural and indeed, political currents.

Architecture's Expanded Field

As the literary critic Peter Bürger argues in relation to the avant-garde, works of art are never received as single entities but instead within the institutional frameworks and conditions that help to determine the functions, meanings and social effects of those works of art.[6] Like great writers, musicians and artists, architects too work within historical, social and cultural contexts. Indeed, critics and theorists of modernism have long noted the hollowness of any modernist movement's claim to artistic autonomy, and as I argue below, what emerged as Sri Lanka's postindependence architectural style sits in close proximity to the mid-twentieth-century emergence of Sri Lanka's modern art movement.[7] The Bawa Archives offer us an insight into the broader terrain of architecture conceived, as I would argue we must, as part of the broader terrain of postcolonial modernism in Sri Lanka, a field of cultural production as much as an autonomous style. To this extent, it is not too much of a leap for the critical imagination to connect the process of rendering, considered as a kind of drawing that helps to produce architectural meaning, to a broader textual field that likewise helps to render the work that architecture does in and through society. For if my argument thus far is that architecture cannot be understood through buildings alone, then it follows that the Bawa Archives can show us the historical, social and cultural contexts through which his work came to mean, and be positioned semantically and symbolically, within postcolonial

4 David Robson, Dominic Sansoni and Michael Ondaatje, *The Architectural Heritage of Sri Lanka: Measured Drawings from the Anjalendran Studio* (London: Talisman/Laurence King, 2016), 35.

5 See Denis Cosgrove, *Social Formation and Symbolic Landscape*, 2nd ed. (Madison: University of Wisconsin Press, 1998).

6 Peter Bürger, *Theory of the Avant-Garde*, trans. Michael Shaw (Minneapolis: University of Minnesota Press, 1984), 12.

7 For example, see Andreas Huyssen, *After the Great Divide: Modernism, Mass Culture, Postmodernism* (Bloomington: Indiana University Press, 1986).

Sri Lanka. As the architect and architectural critic Jeremy Till contends, although the profession of architecture is often thought of as self-contained and internally defined, "the practice of architecture is a set of external networks, and necessarily dependent."[8] Built space was, and is, dependent on myriad other registers including, for example, client demand, political economy, planning and zoning regulations, prevailing religious and political currents, taste, its own heritage industry and, of course, mere happenstance. But to say it is merely dependent on those external networks and factors is to underplay the role that architecture historically plays in shaping those complex assemblages of political economy, prevailing religious and political currents, vagaries of taste, and so on.[9] Indeed, no architecture can be unpicked from the patina of the culture, society and zeitgeist in which it both emerges and participates. In other words, architecture is in and of this world.

Inspired by the art historian Rosalind E. Krauss's seminal attempt to place modernist sculpture of the 1960s in a relationship to other nonsculptural forms, the architectural theorist Anthony Vidler has suggested the value of what he refers to as "not-exactly-architecture" for understanding the broader ecologies of architectural practice.[10] If Vidler, after Krauss, teaches us that architecture necessarily exists in a broader "expanded field," then architecture's archival traces take on huge significance for anyone interested in the archaeological work of placing built space in the broader contextual histories in which it inevitably and invariably participated. Despite Bawa's well-known reluctance to speak or write about his work during his own lifetime, indeed perhaps because of it, the intertextual terrain of his "not-exactly-architecture" in the archives offers valuable material for contextualizing an architectural practice.

This begs a question of methodology: how might we go about this kind of archaeological work? In the next section, I offer a few scattered speculations on this methodological question by turning to the work not of Bawa, but of his contemporary Minnette de Silva, whose architectural innovation we know influenced Bawa, and who was much more public about her process, influences and architectural intention. Before doing so, however, I want to point to some of the rare instances where Geoffrey Bawa did speak about his work, for these tantalizing glimpses should tweak our interest, push us to the archives, toward the broader expanded field of his practice, such that we might begin to situate and read his work contextually. The examples I tease out are from the 1990 book *Lunuganga*, a project largely steered by Christoph Bon and Jean Chamberlin and photographed by Christoph Bon and Dominic Sansoni but is punctuated with Bawa's narrative voice, which at key moments wonderfully elaborates on the aesthetic domain of his estate. Though Bawa, Bon and Sansoni share authorship of this

8 Jeremy Till, *Architecture Depends* (Cambridge, MA: MIT Press, 2009), 161.
9 For an elaboration on this, see Jazeel, *Sacred Modernity*, chapters 5–7.

Front terrace at Lunuganga, gelatin silver print, Christoph Bon, ca. 1988

very beautiful book, fragments in Bawa's own voice dot the text, making its sumptuous content sparkle. Relatively early in the book, for example, Bawa describes the hard and deliberate work of producing atmospheres across the estate; atmospheres that for all intents and purposes appear, as he stresses, both natural and timeless: "Over the years moving through the garden as it grew, one saw the potential of various areas which had inherently different atmospheres. For instance, the long view to the south ended with the temple, but in the middle distance was a ridge with a splendid ancient *moonamal* tree and when I placed a large Chinese jar under it, the hand of man was established in this middle distance. Now the eye stops here, travels to the glimmer of the lake beyond, to the slope across a long stretch of rice fields and to the stupa on the crown of the far hill across the lake. In this view the vision of the lake was too slight to be effective and it soon became obvious that a part of the ridge needed to be lowered a few feet to make this whole composition establish itself with a total finality which has not changed and now looks as if it had been there since the beginning of time."[11]

What Bawa describes is a view that extends through and beyond his estate, one that he has carefully choreographed to appear and feel timeless. In other words, he intimates that a crucial part of the architectural labor at Lunuganga was geared toward seamlessly settling the estate within its historical and geographical contexts. After all, in the composition's "total finality," neither the spatial extent of Bawa's estate nor its historical parameters are in any sense clear. The timeless nature of this view, as well as its spatial fluidity, is precisely the compositional aim. Just a couple of pages earlier, the book remarks that "Lunuganga from the start was to be an extension of its surroundings – a garden within a garden."[12] And much later – in the very last line of the epilogue in fact – in reflecting upon Lunuganga, Bawa defers to the words of a visiting driver who, upon making a delivery, took the opportunity to walk around the estate. Bawa writes, or is quoted as saying, that "when his bricks

10 Anthony Vidler, "Architecture's Expanded Field," *Artforum* 42, no. 8 (2004): 142–48; see also Rosalind E. Krauss, "Sculpture in the Expanded Field," *October*, no. 8 (1979): 30–44.
11 Bawa in Geoffrey Bawa, Christoph Bon and Dominic Sansoni, *Lunuganga* (Singapore: Times Editions, 1990), 13.
12 Bawa, Bon and Sansoni, *Lunuganga*, 11.

were being loaded – [the truck driver] said to me – මේක නං හරි සීදේවි තැනක් (but this is a very blessed place)."[13] In this high-quality, black-and-white English-language book, it is significant that Bawa, Bon and Sansoni leave the last word on the estate to one whom we can reasonably assume to be a working-class truck driver speaking in Sinhalese, for this indicates a folkish endorsement of his gentle modernism. It is, in other words, Lunuganga's very ordinariness in that spatial context that makes it a blessed place. If these fragments of "not-exactly-architecture" hint at Bawa's authorial intention that Lunuganga merge into the environment beyond, they also leave open further questions regarding what kind of ordinariness he aimed at with Lunuganga. From which folk does Bawa seek acceptance and why? And in what historiographical context does Lunuganga's timelessness make sense? In the rest of this essay I elaborate on why and how archives might help us in answering questions of this nature by turning to one of Bawa's contemporaries, Minnette de Silva, an architect who, as I have stressed, was keen to publicly contextualize her own architectural practice.

A Fish Describing the Water in Which It Swims

Minnette de Silva was the first of her talented generation of mid-twentieth-century Ceylonese architects to begin the process of adapting international modernism to the climate and superabundant growth of their native tropical environment.[14] She began to practice in 1948 following her return to Ceylon from London's Architectural Association (AA). Unlike Bawa's portfolio however, the vast majority of de Silva's built work no longer exists. As such, any analysis of de Silva's architecture must negotiate its material absence, and it is in this context that we must turn to the importance of "not-exactly-architecture" for a proper understanding of her practice.[15] Our attempts, therefore, to understand de Silva's practice can teach us a lot about how to approach the Bawa Archives.

Having said this, there is no publicly accessible archive of de Silva's drawings or other textual fragments testifying to her practice. However, before she died, de Silva put together a memoir with the help of architect Ashley de Vos, *The Life and Work of an Asian Woman Architect*, which was eventually published a few weeks after her death in 1998. At once scrapbook, diary, coffee-table book, catalogue raisonné and a compilation of her work and other fragments, it is an invaluable resource for any scholar of her work. It is part bildungsroman, part portfolio, equally committed to documenting family biography, a history of Sri Lanka and her intellectual concerns.[16] It is chaotic, difficult to follow, but also a treasure chest full with de Silva's iterations, thoughts, ideas and glimpses into her main influences, both professional and personal. It remains the only book-length work of nonfiction on Minnette de Silva (at the time of writing) and is a valuable document not

13 Bawa, Bon and Sansoni, *Lunuganga*, 219.

14 For more on Minnette de Silva, see Tariq Jazeel, "Tropical Modernism/Environmental Nationalism: the Politics of Built Space in Postcolonial Sri Lanka," *Fabrications: The Journal of the Society of Architectural Historians, Australia and New Zealand* 27, no. 2 (2017): 134–52; and David Robson, "Andrew Boyd and Minnette de Silva: Two Pioneers of Modernism in Ceylon," *Thinkmatter: Architecture in India* (2015), thinkmatter.in/2015/03/04/andrew-boyd-and-minnette-de-silva-two-pioneers-of-modernism-in-ceylon (accessed May 11, 2020).

15 The combined reasons why much of de Silva's portfolio has not survived materially certainly warrants further and full exploration that is beyond the scope of this essay. While the emergence of a modern architectural heritage in Sri Lanka has overwhelmingly focused on preserving the undeniably important work of Geoffrey Bawa, de Silva's less acclaimed, earlier, and pioneering output has too easily fallen prey to the developer's wrecking ball.

16 For a discussion of the book, see Anooradha Iyer Siddiqi, "Crafting the Archive: Minnette de Silva, Architecture, and History," *The Journal of Architecture* 22, no. 8 (2017): 1299–366.

Spread from *The Life & Work of an Asian Woman Architect*, Minnette de Silva, 1998

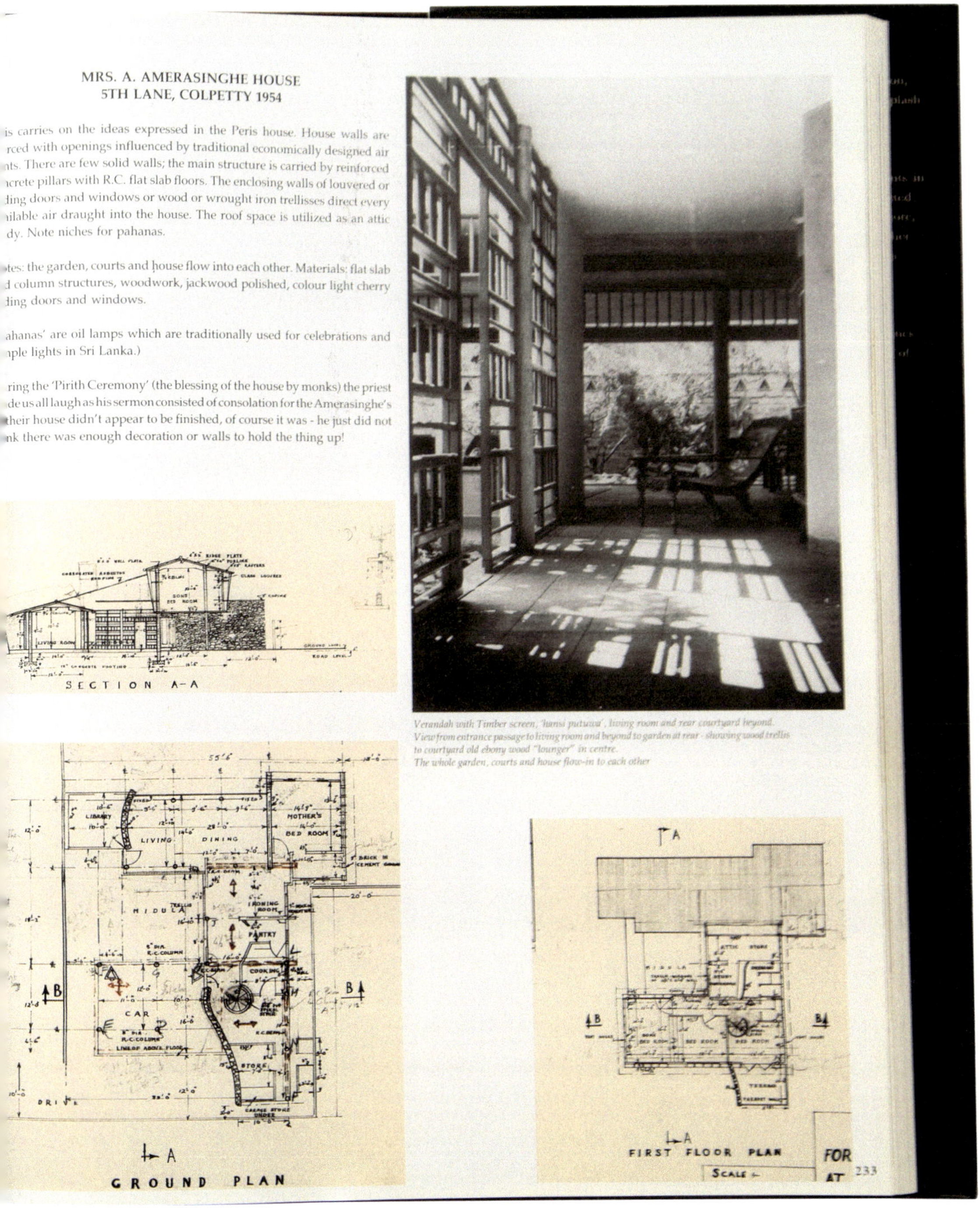

MRS. A. AMERASINGHE HOUSE
5TH LANE, COLPETTY 1954

is carries on the ideas expressed in the Peris house. House walls are rced with openings influenced by traditional economically designed air nts. There are few solid walls; the main structure is carried by reinforced ıcrete pillars with R.C. flat slab floors. The enclosing walls of louvered or ding doors and windows or wood or wrought iron trellisses direct every ıilable air draught into the house. The roof space is utilized as an attic dy. Note niches for pahanas.

ıtes: the garden, courts and house flow into each other. Materials: flat slab d column structures, woodwork, jackwood polished, colour light cherry ding doors and windows.

ahanas' are oil lamps which are traditionally used for celebrations and ıple lights in Sri Lanka.)

ring the 'Pirith Ceremony' (the blessing of the house by monks) the priest de us all laugh as his sermon consisted of consolation for the Amerasinghe's their house didn't appear to be finished, of course it was - he just did not nk there was enough decoration or walls to hold the thing up!

Verandah with Timber screen, 'lumsi putuwa', living room and rear courtyard beyond.
View from entrance passage to living room and beyond to garden at rear - showing wood trellis to courtyard old ebony wood "lounger" in centre.
The whole garden, courts and house flow-in to each other

233

PIERIS HOUSE
ALFRED HOUSE GARDENS, COLOMBO 3 - 1952-56

(Extracts from an article)

High walls enclose the garden and house, shutting out the dust and noise and curious passers-by. The main rooms look into courtyards or *midulas* of the house with a place for games, a place for sitting out, an enclosure for open-air bathing and space for walks and flowers and pools. All this was integrated into one. Few heavy walls block the vista of pillared hall; looking through to an inner courtyard and onto another room or loggia and behind this again to a rear courtyard garden. The air flows through the house and up through the *midula* to upper floors. Fifteen or twenty perches of ground appear double the size. No space is wasted in pretentious inadequate drive ways. You drive straight under or beside your house. All the garden area possible is collected within for the enjoyment of the householder.

The house was carried on reinforced concrete columns with a rei concrete flat slab construction (the first in Sri Lanka) designed by C Wood of Ove Arup and Partners. All rooms were conceived as ve rooms with sliding doors to one or two sides.

The Pieris' were great family friends - Ian used to drive me to schoo me do whatever I liked with the house - he'd argue, but in the end I'd own way. So the house was quite revolutionary at the time - with it and free-flowing spaces. The letters show Ian despairing of my disap act, but I had to get away. The isolation in Ceylon was overbear having grown up in many worlds that of Ceylon and India and Europe, the need to be involved with European civilization too, was Anyway, he commissioned me to do another house next door in 19 can't have been too disastrous.

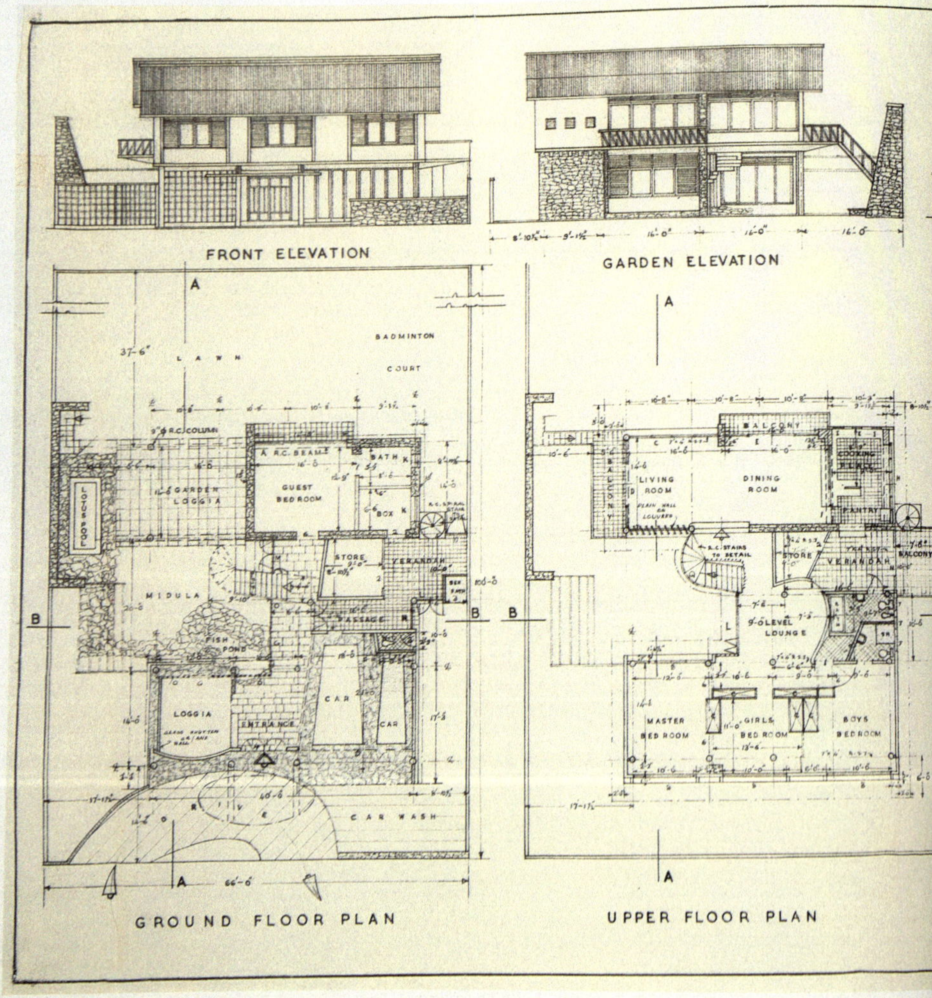

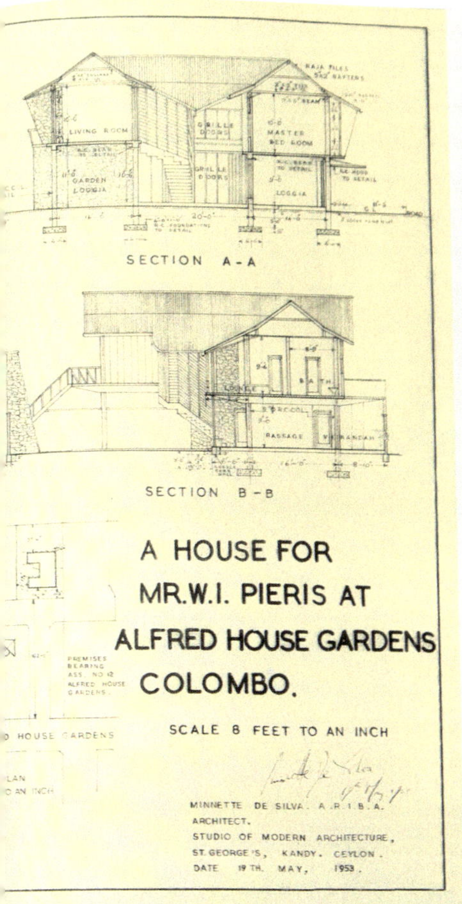

OVE ARUP & PARTNERS CHARTERED CIVIL ENGINEERS

8 FITZROY STREET LONDON W1 TELEPHONE LANGHAM 7781/5

813 JJT/EC 19th November, 1953

Minette de Silva,
Studio of Modern Architecture,
Kandy,
Ceylon.

Dear Madam,

House at Alfred House Gardens - Colombo.

We have forwarded per surface mail two copies of each of our drawings Nos. 813/2, 3 & 4, being reinforced concrete details of the above job, and three copies each of bending schedules 2/1, 2/2, 2/3, 2/4; 3/1, 3/2, 3/3 and 4/3.

If further copies are required would you please let us know.

Yours faithfully,
for OVE ARUP & PARTNERS.

J.J. THOMSON.

U.S.C.per surface mail
813/2,3,& 4. + B.S.

just because of its descriptions, drawings and photographs of buildings long since demolished but also for its collected ephemera that enable us to place her work in its wider field of cultural production. As the architectural historian Anooradha Iyer Siddiqi has written, the book is valuable because it is a rare case of a fish describing the water in which it swims.[17]

Feminist and Subaltern historical methodologies draw attention to the importance of reading archives across and against their grains, looking for the gaps, tensions and anxieties in private or quasi-public collections.[18] This disposition is well rewarded when it comes to orienting oneself to de Silva's book. From de Silva's memoir we are able to locate her practice within Ceylon's broader postcolonial and ethnonational social and political currents. Take, for example, her description of the 1954 house she designed for Mrs. A. Amerasinghe: "House walls are pierced with openings influenced by traditional economically designed air vents. There are few solid walls; the main structure is carried by reinforced concrete pillars with R.C. flat slab floors. The enclosing walls of louvered or sliding doors and windows or wood or wrought iron trellises direct every available air draught into the house. The roof space is utilized as an attic study. Note niches for *pahanas*. Notes: the garden, courts and house flow into each other. Materials: flat slab and column structures, woodwork, jackwood polished, colour light cherry sliding doors and windows. (*Pahanas* are oil lamps which are traditionally used for celebrations and temple lights in Sri Lanka.) During the Pirith Ceremony (the blessing of the house by monks) the priest made us all laugh as his sermon consisted of consolation for the Amerasinghes as their house didn't appear to be finished, of course it was – he just did not think there was enough decoration or walls to hold the thing up!"[19]

De Silva's clients, the Amerasinghes, were a middle-class, professional nuclear family, both Buddhist and Sinhalese, but not implicated in the populist Sinhala Buddhist nationalism of mid-1950s Ceylon. The priest and monks invited to bless the house represent a public institution (the Buddhist clergy) of considerable power and far closer to populist nationalism at the time. As such, what interests me about the excerpt above are the lengths to which de Silva goes to distinguish her modern architectural sensibility from the priest's fear that the house did not appear to be finished. Given de Silva describes an encounter that took place just two years before Ceylon's 1956 ethnic riots and Sinhala-only language bill in a historical conjuncture when there was growing popular dissatisfaction with the pluralist policies of the UNP government, her laughter at the priest's incomprehension of the house's structural integrity performs a kind of distancing from the politicized community he represents. At the same time, by his very presence and the fact of his invitation to perform the Pirith Ceremony, de Silva describes a mis-en-scène wherein the structure's nonsecular

17 Siddiqi, "Crafting the Archive," 1301.
18 On subaltern history writing, see Vinayak Chaturvedi, ed., *Mapping Subaltern Studies* (London: Verso, 2000); and on feminist historical methodology, see Antoinette Burton, *Dwelling in the Archive: Women Writing House, Home and History in Late Colonial India* (Oxford: Oxford University Press, 2003).
19 Minnette de Silva, *The Life and Work of an Asian Woman Architect* (Colombo: Smart Media, 1998), 233. For an extended discussion of this description, see Jazeel, "Tropical Modernism/Environmental Nationalism."

essence is actively inscribed.[20] That the Amerasinghes requested de Silva build a shrine room into the house was, we should note, symptomatic of the growing (postcolonial) normalization of Buddhist aesthetics in the former colonial capital, Colombo. In short then, for de Silva, the house embodied an architected teleology wherein the sacred, Buddhism, is allowed to become modern and cosmopolitan on its own terms, cleaved from the ethnic absolutism that was creeping across 1950s Ceylonese society.

Elsewhere in her memoir, there are clues regarding de Silva's architectural influences. Though we know the universalism of Corbusian classicism inspired her work, she stresses how it was Patrick Geddes's work in India that impelled her toward a genuinely Ceylonese form of architectural modernism. She was inspired by Geddes's notion of *conservative surgery*, which advocated modern improvements sensitized to the roots of regional culture. In conservative surgery de Silva saw a road map for a new, vanguardist Ceylonese architecture offering an avowedly postcolonial departure that walked in step with Ceylon's political ambition toward independence. Conservative surgery held the potential to concretize a rupture with the standardizations of colonial architecture, anticipating many local iterations of modern architecture across the world. And as de Silva put it, Geddes's conservative surgery provided "the perfect counter-balance to the Corbusian classical; the two complementing each other became the foundation for most of my thinking."[21]

De Silva's architecture then was, just like Bawa's efforts at Lunuganga, a search for the ordinary, for the historical, despite its resolute modernism. In this respect, she found architectural inspiration in the ethnicized craft histories and traditions outlined in Ananda Coomaraswamy's seminal 1908 monograph *Medieval Sinhalese Art*, which was a manifesto of sorts for a modern revival of the Sinhala arts and crafts tradition that had much of its historical provenance in the Kandyan Kingdom.[22] (The Kandyan Kingdom being the interior, high-country, monarchical territory where, until the British conquered the kingdom in 1815, a succession of Sinhala kings had held out against European colonization.) Indeed, de Silva's own book pays homage to Coomaraswamy's 1908 text and to his work, such that we can surmise how, for de Silva, her work not only had a geographical foundation in the former Kandyan Kingdom, it was explicitly congruent with Kandyan aesthetic traditions that were at the heart of postcolonial national imaginations. For example, she emphasizes that "[m]y parents had kept our roots intact for my generation, but now I had to interpret this in architecture. I decided to live in Kandy, it being the center of Ceylon and the heart of our *national tradition*."[23]

De Silva's equation of Coomaraswamy's historical narrative about Kandyan Sinhala craft with an understanding of the precolonial nation-state thought retroactively as Sinhalese was not,

20 In Sri Lanka, Pirith ceremonies are a form of ritual blessing involving chants recited by Buddhist monks and the tying of blessed strings. The ceremonies are typically for both protection and blessing, and are commonly performed in new homes.

21 De Silva, *The Life and Work of an Asian Woman Architect*, 100.

22 For a critical discussion of the relevance of Coomaraswamy's book in the context of Sri Lanka's postcolonial history, see Pradeep Jeganathan, "Disco-*very*: Anthropology, Nationalist Thought, Thamotharampillai Shanaathanan, and an Uncertain Descent into the Ordinary," in *Violence*, ed. Neil L. Whitehead (Santa Fe: School of American Research Press, 2004), 185–202.

23 De Silva, *The Life and Work of an Asian Woman Architect*, 100 (emphasis mine).

however, entirely of her own making, and this is where we should be careful to place her work in the broader context of modernist discourse at the time. As her book attests, she was deeply influenced by her association with Sri Lanka's '43 Group, and in particular by her friendship with the painter George Keyt, whom she met through her mother's cousin Lionel Wendt, founder of the group. Through their work, this group of artists advanced their own forms of anticolonial aesthetic expression, which combined distinctively Ceylonese formal and pictorial symbols with European modernist trends such as Cubist pictorial language and Expressionism. Theirs was an attempt to express Ceylonese particularity, but it was a particularity that betrayed the underlying assumption that the contours of the postcolonial nation to come were contiguous with Buddhist (and Sinhala) tradition, whose cultural and geographical kernel was the Kandyan Kingdom. In her book, de Silva reproduces an essay by George Keyt entitled "The Folk Culture of Ceylon," which begins: "The survival of folk culture in a small country like Ceylon is astonishing when we take into consideration the later history of the Island. The occasional raids and invasions from Southern India in ancient times were not culturally destructive [...] because the cultural structure of Ceylon was fundamentally an Indian extension. But destructive forces of an alarming nature made their appearance when [...] Ceylon began to stagnate and was finally subjugated by the sweeping domination of three successive powers from Europe. [...]

Largely responsible for the survival of the Ceylonese folk and classical culture was the Buddhist religion, a faith which was somehow preserved through the centuries since Asokan times."[24]

What Keyt suggests here is that the particularity of Ceylonese folk culture is not just that which preceded "the sweeping domination of three successive [colonizing] powers from Europe" but also that which can be parsed from the much more entangled and historically entrenched confluence of South Indian culture. Though benign, this too lives under the sign of "invasion." For Keyt, Tamil cultural, artistic and formal presence in the Ceylonese polity is marked as arrival and accommodation into a notion of Ceylonese folk culture that he explicitly names as Buddhist. It is important to remember here that historically, island-wide territorial coherence was only achieved when the British conquered the Kandyan Kingdom in 1815, thus bringing for the first time the whole island under a single political administration. Prior to that, the very notion of Ceylon – and by extension Ceylonese folk culture – was politically and culturally chimerical at best. What Keyt, de Silva and other modernists did was to allow the particularity of Kandyan Buddhist and Sinhalese culture to slide over, subsume and discursively territorialize the emergent post- and anti-colonial nation.

What de Silva's own archive of sorts tells us then is that for her the ordinariness that postcolonial Ceylonese conservative surgery

24 George Keyt in de Silva, *The Life and Work of an Asian Woman Architect*, 144.

219

EPILOGUE

Looking back on the making of the garden, seeing it as it is now, it seems to me to be almost inevitable that it should be there. The first decision to make a garden was taken at a time when — to me — the world seemed stable, almost anything one wanted to do seemed possible and the time was there to do it.

In my travels I had seen many splendid gardens as well as a great deal of beautiful natural landscape in many countries. I have always enjoyed visual pleasures and nature had often provided marvellous scenes and settings, but equally often human imagination and invention had emphasized this beauty with the line of a balustrade or the formation of a lake. Water was enormously important in any view — water and the play of light and shade were what gave me most pleasure and that pleasure enhanced by a line of wall or building — geometry with nature — colour being secondary, almost intrusive in the larger composition. The area one was dealing with was about twenty-five acres but with its surrounding lakes the land beyond seems to go on for ever.

For many years the garden had grown gradually into a place of many moods, the result of many imaginings, some simple, some complex, offering me a retreat to be alone or to fellowfeel with friends, whilst an added pleasure is one of seeing and feeling the reactions to this place, from puzzlement to the silence of contentment, from the remarkable comment of a friend of a friend "This would be a lovely place to have a garden"! to the words of the lorry driver who walked around the garden recently — when his bricks were being unloaded — and then said to me " මේක නං හරි සිදේවි තැනක් " (but this is a very blessed place).

Epilogue from *Lunuganga*, Geoffrey Bawa, Christoph Bon and Dominic Sansoni, 1986

aimed at recuperating following the architectural standardizations of the colonial period had particular historiographical and cultural coordinates. In envisioning a future for postcolonial Ceylon that was fashioned from the cultural afterlives of Kandyan Sinhala craft, as well as from historical narratives of precolonial Buddhist purity that accommodated and tolerated difference in the forms of "invasion" and "arrival," she was part of a broader vanguard imagination shared by, and perhaps most closely associated with, the '43 Group. Despite the many differences between de Silva's and Geoffrey Bawa's styles, I want to suggest the similarities between the historical and environmental imaginations upon which their differing architectural praxes depended. For when Bawa frames the view across his estate by the stupa that lies beyond – that is to say, the gleaming white dome of the neighboring Katakuliya temple – he situates this view within a low-country translation of de Silva's Kandyan vernacular. That the lorry driver's compliment to Lunuganga is reproduced and preserved in the Sinhala script in which it was uttered hints also toward the importance of this low-country vernacular, a vernacular that is as aesthetic as it is linguistic.

Let me be clear in closing that my argument is not to impugn de Silva and Bawa nor to align their work with Sinhala Buddhist nationalism. This would be a clumsy misinterpretation of my reading here. Rather, it is to suggest that contrary to much of the rhetoric around postindependence Sri Lankan architecture, their work was never simply outside politics. As forms of artistic modernism – and de Silva and Bawa were certainly among the greatest authors of modern postindependence Sri Lanka – their work was inescapably part of the weft and warp of postcolonial nationhood, despite their own claims to be working beyond the squabbles of nationalist politics. Both were articulating visions of a uniquely Ceylonese modernism. My argument here is that it is only by paying attention to the "not-exactly-architecture" that surrounds de Silva and Bawa's built work that we are able to begin to do the work of placing their architecture, contextually so, within these wider currents and debates. In fact, the Bawa Archives may even reveal to us the editorial decisions that went into the composition of the 1990 book *Lunuganga* upon which I have drawn in this essay. Paying attention to such intertexts, to such ephemera, to this broader textual field enables us to pose important questions concerning not just what their influences were but also what the effects of their work were. What broader social and political debates did the narrative dimensions of their architecture and their building practices participate in, even as we acknowledge their own desire to sidestep politics, or in Bawa's case to refrain from talking about his practice? These are important questions, especially in the context of some of the larger commissions that Bawa particularly was involved in: the Parliament building and the University of Ruhuna, for example. Archives can help us along with these questions, and thus the opening of the Bawa Archives is an invaluable resource for historians of postcolonial Sri Lanka as much as it is for architectural historians.

Conclusion

Insofar as rendering is a process of drawing, I have suggested in this essay that we can also usefully think of it as a process of drawing out from the archives the manifold ways that architectural meaning is made. Architecture's intertextual ephemera are not incidental to its meaning. All artistic process is in and of the world, and the opening of the Bawa Archives offers an exciting opportunity for the careful historical and archaeological work of excavating and locating the practice of an architect, Geoffrey Bawa, who was famously restrained when it came to talking or writing about his work. The archives offer an opportunity to demystify what so often are his work's unexplainable qualities and sumptuous pleasures. Explanation though is probably not what we should demand. I have an intuition that we should also be content to continue to let his architectural practice delight our senses and still our souls. After all, unlike Minnette de Silva's practice, much of Bawa's work remains and has been preserved. Among others who have been involved in the tireless work of architectural heritage in Sri Lanka, we have the Bawa Trust to thank for the preservation work that means we can, and should where possible, continue to experience his built space for ourselves. But through a reading of Minnette de Silva's practice, and more specifically her 1998 book, I have tried to show in this essay that the Bawa Archives might open toward ways of locating, contextualizing and situating his practice and process in the broader cultural and social terrains from which it emerged, was commissioned and developed through the course of his long career.

But archives, we should remember, are made by humans. They are the result of decisions; decisions about what to preserve, what to discard, what to hide and what to celebrate. They are thus not only powerful resources for writing history. They are also riven through with power themselves insofar as they are the result of all those decisions taken that bear upon their eventual shape. To this extent, we should approach the Bawa Archives with something like a forensic disposition, attuned to questions about what it contains, why, and what its gaps, silences, connections and disconnections might be. Equally, however, just as I have drawn upon published work on, and by, Minnette de Silva, there is a vast textual field of writing on Bawa and modernism that we can and should also consider an archive of sorts.

St. Bridget's Montessori, Colombo

1963–64

Facade corner detail, gelatin silver print,
Geoffrey Bawa, ca. 1963 GB/DOC/142/001

View of half-height walls with murals by Barbara Sansoni, gelatin silver print, Geoffrey Bawa, ca. 1963 GB/DOC/142/002-003

First-floor plan, ink on tracing paper GB/DA/045/003

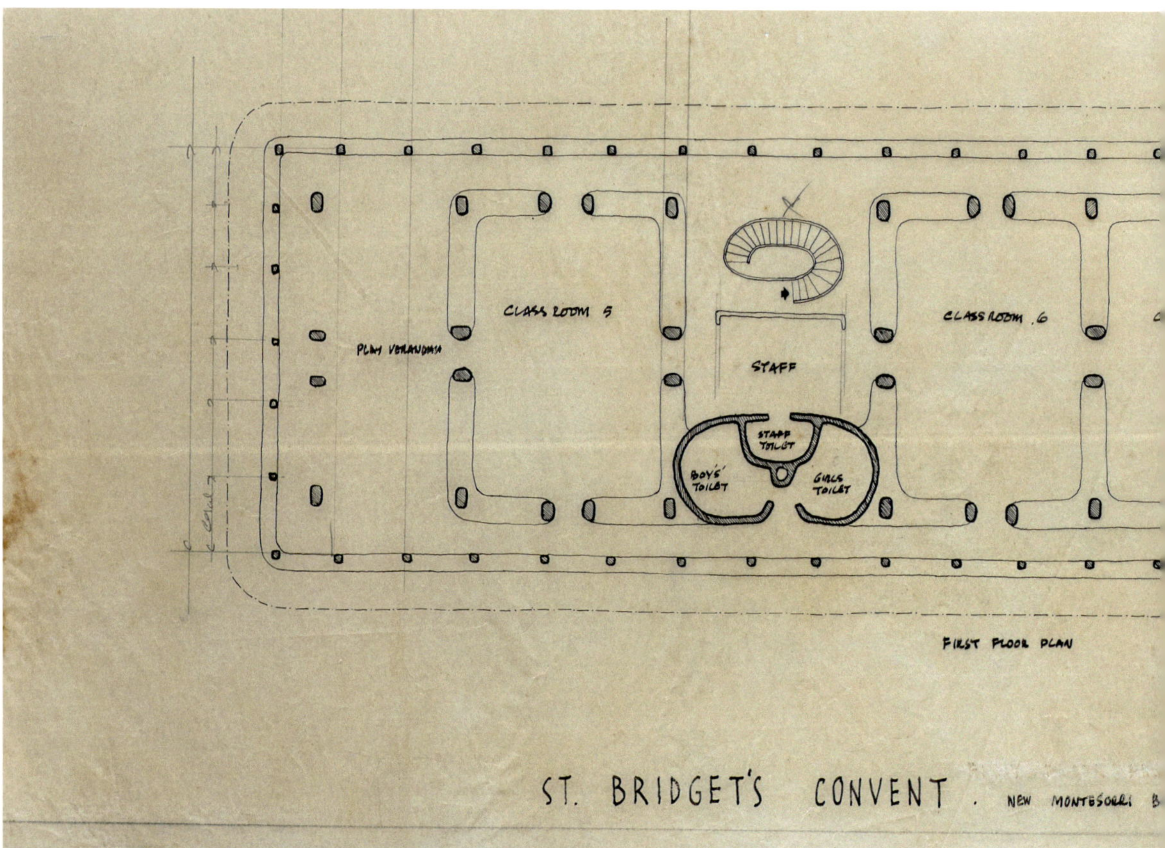

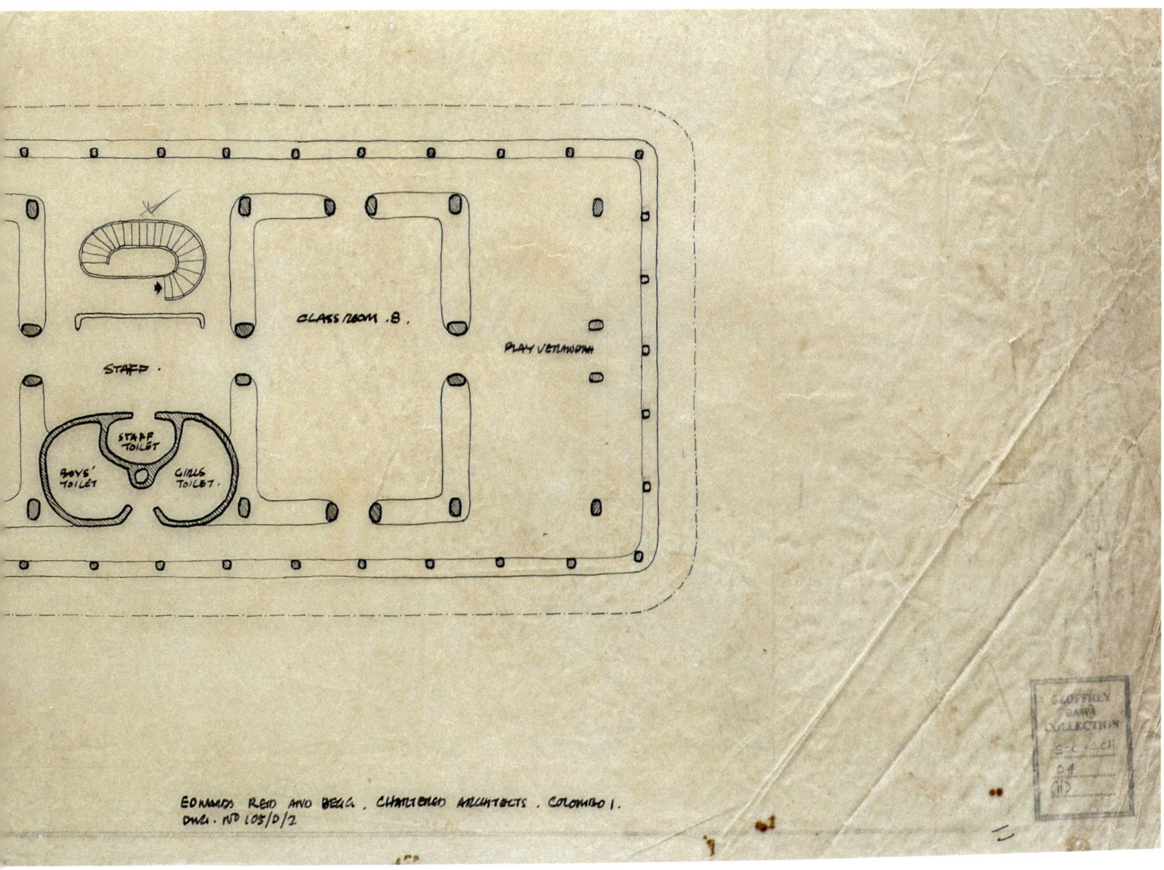
CLASSROOM . 8 .
PLAY VERANDAH
STAFF .
STAFF TOILET
BOYS' TOILET
GIRLS TOILET .
EDWARDS REID AND BEGG . CHARTERED ARCHITECTS . COLOMBO 1.
DWG . NO 105/D/2

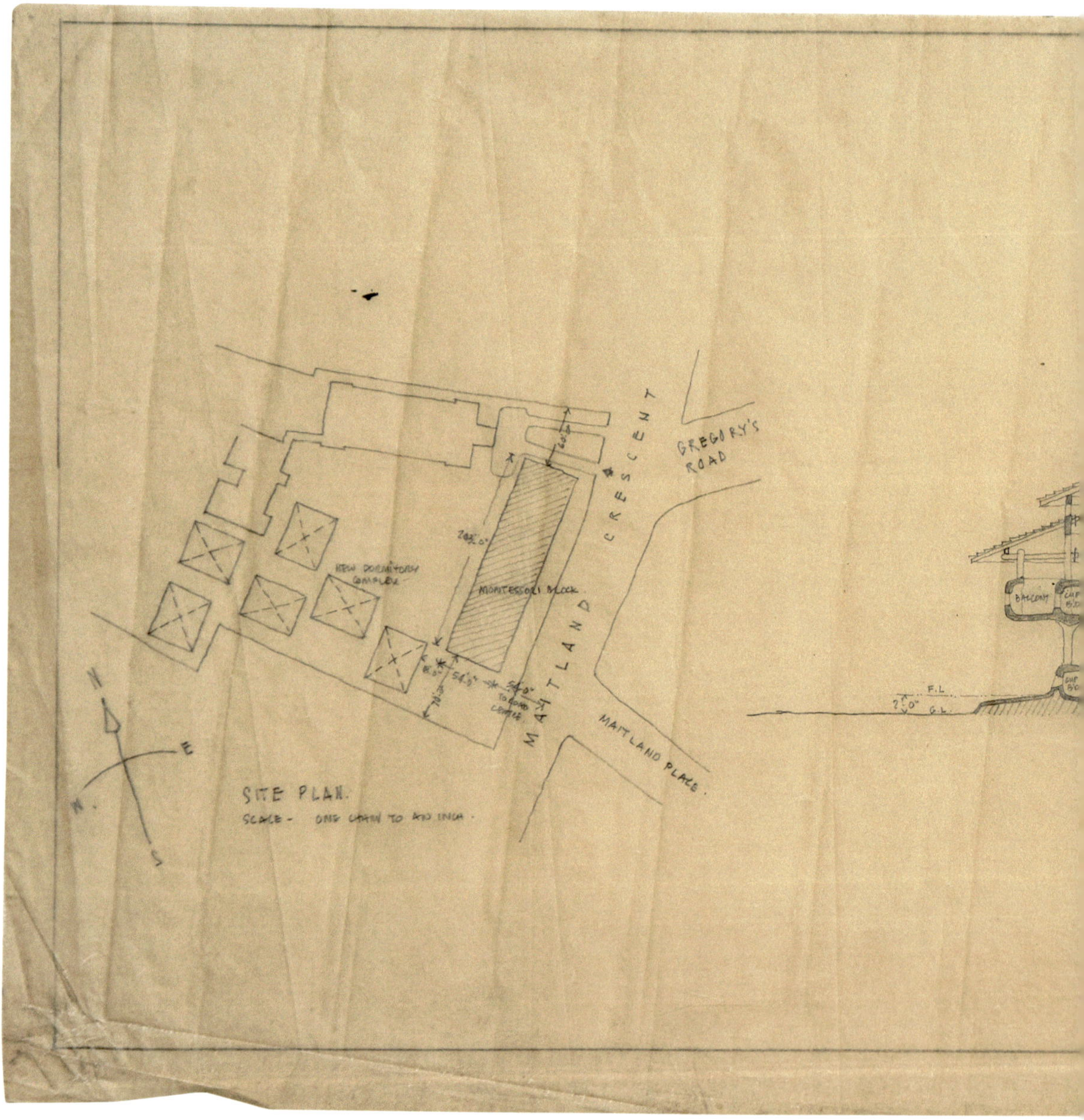

Site plan and section, graphite on tracing paper, ca. 1963 GB/DA/045/006

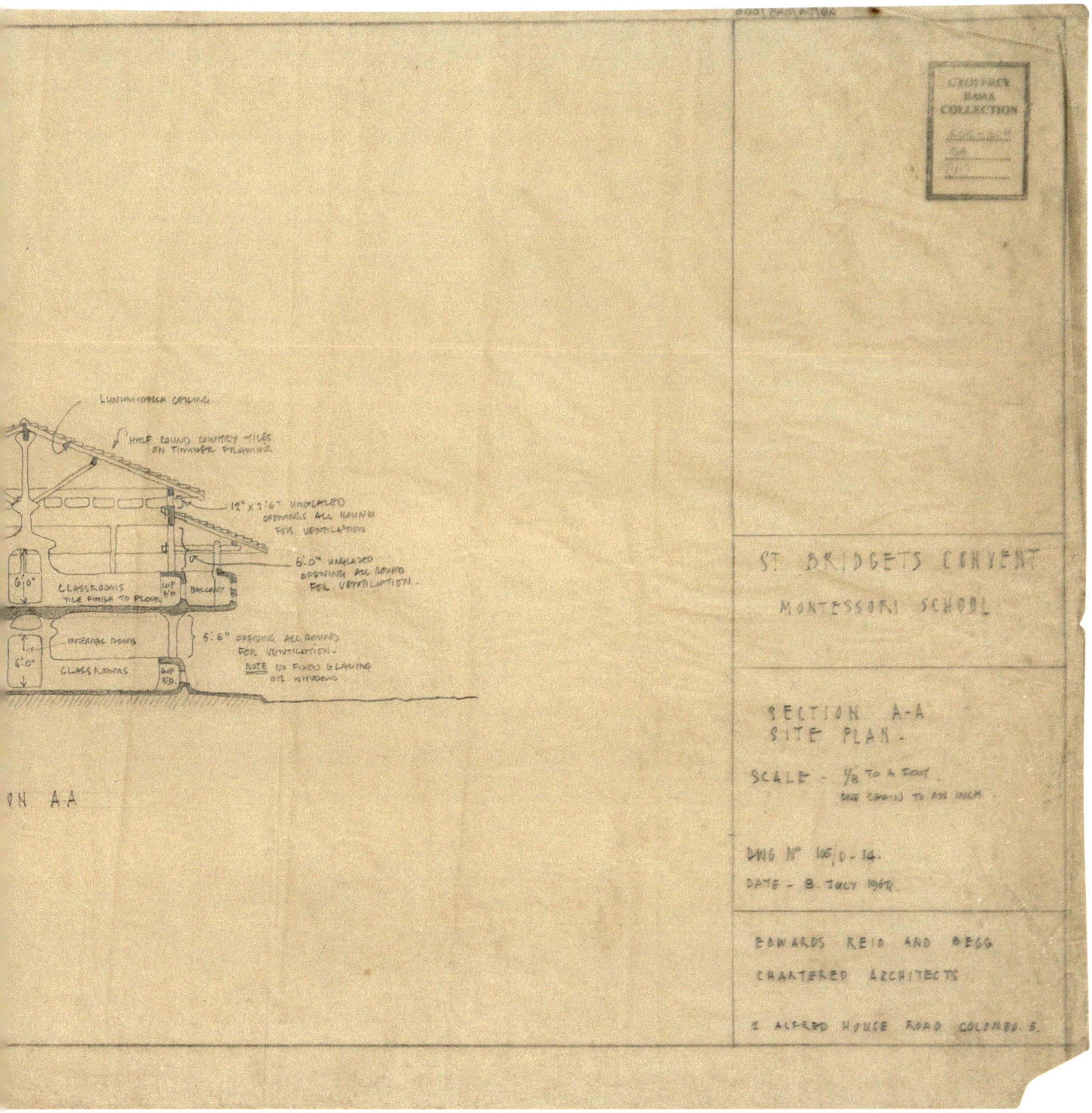
GEOFFREY BAWA COLLECTION
HALF ROUND COUNTRY TILES ON TIMBER FRAMING
12" x 2'6" UNGLAZED OPENINGS ALL ROUND FOR VENTILATION
6'0" UNGLAZED OPENING ALL ROUND FOR VENTILATION.
6'0"
CLASSROOMS TILE FINISH TO FLOOR
BALCONY
INTERNAL DOORS
5'6" OPENING ALL ROUND FOR VENTILATION.
NOTE NO FIXED GLAZING OR WINDOWS
CLASSROOMS
ON AA
ST BRIDGETS CONVENT
MONTESSORI SCHOOL
SECTION A-A
SITE PLAN.
SCALE - 1/8" TO A FOOT.
ONE CHAIN TO AN INCH.
DWG Nº 105/D-14.
EDWARDS REID AND BEGG
CHARTERED ARCHITECTS
2 ALFRED HOUSE ROAD COLOMBO. 3.

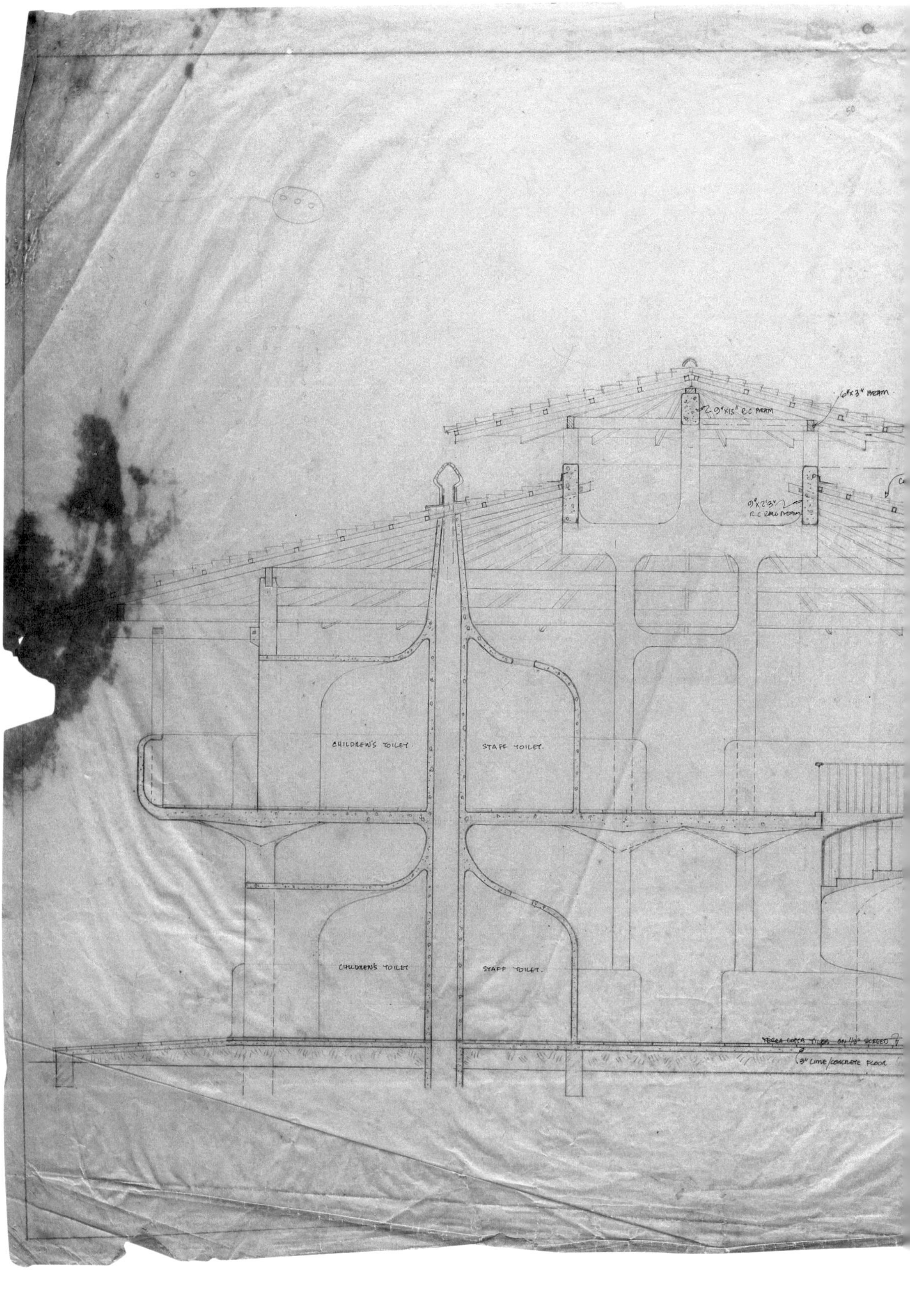

Section through (unbuilt) scheme with monitor roof, graphite and ink on tracing paper, ca. 1963 GB/DA/045/007

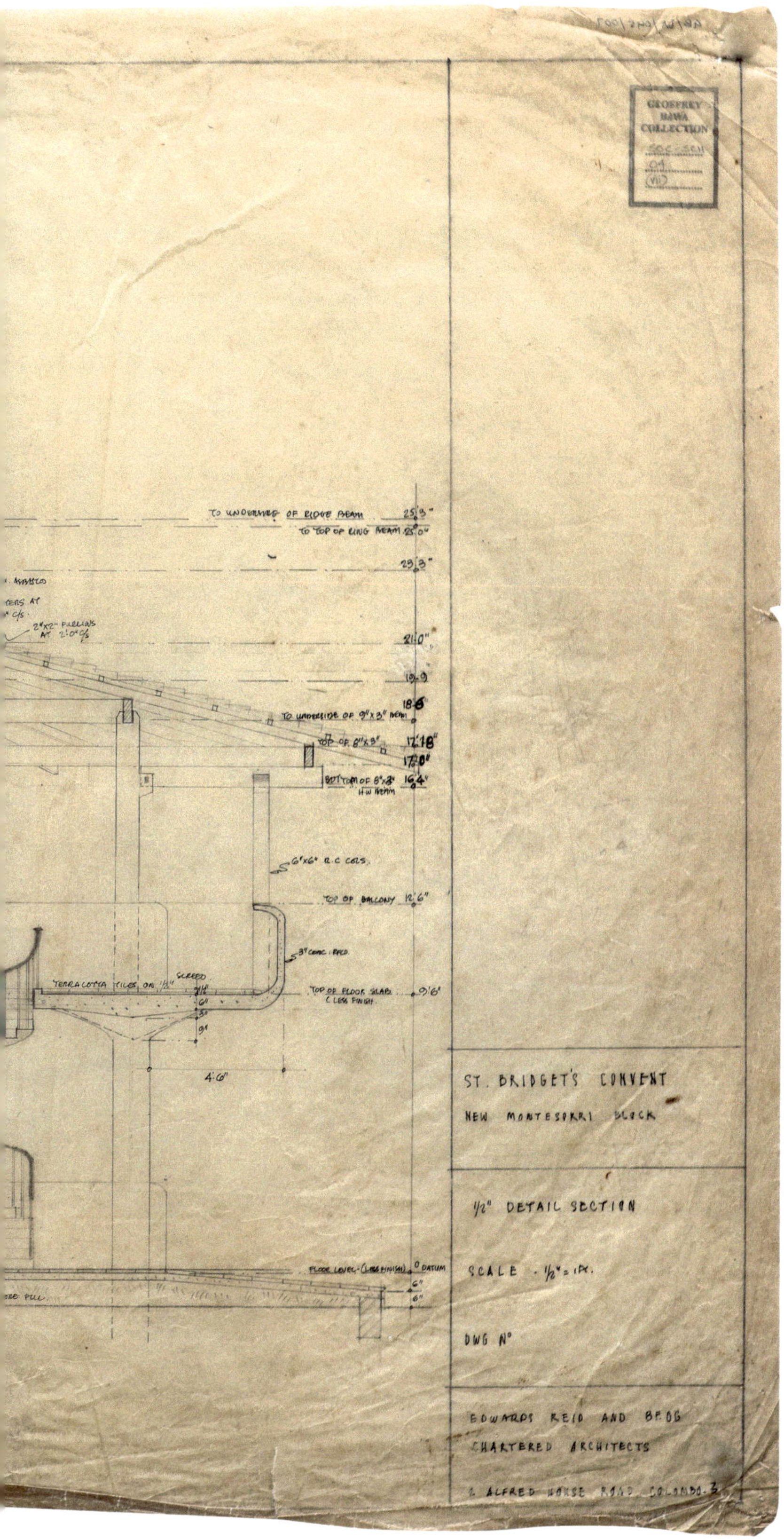
GEOFFREY BAWA COLLECTION
ST. BRIDGET'S CONVENT
NEW MONTESORRI BLOCK
1/2" DETAIL SECTION
SCALE - 1/2" = 1FT.
DWG Nº
EDWARDS REID AND BEGG
CHARTERED ARCHITECTS
TERRACOTTA TILES ON 1/2" SCREED
6"x6" R.C COLS.
TOP OF BALCONY 12'6"
TOP OF FLOOR SLAB 9'6"
FLOOR LEVEL 0 DATUM

Exterior view showing rounded edges and windows at toddler height, gelatin silver print, Geoffrey Bawa, ca. 1963 GB/DOC/142/004

Elevation, ink on tracing paper GB/DA/045/008

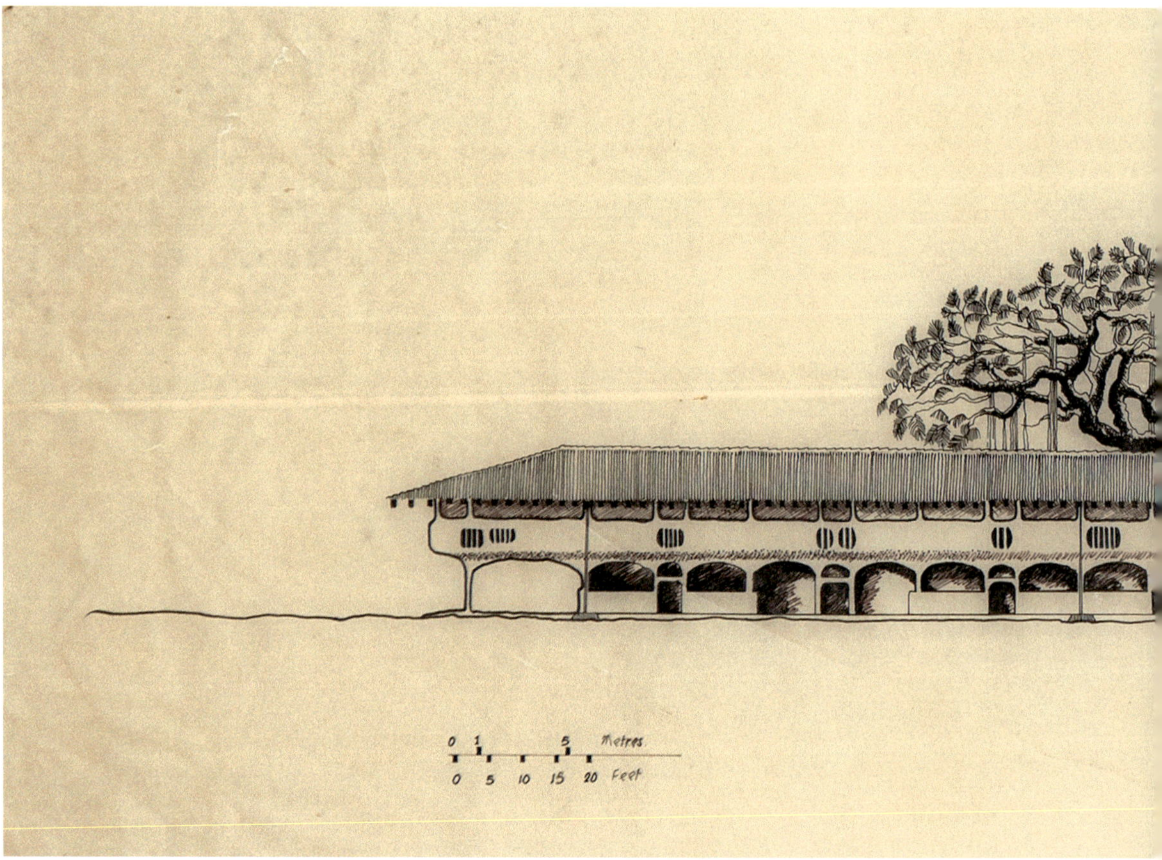

Exposed concrete spiral staircase with murals by Barbara Sansoni, gelatin silver print, Geoffrey Bawa, ca. 1963 GB/DOC/142/005

April 27, 1978

H.E. Mr. J.R. Jayewardene
President
Office of the President
Janadipathi Mandiriya
COLOMBO 1

Dear Mr. President:

I was invited to be on the Committee for the improvement of the Galle Face Green but unfortunately owing to lack of time was not able to be at the first meeting. However, the Convenor, Mr. Nimalasiri de Silva of the Tourist Board, met me and gave me the file of the proceedings of this meeting, and asked me for my suggestions and views.

As I was given to understand that my presence on the Committee was at the instance of the Prime Minister, I am sending him a copy of my report, and I take this opportunity to send you a copy too as I know you are interested in restoring our city to some order and beauty.

The Galle Face Green is such an important part of Colombo that a good deal of thought must be given to any drastic changes made to it, and my report, although partially at variance with the earlier findings of the Committee, is at least a sincere contribution which I thought you might like to read.

Yours sincerely,

Geoffrey Bawa

Encls. Copy of Report dated 27th April, 1978
Sketch - Development of Galle Face Green

Typewritten correspondence from Geoffrey Bawa to J. R. Jayewardene, ink on paper, 1978

The Most Important Open Space in Colombo

Meghal Perera

Galle Face Green is an urban park at the very heart of Colombo, a 5-hectare strip of grassy land wedged between the city's commercial district and the Indian Ocean, a stone's throw away from the prime minister's residence. It is a place where Colombo's colonial past meets its visions of the future, watched over by the Old Parliament Building turned Presidential Secretariat and a row of new luxury hotels and malls in various stages of completion. The park's rhythms ebb and flow daily. In the evenings, office workers and families stream out onto the green to watch the sun set over the ocean; vendors offer everything from sliced pineapple to kites to inflatable monkeys, and couples enjoy the bracing sea breeze from the benches on the promenade. At dawn armed forces personnel raise a giant Sri Lankan flag over middle-aged joggers and wedding photographers capitalizing on the theatrical effect of the morning light and crashing waves. The park's activities take a seasonal turn as well; it is the stage for Independence Day parades in February, rallies in May and kite festivals in August.

Laid out by British Governor Henry Ward in 1859, Galle Face Green was designated as a space for ladies and children to take in the air and for the new native elite to practice colonial ways of life. Ward's intentions are inscribed in the space itself, engraved on a stone tablet that stands on the promenade, declaring that it is "recommended to his successors in the interest of the Ladies and Children of Colombo." Archival records underscore its significance as a public space, as Governor Ridgeway West writes in 1899: "Galle Face is the esplanade and principal place of recreation of the people of Colombo. It borders the sea, is traversed by public roads, and the people, from time immemorial, ride, walk, play football, golf and other games on the many acres of grass within its limits. [...] The public have thus acquired a prescriptive right of use, and even if it were legal [...] to enclose the ground and exclude the public from it, it would be most inexpedient, indeed cruel."[1]

Cities are repositories of social meaning. To Roland Barthes, the city is a discourse, and "the city speaks to its inhabitants, and

1 Governor Ridgeway West to Colonial Office, January 20, 1899, WO 33/176, War Office: Reports, Memoranda and Papers (O and A Series), The National Archives, London, 2.

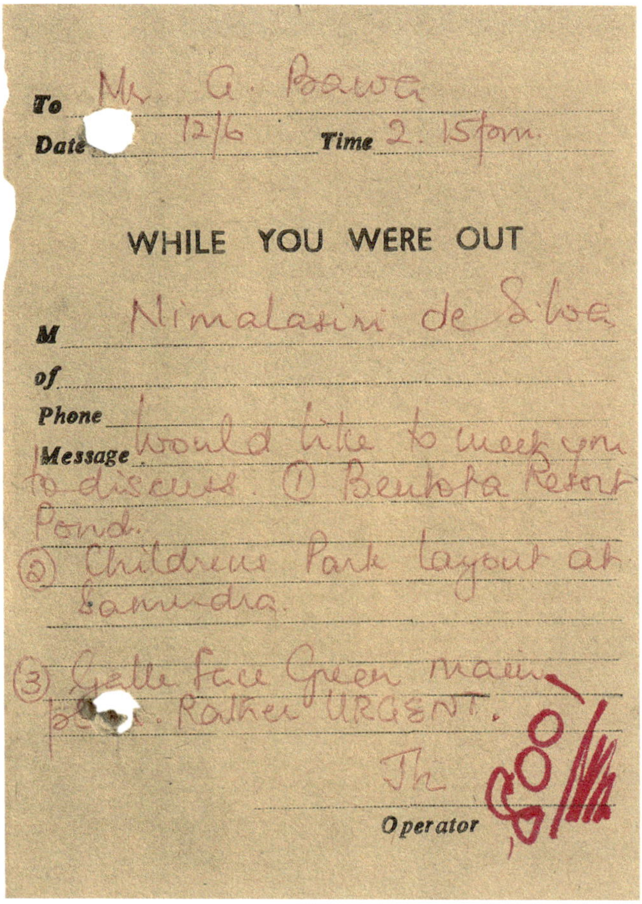

To Mr. G. Bawa
Date 12/6 Time 2.15pm.

WHILE YOU WERE OUT

M Nimalasiri de Silva
of
Phone
Message would like to meet you to discuss. (1) Bentota Resort Pond.
(2) Childrens Park layout at Samudra.
(3) Galle Face Green main p... Rather URGENT.
Jh
Operator

Handwritten memorandum from the office of Geoffrey Bawa setting up a meeting with Nimalasiri de Silva regarding the Galle Face Green Development, Colombo, ink on paper, ca. 1978

Typewritten correspondence from Chelvadurai Anjalendren to Marasinghe Perera, ink on paper, 1978

we speak to our city, the city where we are, simply by inhabiting it, by traversing it, by looking at it."[2] The city, both in its built environment and representational forms, is littered with signs that hold multiple and conflicting meanings for various readers. The city can be seen as a text that is authored by power, as James Duncan posits when examining another Sri Lankan city – Kandy in the nineteenth century.[3]

Galle Face Green offers a rich mine from which such meanings can be extracted and explored. It is also a space upon which Colombo's global aspirations are pinned and projected: foreign investment and State initiatives are keen to capitalize waterfront-adjacent property. Visions for what kind of space Galle Face Green should be have been contested in this context. In 2004 the Urban Development Authority of Sri Lanka sought to hand over the management and control of Galle Face Green to a private company, with plans to turn the green into a "mega leisure complex." These plans were challenged successfully in the Supreme Court, and in their judgment the Justices ruled that the government had to manage the Green for public use in the spirit in which it was intended, citing the stone tablet as proof.[4]

Barthes writes that "architecture is always dream and function, expression of utopia and instrument of convenience."[5] Successive governments have attempted to balance the weight of history with the desire for development and convenience. The Galle Face Report offers insight into one such nascent negotiation, as drafted and envisioned by the architect Geoffrey Bawa. In April 1978 Bawa was invited to serve on a special committee on the Landscaping

2 Roland Barthes, *The Semiotic Challenge* (Oxford: Blackwell, 1988) 195.
3 See James Duncan, *The City as Text: The Politics of Landscape Interpretation in the Kandyan Kingdom* (Cambridge: Cambridge University Press, 2005).
4 *Environmental Foundation Limited* v *Urban Development Authority* (2005), *Sri Lanka Law Reports* 2009 (1).
5 Roland Barthes, *Mythologies*, trans. Annette Lavers (New York: Hill and Wang, 1972), 239.

8th November, 1978

Mr. Marasinghe Perera,
Chief Municipal Engineer,
Colombo Municipal Council,
Town Hall,
Colombo 7.

Dear Mr. Perera,

GALLE FACE GREEN DEVELOPMENT

I have tried to get you on the phone many times without success regarding the above matter. Also, when I came to the Municipality on another matter I was disappointed to find that the working drawings on the sketches submitted by us, have been finalised and sent for tender without our approval as agreed by you previously. It was also found that some of these details were not according to specifications and in the case of the seat, not in accordance with the sketch submitted by us.

Please do not hesitate to call me up and clarify any details or amendments as would be required.

Hoping to hear from you soon,

Yours sincerely,

C. Anjalendran.

and Beautification of the Galle Face Green Area, alongside representatives from the Ceylon Tourist Board and the Ministry of Local Government, Housing and Construction.[6] Unable to attend the first meeting of the committee, he outlined his recommendations in a brief four-page document entitled "Report on the Landscaping and Beautification of the Galle Face Green Area."[7]

At this point in time, Bawa was a significant shaper of the city's urban landscape. Bawa's office, Edwards, Reid and Begg, had designed several public buildings, such as offices and house staffing for the Steel Corporation at Oruwela, the State Mortgage Bank Building on Darley Road and the Agrarian Research and Training Institute on Wijerama Mawatha. His designs were also changing public spaces such as the Beira Lake with the design of the Seema Malaka Temple that juts into the lake, which was completed in 1978 – the same year that this report is dated. Bawa would continue to sit on urban development committees concerned with the beautification of Colombo, designing smaller public spaces in the form of roundabouts and triangles that dotted the city in 1979. His most significant State projects would be outside Colombo's urban limits – the Parliament building in Sri Jayawardenepura Kotte and the Ruhuna Campus in the south of the country, both projects embedding him in the nation-building project of the State.[8] The Galle Face Report and its related correspondences underline the growing recognition of Bawa and his role as an architect of the State.

Proposals to redevelop Galle Face Green were put forward soon after the UNP government assumed power in 1977. The UNP government was responsible for the liberalization of the economy as well as the introduction of a new constitution, both of which had immense significance for Colombo. Sri Jayawardenepura Kotte was selected as the new capital, marking a break from the country's colonial past. Nihal Perera notes that plans for Colombo to be upgraded as a modern central business district also supposedly influenced the decision to shift the parliament.[9] The old Parliament Building, which overlooks Galle Face Green, was too bound up with the colonial past and too adjacent to a cosmopolitan and economic powerhouse. Bawa was involved in these dual processes of urban change, consulting on how to conceptualize the space of old power while helping to forge its new seat as well.

Urban landscapes are constantly transforming, layers of history and change ossifying into the physical environment, only to be erased in a day. Making sense of the ephemeral reality of the city is difficult, and turning to representations of the built environment offers a glimpse into a vanished urban form and way of life.[10] The fact remains that the bulk of the recommendations in Bawa's report were never implemented, and none have survived the passing of four decades. Many features of Galle Face Green's design today are antithetical to the report's clear and emphatic

6 Chandra De Soyza to Geoffrey Bawa, April 3, 1978, GB/DOC/003/03, Box 01, Bon Chamberlin fonds, Geoffrey Bawa Archives, Colombo, Sri Lanka.

7 Geoffrey Bawa, "Report on the Landscaping and Beautification of the Galle Face Green Area," 1978, GB/DOC/003/02, Box 01, Bon Chamberlin fonds, Geoffrey Bawa Archives, Colombo, Sri Lanka.

8 See Tariq Jazeel, *Sacred Modernity: Nature, Environment, and the Postcolonial Geographies of Sri Lankan Nationhood* (Colombo: Social Scientists' Association, 2014).

9 See Nihal Perera, "The Making of a National Capital," in *National Symbols, Fractured Identities*, ed. Michael Geisler (London: Middlebury College Press), 241–71.

10 See Jane M. Jacobs, "The City Unbound: Qualitative Approaches to the City," *Urban Studies* 30, no. 4–5 (1993): 827–48.

suggestions. What value then, apart from intellectual novelty, does Bawa's report have for the contemporary urban citizen?

By only reading the built environment, competing visions of the past are ignored. Just because these alternate plans did not win out, it does not follow that they have nothing valuable to contribute to the understanding of a city's past and future.[11] Documents such as the Bawa report make up what Katheryn Oberdeck calls "the unbuilt environment," planning histories documented in archival records of unrealized projects, plans and designs.[12] These are abundant because architects and planners often make multiple versions and sketches before a project is finalized, and the politics of planning itself means that many plans are never implemented in stone and concrete. The existence of these documents evinces the messy and political process of planning urban spaces. When the committee took up "Mr. Bawa's Plan" a month later, only his recommendations for tree planting and the creation of "irregular shaped (snake-like formation) concrete seats of very low height" were approved.[13] In November a letter from Bawa's office to the chief municipal engineer conveys terse disappointment at the Colombo Municipal Council's finalized deviation from Bawa's plan.[14] He notes the difficulty he has had trying to contact the chief municipal engineer, that working drawings have been finalized without the approval of the Bawa office and that many specifications are "not in accordance to the sketch submitted by us."

The unbuilt environment constructed by these documents contains visions of public space, identities and values.[15] They contribute to a collective idea of what might have been, an imagination of space that is in some ways no different or no more unreal than a depiction of the city in a film or novel or even a tourist brochure.

Bawa himself adopts a position of caution when considering the beautification of the green, understanding the importance of the place in the city and to the public. His reserved approach is antithetical to the rapid visionary and large-scale change that many planners seek to implement when given a chance to restructure the chaos of the city. In his letter to President J.R. Jayewardene in 1978, he notes that "the Galle Face Green is such an important part of Colombo that a good deal of thought must be given to any drastic changes made to it."[16] He sees the need to place Galle Face Green in congruence with its urban landscape, noting that the urban aesthetics applied to Galle Face Green must be consistently extended to the surrounding areas. The need to design with the environment rather than against it, albeit in this case the urban one, is consistent with Bawa's architectural practice. But it is also a reflection of the value he places on the park. He urges that "we do not do anything in any piecemeal way as the Galle Face Green always has been, and always will be, the most important open space in Colombo."[17]

11 See Jacobs, "The City Unbound."

12 See Katheryn Oberdeck. "Archives of the Unbuilt Environment: Documents and Discourses of Imagined Space in Twentieth-Century Kohler, Wisconsin," in *Archive Stories: Facts, Fictions, and the Writing of History* (Durham: Duke University Press, 2006), 251–73.

13 Special Committee Meeting Minutes, May 16, 1978, GB/DOC/003/03, Box 01, Bon Chamberlin fonds, Geoffrey Bawa Archives, Colombo, Sri Lanka.

14 C. Anjalendren to Marasinghe Perera, November 8, 1978, GB/DOC/003/00, Box 01, Bon Chamberlin fonds, Geoffrey Bawa Archives, Colombo, Sri Lanka.

15 C. Anjalendren to Marasinghe Perera, November 8, 1978.

16 Geoffrey Bawa to President J. R. Jayewardene, April 27, 1978, GB/DOC/003/00, Box 01, Bon Chamberlin fonds, Geoffrey Bawa Archives, Colombo, Sri Lanka.

17 Bawa, "Galle Face Report," 2, GB/DOC/003/02, Box 01, Bon Chamberlin fonds, Geoffrey Bawa Archives, Colombo, Sri Lanka.

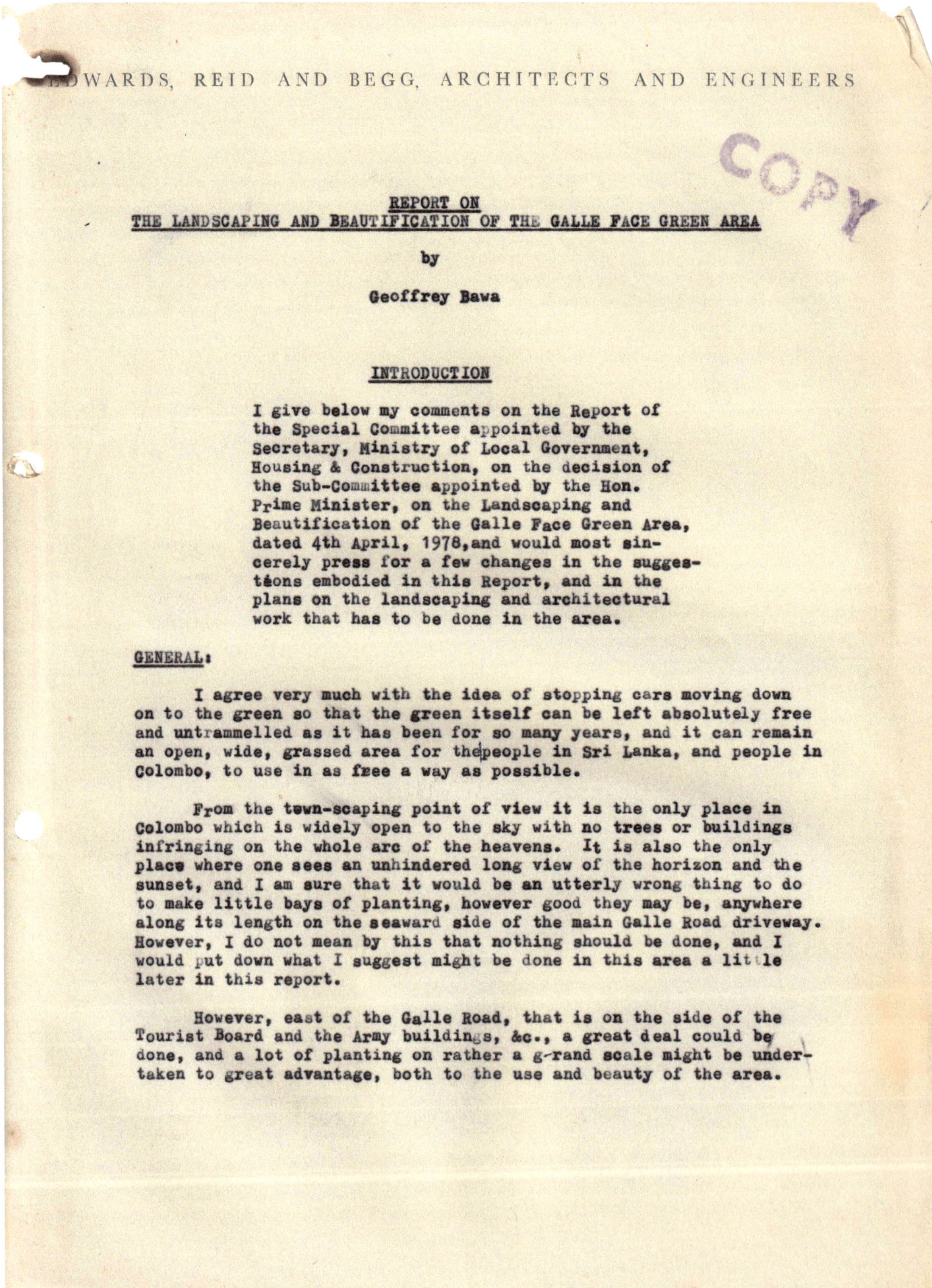

EDWARDS, REID AND BEGG, ARCHITECTS AND ENGINEERS

COPY

REPORT ON
THE LANDSCAPING AND BEAUTIFICATION OF THE GALLE FACE GREEN AREA

by

Geoffrey Bawa

INTRODUCTION

I give below my comments on the Report of the Special Committee appointed by the Secretary, Ministry of Local Government, Housing & Construction, on the decision of the Sub-Committee appointed by the Hon. Prime Minister, on the Landscaping and Beautification of the Galle Face Green Area, dated 4th April, 1978, and would most sincerely press for a few changes in the suggestions embodied in this Report, and in the plans on the landscaping and architectural work that has to be done in the area.

GENERAL:

I agree very much with the idea of stopping cars moving down on to the green so that the green itself can be left absolutely free and untrammelled as it has been for so many years, and it can remain an open, wide, grassed area for the people in Sri Lanka, and people in Colombo, to use in as free a way as possible.

From the town-scaping point of view it is the only place in Colombo which is widely open to the sky with no trees or buildings infringing on the whole arc of the heavens. It is also the only place where one sees an unhindered long view of the horizon and the sunset, and I am sure that it would be an utterly wrong thing to do to make little bays of planting, however good they may be, anywhere along its length on the seaward side of the main Galle Road driveway. However, I do not mean by this that nothing should be done, and I would put down what I suggest might be done in this area a little later in this report.

However, east of the Galle Road, that is on the side of the Tourist Board and the Army buildings, &c., a great deal could be done, and a lot of planting on rather a grand scale might be undertaken to great advantage, both to the use and beauty of the area.

Report on the Landscaping and Beautification of the Galle Face Green Area, ink on paper, Geoffrey Bawa, 1978

[ED]WARDS, REID AND BEGG, ARCHITECTS AND ENGINEERS

- 2 -

Another question to raise, is that whether when one says "Galle Face area", one should not examine at the same time the full length of the promenade roadway from the Galle Face Hotel, right along the green, past the lighthouse, and up to the elevated dagoba at the entrance to the port. I mean the same planning and rules of urban aesthetics that we attempt on the Galle Face Green should apply throughout, and no attempt made at a piecemeal development.

I would willingly, and in an honorary capacity, give your Committee detailed plans of the whole area, and would give you with this report an itemised summary of what I think should be done, plus a sketch scheme as I have not got an accurate plan of the present Galle Face Green (the Municipal plans in my present possession still show the old form of the roadway). But when work comes to be done, the work should be carefully pre-planned and considered, obviously as fast as possible, as this work is urgent, but I do urge that we do not do anything in any piecemeal way as the Galle Face Green always has been, and always will be, the most important open space in Colombo.

1. <u>The Pedestrian Promenade from the Galle Face Green to the Lighthouse:</u>

This promenade should be evenly surfaced with either tar macadam or a mixture of tar and road gravel, possibly with a pattern of pre-cast concrete blocks, and all this laid absolutely level so that people taking their evening walks should find the premenade easy and safe. Along this whole length we could provide bays of seats and long, continuous walls, none of them, however, higher than 18" sitting height, and the backs of the seats 2'6" so that in no way would the view of the sea be impaired for people walking on the green or enjoying the open view from their motor cars parked at the top end of the green. The green itself should be levelled and turfed as suggested in your report, and the curb to prevent cars moving onto the green is a very good idea. However, this curb too should be as unobtrusive as possible while yet serving the purpose it sets out to serve. Along the whole promenade these should be suitable lighting installed but this can be done in close designed coherence with whatever seats and wide walls we plan for the paved promenade below the green. This is all shown in the accompanying sketch.

2. On the eastern side of the Galle Road, starting at the Galle Face Hotel end, and after examining the wind pattern, a planting programme should be undertaken to beautify and shade the continuous length of the roadside from the Galle Face Hotel and up to the new area where the Saturday Night Fair is held. The planting of this area will also provide a length of shaded walk so that people during the heat of the day would find greater comfort if they walk from the Galle Face Hotel end to the Fort. A careful selection of trees here is essential -- trees whose shape is not affected by the wind to a

very great extent can be planted where there is no back-up of building, and other trees and shrubs could be grouped where there is some protection for them.

3. Where the Galle Face Centre Road runs near the s-ea, with the sea on the west, and the lake on the east, and the buildings of the Fort in front, no trees should be planted, and the view should be an all-round one for anyone moving through that area either by car or walking. This is because the views from there put the whole perspective of Colombo clearly, and the view gives the proper urban perspective. I am told that a fountain is suggested in the basin of the lake -- this would be a good idea provided that only the jets of water are visible and are high and powerful enough to be in scale with this area, for example, like the high jet in Lake Geneva. Perhaps this fountain could replace the fountain already in position at the bottom of Janadhipathi Mandiriya as that fountain has the disadvantage of obscuring the view of the sea and the opening up of the wide view of Colombo as you leave the Fort. Even if this fountain is kept in position it could be altered to make the base very much wider and provide this fountain with a greater volume of water so that great sheets of water pour over the large basin in a low-level flat pool almost the size of the roundabout. The small-scale details of planting too, in this rea, are unsuitable, as the plants themselves cannot possibly thrive in so wind blown and bare a locale. This can all be thought of in detail when plans are being made for the whole area. I cannot emphasize too much that the whole area from the Fort to the Galle Face Hotel should be treated as one wide, cohesive, urban area, and small, individual design efforts, however well planned in themselves, should be avoided.

4. Lighting:

The lighting along the sea front promenade should not be too bright but must obviously give sufficient light to make the length of walkway safe and agreeable. These lights should be shaded from the east so that parked cars looking across the green even at night could see the width of horizon without visual disturbance. The centre roadway lights would be much brighter and probably remain as they are, but even this would be improved if they were shaded so that they were trained on the roadway, causing no glare.

5. Toilets:

This is a great necessity and must be so planned that they are virtually invisible, and this could be done possibly by placing them under the sea front walkway, and entered from the beach itself, with stairways going down to them. It would be a necessity to staff these toilets and keep them in a clean and wholesome state, and the ventilation of the toilet area should be ensured, possibly with a forced-drive ventilation system.

EDWARDS, REID AND BEGG, ARCHITECTS AND ENGINEERS

- 4 -

CONCLUSION:

The main thought underlying all these suggestions is that the Galle Face Green, as it is now, should remain open and free as it has always been, and that whatever we do to improve it should be done with great discretion, and in sympathy with its age old ambience of a public open space with a wide range of use.

Geoffrey Bawa

Colombo,
April 27, 1978

At the core of the report is a firm belief that Galle Face Green's significance is derived from its unspoiled views and the freedom and access to public space it affords to the people of Colombo. Bawa articulates the uniqueness of this particular space, and all his interventions aim to preserve and enhance these features. He offers us a few timeless attributes that make Galle Face Green unique as the "only place in Colombo which is widely open to the sky with no trees or buildings infringing on the whole arc of the heavens"[18] and "it is also the only place where one sees an unhindered long view of the horizon and the sunset."[19]

Preserving this view by removing obstructions and ensuring access is the central thread that ties all the suggestions in the report together. He recommends that the space should be kept "absolutely free and untrammeled as it has been for so many years, and it can remain an open, wide, grassed area for the people in Sri Lanka and the people in Colombo to use in as free a way as possible."[20] Bawa's vision for the space is conservative in that it seeks to make few changes and largely wishes to retain the status quo. Its ethos revolves around preserving the heritage and essence of a place and that "the Galle Face Green, as it is now, should remain open and free as it has always been, and that whatever we do to improve it should be done with great discretion, and in sympathy with its old age ambience of a public open space with a wide range of use."[21]

To Bawa, the view of the sea is sacred. He finds fault with the fountain at the bottom of Janadhipathi Mandiraya, the president's residence to the north of Galle Face Green, as it obstructs the view of the ocean as one leaves the green. This edge of the green is special to him, because "the views from there put the whole perspective of Colombo clearly, and the view gives the proper urban perspective."[22] He provides two alternatives to this: one, to replace the fountain with a jet in the middle of Beira Lake, similar to Lake Geneva; and two, to widen the existing fountain. Both ideas gained traction in the following months. On July 3, Dr. Poologasundram, engineer and partner at Edwards, Reid and Begg, dispatched an associate to measure the fountain at Janadhipathi Mandiraya – and sketches developed in July offer a snapshot of the original design, before further alterations were made.[23]

Many of Bawa's recommendations fall in this register of preserving both free access and views and ensuring that one does not despoil the other. Utilities, from lighting to seating, must serve their purpose in as discreet a way as possible. He notes that cars should not be allowed to drive onto the green but also that any curb designed to stop this should be as unobtrusive as possible and allow for cars parked on the side to look down at the green and ocean without interference. Similarly, the report specifies that any seating built on the promenade should not be taller than 30 inches and that lighting for the walkway should be shaded from

18 Bawa, "Galle Face Report," 1, GB/DOC/003/02, Box 01, Bon Chamberlin fonds, Geoffrey Bawa Archives, Colombo, Sri Lanka.

19 Bawa, "Galle Face Report," 1, GB/DOC/003/02, Box 01, Bon Chamberlin fonds, Geoffrey Bawa Archives, Colombo, Sri Lanka.

20 Bawa, "Galle Face Report," 1, GB/DOC/003/02, Box 01, Bon Chamberlin fonds, Geoffrey Bawa Archives, Colombo, Sri Lanka.

21 Bawa, "Galle Face Report," 4, GB/DOC/003/02, Box 01, Bon Chamberlin fonds, Geoffrey Bawa Archives, Colombo, Sri Lanka.

22 Bawa, "Galle Face Report," 3, GB/DOC/003/02, Box 01, Bon Chamberlin fonds, Geoffrey Bawa Archives, Colombo, Sri Lanka.

23 Dr. Poologasundram to the officer-in-charge of the fountain at Galle Face Roundabout, July 3, 1978, GB/DOC/003/00, Box 01, Bon Chamberlin fonds, Geoffrey Bawa Archives, Colombo, Sri Lanka.

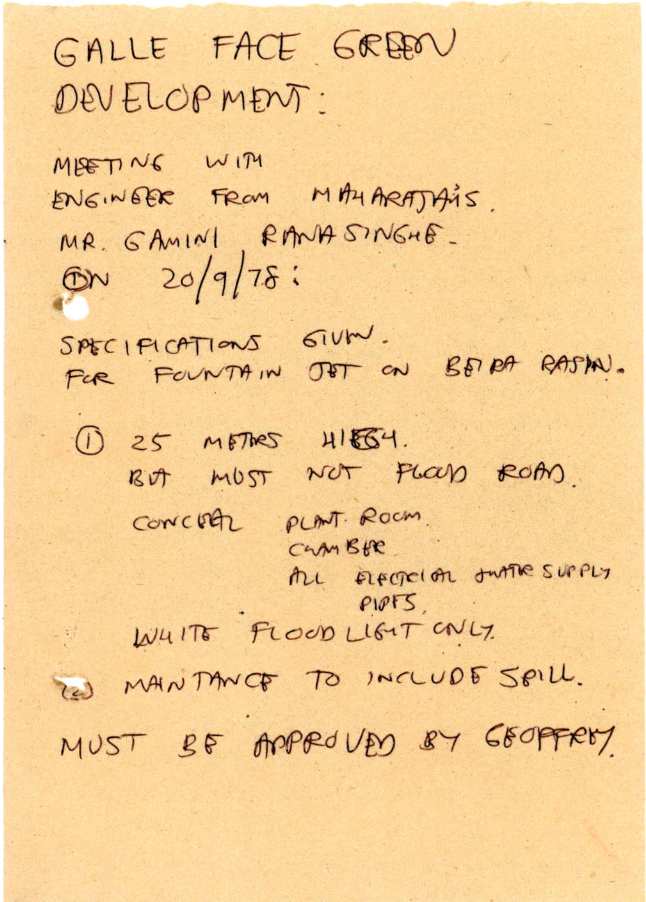

GALLE FACE GREEN
DEVELOPMENT:

MEETING WITH
ENGINEER FROM MAHARAJAH'S.
MR. GAMINI RANASINGHE.
ON 20/9/78:

SPECIFICATIONS GIVEN.
FOR FOUNTAIN JET ON BEIRA BASIN.

(1) 25 METRES HIGH.
BUT MUST NOT FLOOD ROAD.
CONCEAL PLANT ROOM.
CHAMBER.
ALL ELECTRICAL & WATER SUPPLY
PIPES,
WHITE FLOOD LIGHT ONLY.
(2) MAINTANCE TO INCLUDE SPILL.

MUST BE APPROVED BY GEOFFREY.

Handwritten memorandum from the office of Geoffrey Bawa regarding the Galle Face Green Development, Colombo, ink on paper, ca. 1978

the east so that the glare does not cause a visual disturbance. There is also an ingenious scheme to place public toilets under the seafront walkway so that they would be completely invisible and accessed only from the beach – here Bawa helpfully adds, "It would be a necessity to staff these toilets and keep them in a clean and wholesome state."[24]

The drawing that accompanied the Galle Face Report is lost, as are the other plans and reports made for the committee. This partial archive is due to wider circumstances as much as to personal idiosyncrasy.[25] Writing to Nimalasiri Silva, deputy director of the Tourist Board, who also sat on the beautification committee, Bawa bemoans the fact that "this country is very short of printing paper," allowing him to make only one set of plans to be circulated.[26]

The objects in the report offer a chance to examine how landscapes hold multiple signs and meanings. They are encoded with Bawa's attitudes and values, but they also offer conflicting meanings. Consider how trees in the plan signify visual disturbance – Bawa insists that "it would be an utterly wrong thing to do to make little bays of planting, however good they may be, anywhere along its length on the seaward side of the main Galle Road." However, he acknowledges that trees can provide valuable shade and again, balancing utility and aesthetics, suggests that trees be planted on the eastern side of the Galle Road. He is designing with the landscape and its climate rather than against it, in keeping with the practices of tropical modernism architecture, where designs are based around the climatic extremes and realities of a varying

24 Bawa, "Galle Face Report," 2, GB/DOC/003/02, Box 01, Bon Chamberlin fonds, Geoffrey Bawa Archives, Colombo, Sri Lanka.
25 This fragmentation of the Bawa Archive is described by other authors in this volume.
26 Geoffrey Bawa to Nimalasiri Silva, June 19, 1978, GB/DOC/003/03, Box 01, Bon Chamberlin fonds, Geoffrey Bawa Archives, Colombo, Sri Lanka.

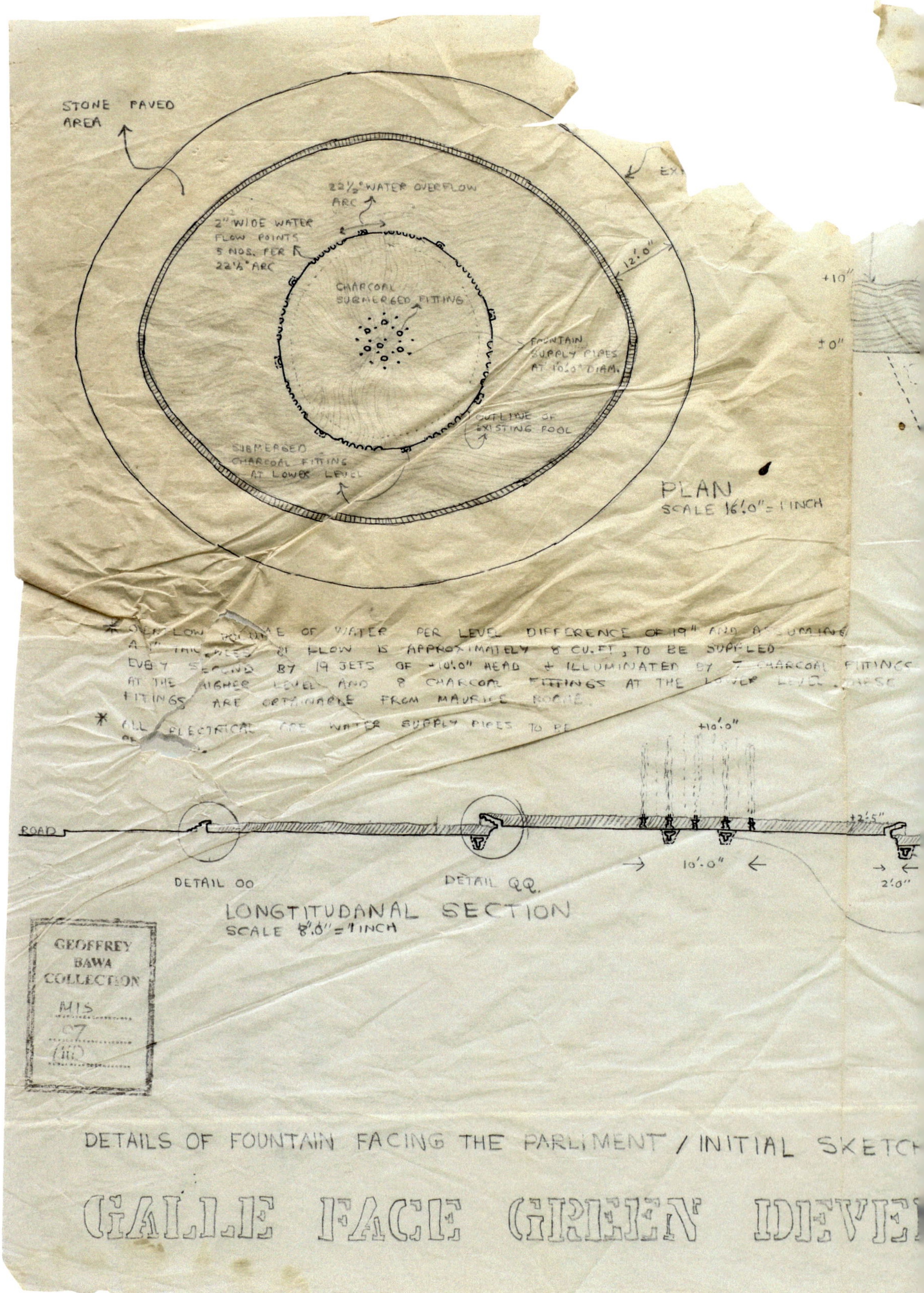

Galle Face Green Development, Colombo, Details of fountain facing the Parliament; initial sketch, graphite and ink on tracing paper, 1978

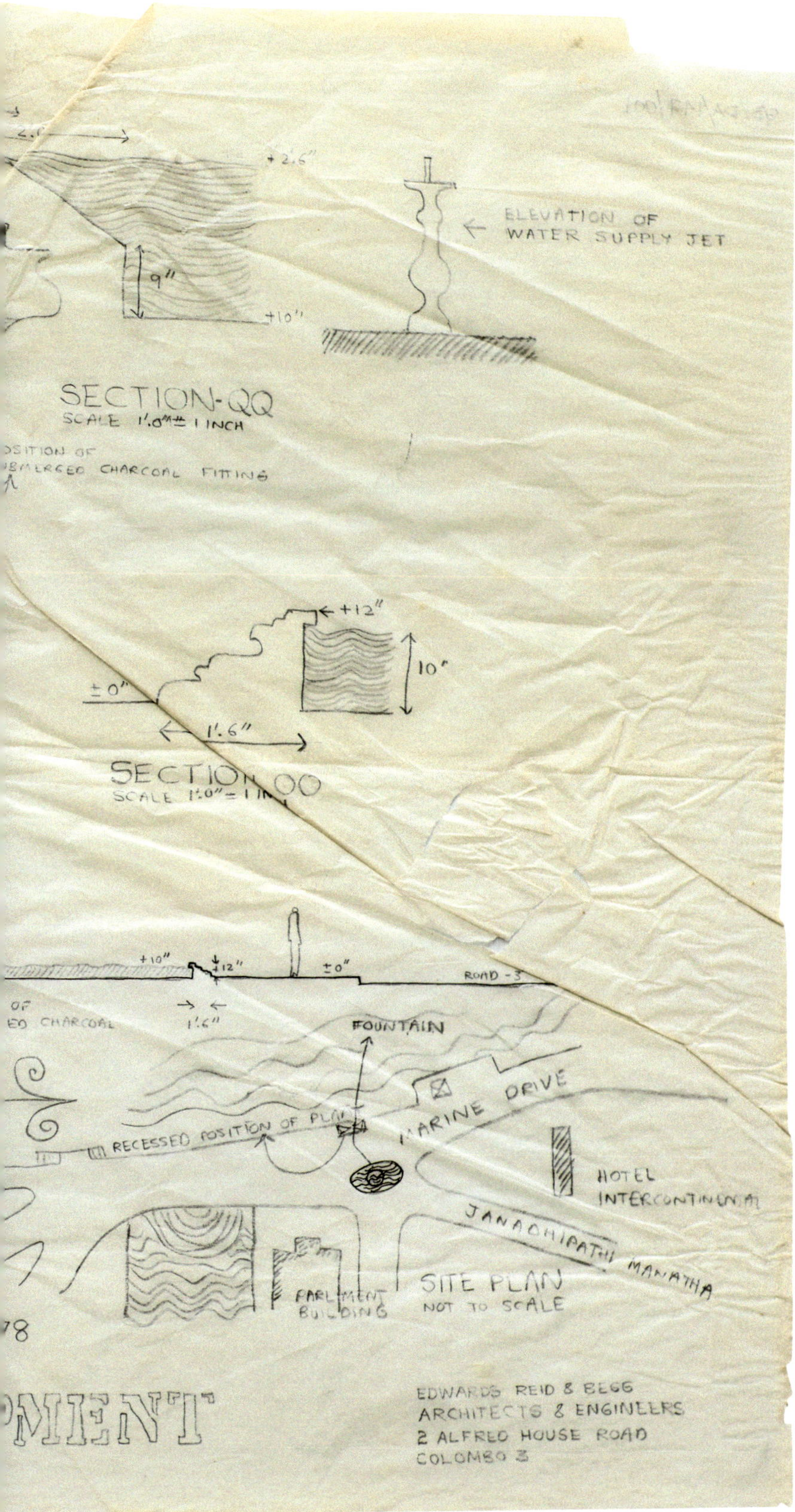

ELEVATION OF
WATER SUPPLY JET
SECTION-QQ
SCALE 1'.0"± 1 INCH
SUBMERGED CHARCOAL FITTING
+12"
10"
±0"
1'.6"
SECTION OO
ROAD - 3
FOUNTAIN
MARINE DRIVE
RECESSED POSITION OF PLAN
HOTEL
INTERCONTINENTAL
JANADHIPATHI MAWATHA
PARLIAMENT
BUILDING
SITE PLAN
NOT TO SCALE
EDWARDS REID & BEGG
ARCHITECTS & ENGINEERS
2 ALFRED HOUSE ROAD
COLOMBO 3

Sri Lankan climate. He displays a similar sensitivity to climate here, asserting that only trees whose shape is unaffected by the wind should be chosen. Any attempt to green the fountain at the base of Janadhipathi Mandiraya is doomed because "the plants themselves cannot possibly thrive in so wind blown and bare a locale."[27]

Tree planting is one of the more obvious ways in which past and recent beautification efforts deviate from Bawa's recommendations. Again, this is perhaps due to semiotic difference, a clash in how planners view trees that encode beauty and shade rather than visual disturbance. Bawa's criteria for the selection of tree species is based on utility or sensitivity to climate, and this was appreciated by the decision-makers of the time, with the minutes of the meeting recording that "All tree planting should be done on the land side of the Galle Face Centre Road i.e. from the wall sides of the buildings such as Ceyfish, Tourist Board Premises, Army Headquarters Military Sports Ground etc. with sea ozone resistant plants such as Casuarina, Mudilla, Vettekeya etc. as per Mr. Bawa's Plan."[28]

Changes to the foliage at Galle Face Green is now based on a vastly different understanding of what trees mean and symbolize. For instance, palm trees planted along Galle Face Green were uprooted in 2012, partly because of their association with regions in the northern and eastern parts of the country, which are occupied by ethnic minorities.[29] They were replaced not only by coconut palms, but also with lightweight fiberglass pillars similar to those found in the Anuradhapura Kingdom, an ancient Sinhalese civilization.[30] The most recent wave of beautification has seen coconut trees remain in bays along the green, which double as seating. These instances of deliberate urban change reveal that the semiotics of landscape is not merely an abstract pedantic exercise but that the iconography and associations behind an object inform decision-making in tangible ways.

It also underscores the idea that planning in cities is more than the mere competition of architectural aesthetics; rather, it is a struggle over space by differing ideological projects that can be based on gender, class, race and religion.[31] The trees remind us of the failure of Bawa's report, emphasizing the wildly different trajectory that urban development took.

It is difficult when reading the report and chancing on such instances to avoid reductive before-and-after comparisons, thinking of the space as a time lapse seen on Google Earth. Part of the allure of unbuilt environments is the nostalgia they evoke. It is a nostalgia not for the past but for the future possibilities it once held.[32] Given the rapid transformation that has occurred at Galle Face Green in the last ten years, it is easy to give in to the siren's call of nostalgic reminiscing. Dutch colonial-era cannons that were intended to guard against the vanquished Portuguese now

27 Bawa, "Galle Face Report," 2, GB/DOC/003/02, Box 01, Bon Chamberlin fonds, Geoffrey Bawa Archives, Colombo, Sri Lanka.

28 Special Committee Meeting Minutes, May 16, 1978.

29 Mandana Ismail Abeywickrema, "SLPA Uproots Trees to Beautify Galle Face," *The Sunday Leader*, February 5, 2012, www.thesundayleader.lk/2012/02/05/slpa-uproots-trees-to-beautify-galle-face.

30 Abeywickrema, "SLPA Uproots Trees to Beautify Galle Face."

31 Jacobs, "The City Unbound," 832.

32 See Ashley Carse and David Kneas, "Unbuilt and Unfinished: The Temporalities of Infrastructure," *Environment and Society* 10, no. 1 (2019): 9–28.

watch over a sandy stretch of land reclaimed from the ocean, the city of a future international hub. A bronze statue of S. W. R. D. Bandaranaike, a former prime minister of Sri Lanka, gifted by the Soviet Union in 1976 only two years before Bawa's report, now rests in the shadow of a Shangri-La Hotel.[33] Many will continue to remember the Shangri-La Hotel for a different reason – it was one of the hotels affected by the Easter Sunday attacks in 2019. The space continues to accrue signs, and meanings converge and refract. In April 2022 Galle Face Green became the primary site of continuous protests over the ongoing economic crisis, as well as a larger call for political accountability.

Nostalgia for a past pregnant with prosperous futures or to retreat to a seemingly simpler way of life comes at the expense of more radical readings of this document. Change is inevitable, and Bawa's recommendations need not be viewed as perfect, desirable or aesthetically pleasing merely because they were never realized. Neither are they examples of design that should be blindly applied to the space immediately as if to rectify a past wrong. Rather, the report offers a counterfactual, untaken pathway and with it a chance to consider the fluid and uncertain process of planning, as well as how symbolism, values and ideology play out in space and time.[34] It is about opening the possibility of an alternative urban form through examining the shadow histories and untaken paths. This challenges the tyrannical inevitability of urban development and the immutability of the present. The landscape is instead a malleable fabric, shaped before, shaped now and reshaped continually.

33 Zahran Imtiaz, "Sculpting SWRD 'Larger than Life,'" *The Sunday Observer*, October 2, 2016, archives.sundayobserver.lk/2016/10/02/fea06.asp.

34 Carse and Kneas, "Unbuilt and Unfinished," 17.

Batujimbar Estate, Bali, cover of sales catalog, printed ink on coated paper, illustrated by Ida Bagus Nyoman Rai, 1975

Place, Flows and Transformations: Bawa in Bali

Shirley Surya

The Batujimbar Estate in Bali – Bawa's second project outside Sri Lanka – has been touted as an early exemplar of the "Bali style" resort; but it has also been critiqued as a speculative development of holiday homes and a superficial translation of indigenous architecture for elites seeking intimacy with Bali without sacrificing their air-conditioned lifestyle. Such views, coupled with a site visit to Bali and an analysis of the project's conception – including its diverse intentions and locally engendered conditions of difference – form this essay's premise to reconsider Bawa's work in Bali along the lines of a more networked signification of place across local, national and regional contexts.

Place and Flows

The study of architectural production that does not consider the specific sociocultural landscapes from which it emerged results in the flattening, or stylistic labeling, of projects arising from disparate contexts. In assessing a design's relevance to its context, projects like Batujimbar Estate need to be understood beyond formalist readings.[1] This requires considering agents – other than architects – who shaped conditions that led to the conception of Bali's holiday-home-by-the sea. It entails the knowledge of Batujimbar Estate as part of a transnational flow of commodities between Bali and other sites of globalized modernity, as well as the "transcendent consciousness" of the cosmopolitan leisure class involved in the project.[2]

In 1967 Dutch-Indonesian collector-entrepreneur-hotel owner Wija Waworuntu and Australian artist-collector Donald Friend each bought land in Batujimbar to construct properties of their own.[3] The idea for the Estate, with Bawa as the project's architect, was developed in 1973, when Waworuntu and Friend realized that wealthy locals, expatriates in Indonesia and foreigners were all in search of congenial get-away homes in Bali.[4] It was planned as an estate of luxurious villas along a 500-meter strip of beach frontage, though an earlier master plan indicated a more ambitious

1 On the need for discussions on critical regionalism to pay attention to the "voices of those responsible for building particular cultures" so as to understand the "richness of internal, local discourses," refer to Keith L. Eggener, "Placing Resistance: A Critique of Critical Regionalism," *Journal of Architectural Education* 55, no. 4 (May 2002): 235.

2 On Bali's being "simultaneously enmeshed in local worlds and transnational commodity relations," see Linda Connor and Adrian Vickers, "Crisis, Citizenship, and Cosmopolitanism: Living in a Local and Global Risk Society in Bali," *Indonesia*, no. 75 (April 2003): 155. On the "transcendent consciousness" of the touristic international middle class, see Dean MacCannell, *A New Theory of the Leisure Class* (Berkeley: University of California Press, 1999), 13.

3 On Wija Waworuntu's role in conceiving Tandjung Sari and Batujimbar Estate, see Diana Darling, *Tandjung Sari: A Magical Door to Bali* (Singapore: Editions Didier Miller, 2012), 28. On Donald Friend's role in conceiving Batujimbar Estate, see Donald Friend, *The Diaries of Donald Friend*, vol. 4, ed. Paul Hetherington (Canberra: National Library of Australia, 2006), 59. Friend's diaries reveal both his ethically questionable living and his contributions to the development of the arts and architecture in Sri Lanka and Bali.

4 Friend, *Diaries*, 292–93. On May 2, 1973, Friend noted investors' interest in Batujimbar Estate and his "plugging hard for Geoffrey Bawa" as architect for the Estate.

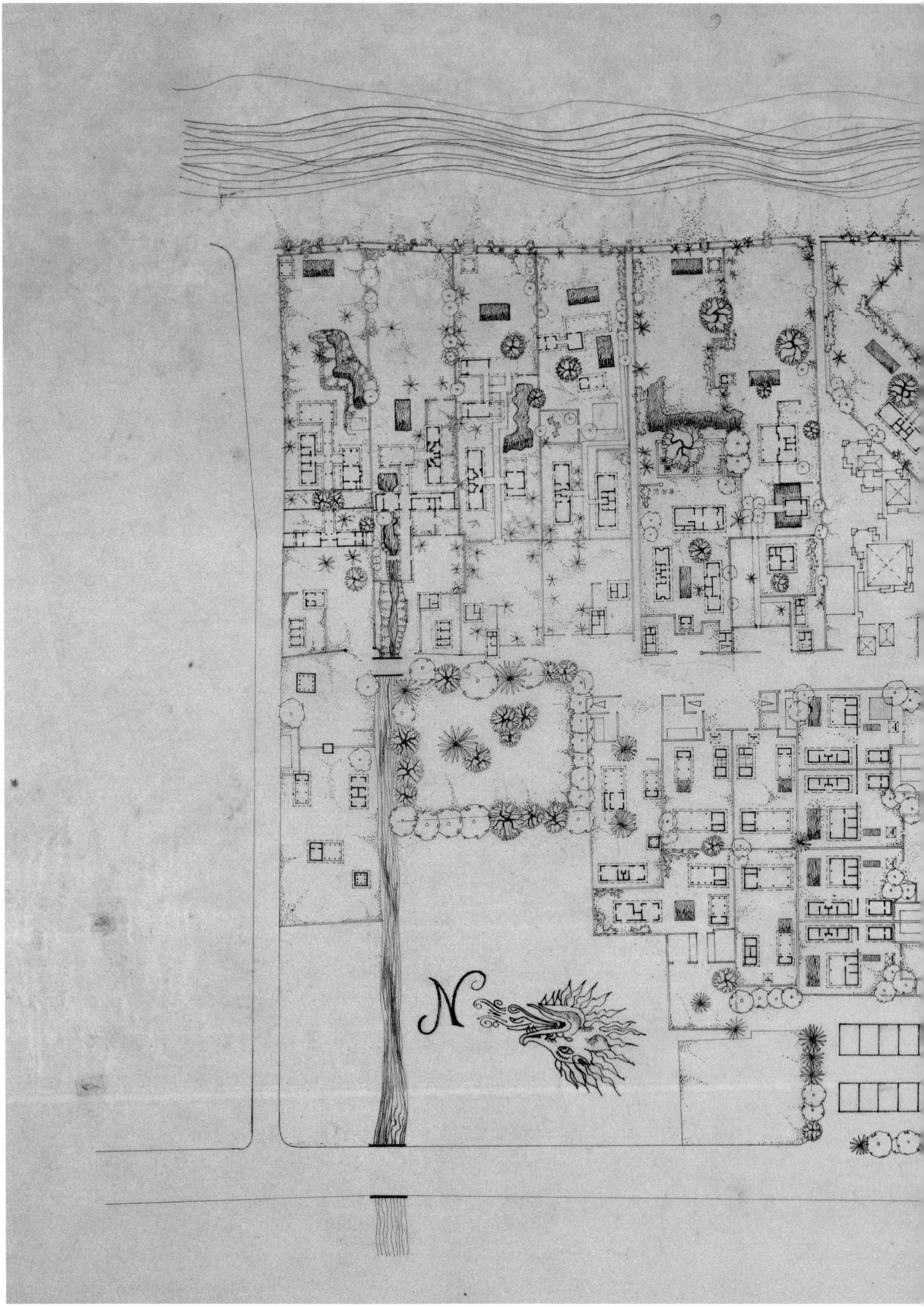

Batujimbar Estate, Bali, early unpublished master plan, ink on tracing paper

0 5 10 20 30 40 50 60 70 80 90 100 Metres

development.[5] Bawa's arrangement of pavilions was varied and asymmetrical, with different hierarchies of privacy. Between 1973 and 1974, Bawa provided individual designs for eight out of the fifteen designated plots, though he only saw through the completion of buildings on three. Nevertheless, Bawa's built and unbuilt designs were considered influential in shaping the scale and style of subsequent "tropical resorts" in Bali, with their mastery of an architectural language that drew from local Balinese architecture and materials while providing a vision of modernity and comfort for well-heeled tourists.[6] The entire development ran out of financial steam by late 1974 and the plots were eventually sold to different owners to build their own homes. By the late 1970s, the Estate was Bali's most expensive residential neighborhood and a "magnet for celebrities."[7]

The project's appeal to the outsider elite's specific interpretation of tradition packaged in modernity has inevitably cast doubt on its local or regional relevance – similar to how Bawa's projects have been viewed in Sri Lanka.[8] Yet to dismiss it on such grounds neglects the realities of the middle-to-upper-class cosmopolitan leisure class whose "eclectic methodology" had led to the production, consumption and mediation of Bali's holiday-home-by-the-sea – a building type that still reverberates.[9] Bali, as a site for Indonesians and foreign tourism, is also as tightly bound to an international web of capital as Batujimbar Estate, which was elaborately financed by British developer Bowaters. This was even more so during the pivotal years of touristic development in Bali in the 1970s, when foreign investments brought about external cultural influences.[10] Bali's identity became mutable and conditional, shaped by the consumption and imagining of a touristic Bali by international middle-class tourist-like expatriates – just as the definition of *Balinese* had been sharpened by the advent of tourism since the early twentieth century. As travelers of a certain type, they systematically discover and employ new and differing experiences, weaving them into a collective and touristic version of other peoples and places aligned to their "values, industry and future

5 Friend, *Diaries*, 285.
6 David Robson, *Beyond Bawa* (London: Thames & Hudson, 2007), 83.
7 Darling, *Tandjung Sari*, 31.
8 For an example of such criticisms, see Anoma Pieris, *Architecture and Nationalism in Sri Lanka: The Trouser under the Cloth* (London: Routledge, 2013), 147.
9 On the "eclectic methodology" of the cosmopolitan middle class, characterized by a combination of an imagined "tourist Bali" with a transcultural sophisticated lifestyle – particularly in the form of "tropical style" holiday houses in Bali – see Connor and Vickers, "Crisis, Citizenship, and Cosmopolitanism," 155, 159–60 and 169.
10 Darling, *Tandjung Sari*, 22–26.

Batujimbar Estate
Bali, Wija Waworuntu looking at drawings, gelatin silver print, Geoffrey Bawa

Composite drawing of materials and structural features in vernacular Balinese architecture, ink on paper

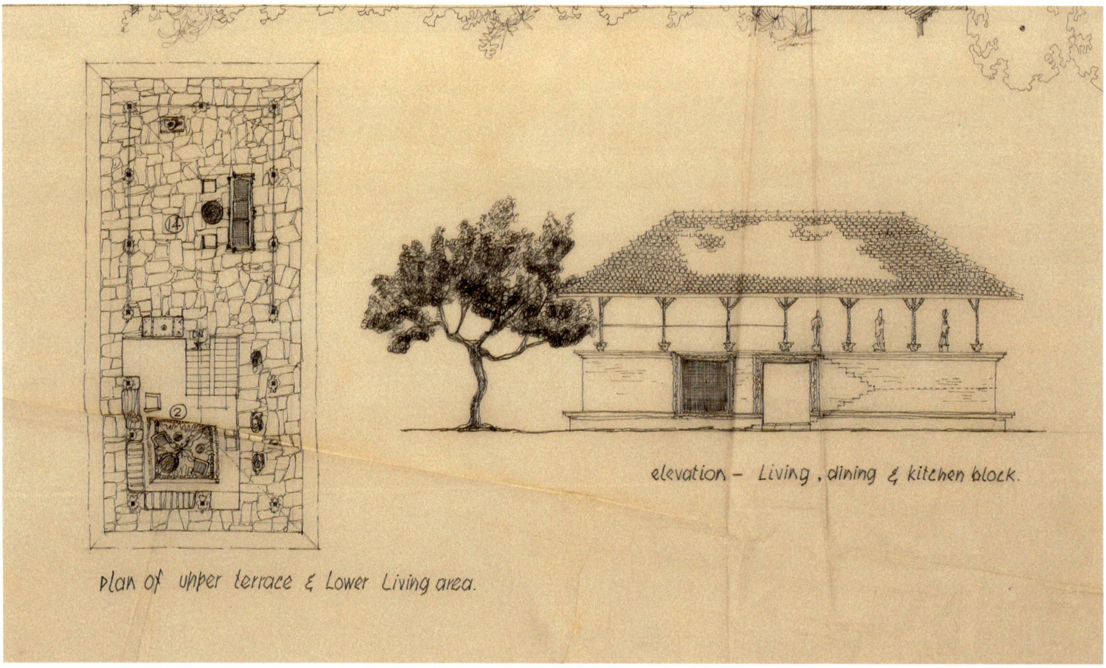

Batujimbar Estate, Bali, plan and elevation of living, dining and kitchen block, ink on tracing paper

designs."[11] While they could seem to encroach on the local, they can also be seen as purveyors of disruptive values and lifestyles, including building one's abode or hotels by the sea, which the locals shunned as Balinese cosmology frames the sea as lurking with danger.[12] Jimmy Pandy, a Dutch-Indonesian expatriate art dealer, built a home on Sanur beach as early as in the 1940s, which was known to inspire Waworuntu to construct his house-turned-hotel Tandjung Sari in 1962.[13] Its success as Bali's first boutique hotel was due to Waworuntu's foresight in understanding tourists' desire to live in what they imagined was a Balinese way, with modern comforts.[14] This resulted in the use of local materials, building techniques and building types – including a *wantilan* (two-tiered open-roof pavilion) under a soaring roof as a restaurant – plus modern amenities like swimming pools, bars and gardens. Waworuntu's "beach bungalows" and "thatched tiny residences" made of bamboo in turn inspired Donald Friend to move to Bali and build his own *wantilan* house.[15] As a product of Waworuntu's and Friend's vision of a local yet transcultural Bali, Batujimbar Estate is thus a legacy of this line of expatriates whose "ethnographic conscience" of investigating and preserving some aspects of locality while simultaneously weaving them into a contemporary mode of living led to their catalytic roles as interpreters of change in the Balinese way of living. Similar "eclectic methodologies," which characterized Bawa's work, bolstered a change in decision to work with Bawa. This was enhanced after Friend's and Waworuntu's visit to residences and hotels Bawa designed, like the Bentota Beach Hotel (1967–69) in Sri Lanka. Built on a massive stone fortification, it reflected a combined sense of medieval forts and colonial bungalows of the past, while equipped with facilities for the modern traveler.[16]

The conception of Batujimbar Estate could also be attributed to its being part of a "metropolitan superculture"[17] of Bali and Southeast Asia in the 1970s – a multidirectional and transnational traffic of human, capital and commodity along an urban corridor

11 MacCannell, *A New Theory of the Leisure Class*, 13.
12 On spatial and spiritual orientation according to Bali's Hindu cosmology – in which a seaward direction is associated with *kelod* (impurity) in contrast to a direction toward the holy mountain of Gunung Agung as *kaja* (sacredness) – see Fred B. Eiseman, *Bali: Sekala & Niskala*, vol. 2, *Essays on Society, Tradition and Craft* (Singapore: Periplus Editions, 1992), 3. On foreign expatriates' role of building Bali's first beachside dwellings since the 1920s, see Darling, *Tandjung Sari*, 12–17.
13 Darling, *Tandjung Sari*, 40–44.
14 Darling, *Tandjung Sari*, 28.
15 Friend, *Diaries*, 2 and 25. Friend first experienced Tandjung Sari in 1966, which led him to consider buying land and building a similarly thatched beach bungalow nearby in 1967.
16 Friend, *Diaries*, 293; Brian Brace Taylor, ed., *Geoffrey Bawa: Architect in Sri Lanka* (Singapore: Mimar with Concept Media, 1986), 126–31; Robson, *Beyond Bawa*, 67.
17 Connor and Vickers, "Crisis, Citizenship, and Cosmopolitanism," 160 and 167–69.

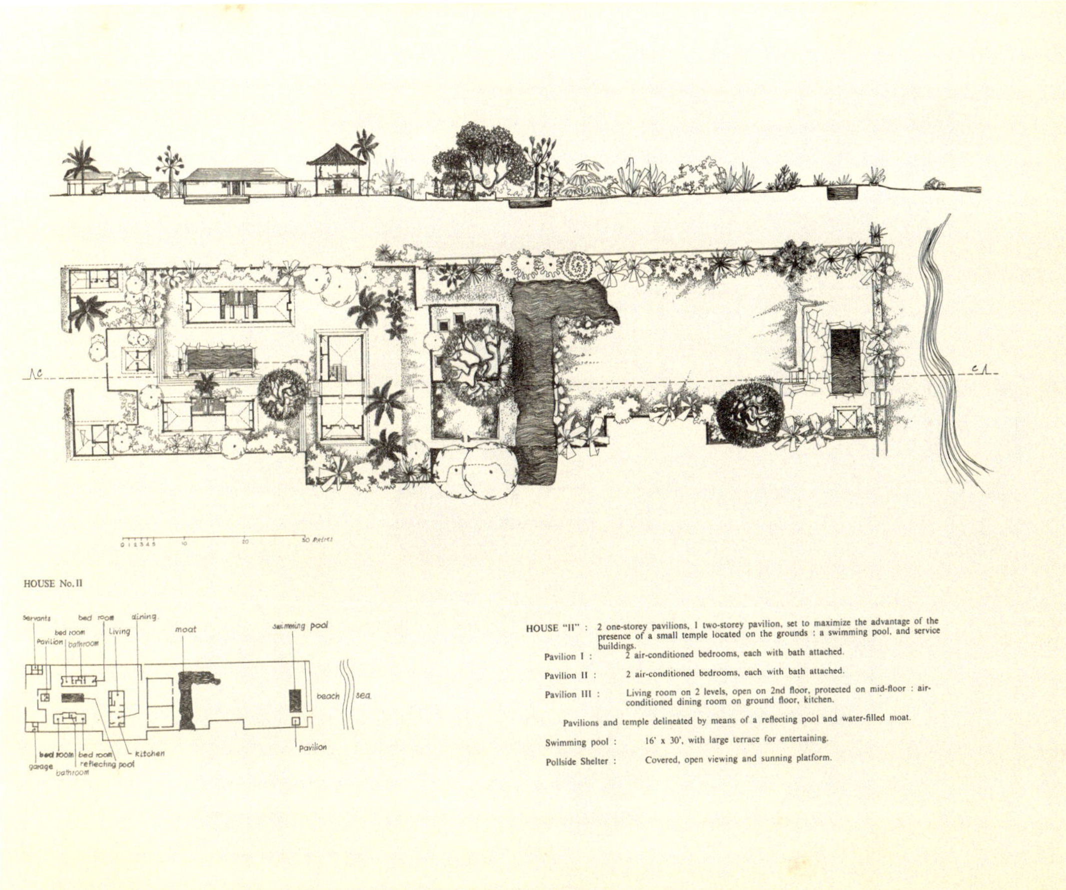

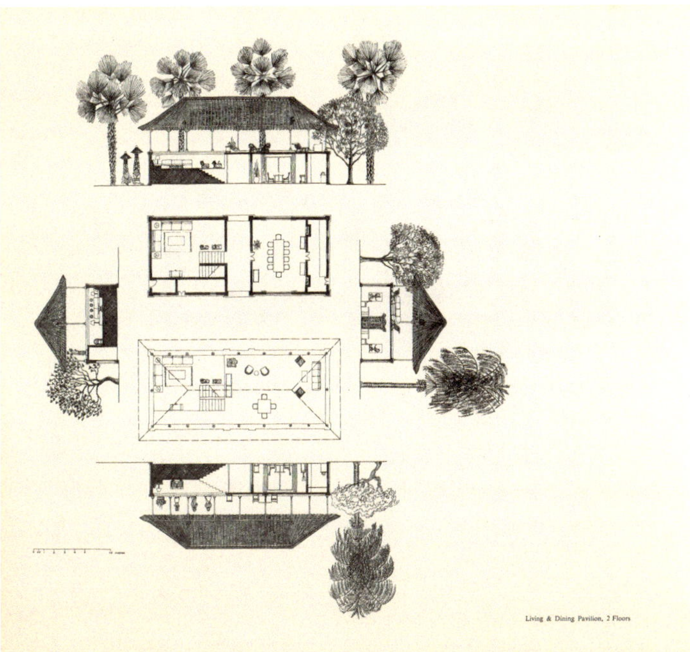

Batujimbar Estate, Bali, site plan and sectional elevation of house no. 11 (top) and plan and elevations of living and dining pavilion on plot 11 (bottom), printed ink on coated paper, 1975

Batujimbar Estate, Bali, interior view of pavilion, digital photograph, color, Shirley Surya, 2019

connecting smaller cities like Bali with other cities, such as Hong Kong and Singapore, considered to be "paradigmatic locations of Asian modernity." Characterized by political and aesthetic leanings that influenced choices of lifestyle and material consumption, this superculture included the jet-setting expatriate bourgeoisie who made Bali the corridor's relaxation center by having their holiday and second houses there. They were the investors, designers and homeowners involved in the production and consumption of Batujimbar Estate. This was reflected in Donald Friend's description of the Estate: Bali as part of the "metropolitan corridors" of Hong Kong, Bangkok and Singapore, while its villas were "small pleasure palaces where princes might retire from burdensome duties."[18] These descriptions generate fantasies of Batujimbar Estate and Bali as a material paradise, demonstrating Bawa's continuity in developing spaces that are "rich, expansive and deeply pleasurable," just as he did in Sri Lanka.[19] This meant designing the Estate with the Balinese way of living in which art was considered a "daily necessity," with the villas demanding "an active enjoyment of Art and Life" from the dwellers. Their design thus focused on local craftsmanship, materials and forms of ornamentation, while incorporating modern amenities to "ensure complete ease of living and maximum comfort."[20] While it is easy to satirize such homes as pretensions of the nouveaux riches, these luxury houses have become hallmarks of modernity and prestige, which the middle class in Bali and other parts of Indonesia aspire to. The seemingly conflicted nature of Batujimbar Estate – with its equal leveraging of Bali's local distinctiveness and contemporary

18 Donald Friend and Geoffrey Bawa, *Batujimbar Bali* (Colombo), 20.

19 On associating Bawa's work with a material paradise, refer to Shanti Jayawardene, *Geoffrey Manning Bawa: Decolonising Architecture* (Sri Lanka: National Trust Sri Lanka, 2017), 218; and Channa Daswatte, "The Architecture of Paradise," *The Sri Lanka Architect* 101, no. 20 (December–February 1997/98): 13–21, 28–33.

20 Friend and Bawa, *Batujimbar Bali*, 3, 8 and 23.

aspirations of the cosmopolitan group – is aligned with an identity that is "worldly," "urbane" and "sophisticated."[21]

Nevertheless, the design of Batujimbar Estate represented Waworuntu's and Friend's ongoing commitment to Balinese culture – even if their "ethnographical conscience" was based on subjective perceptions.[22] Friend and Waworuntu attempted to identify, preserve and revive traditional Balinese art forms and practices deemed under threat from an increasingly commercial tourist industry. They studied "architectural fantasies in the villages;" admired the skills of masons, carpenters and artisans and hired them for their projects; collected bronzes, woodcarvings and paintings; built their own kilns to make local clays; and paid high prices for antique doors, windows and local materials to be incorporated into new buildings designed to echo traditional Balinese architecture.[23] Upon Bawa's arrival, they arranged for him to "scan the site" and get "insights" on architectural possibilities, local materials and capabilities of craftsmen they worked with.[24] The Estate's sales brochure – which reads like a cultural guide rather than a commercial brochure – was also a product of such "ethnographical conscience." Its introductory texts and illustrations – of thatched roofs, carved pillar columns, carved gateways opening onto gardens and outrigger canoes – conjure up Bali's everyday scenes, materiality and planting through the lens of an explorer's imagination, similar to Friend's 1972 book *Donald Friend in Bali*.[25] In many ways, Friend and Waworuntu were akin to Bawa's network of designers and sympathetic clients in 1960s postcolonial Sri Lanka, who studied and embraced the aesthetic, structural and functional potential of indigenous architecture.[26]

In 1970s Bali, such emphasis on a filtered sense of locality was more than an exercise of nostalgia or symbolic nationalism, with implications for Bali's urban socioeconomic development amid incoming pressure of foreign investment in the bid of economic growth. The aesthetic ambition of a project like Batujimbar Estate – which could seem relegated to the trivial pursuit of class distinction and conspicuous consumption – presented a creative potential of developing new forms of social values, organization and action.[27] While the 11-story, 300-room Bali Beach Hotel (1963) was backed by Indonesia's first president, Sukarno, Waworuntu chose to turn his holiday home in Sanur into a group of bungalows akin to a Balinese village in the belief of developing high-quality tourism in Bali while stewarding and guarding its intrinsic local qualities and traditions. Bali Beach Hotel provoked a public outcry, which led the government to pass a decree limiting all future developments to the height of a 15-meter-tall coconut palm – and some give the credit for the adoption of this rule to Waworuntu.[28] He actively took part in a constituted corporation backed by civil and military government, with power to approve or reject hotel building, tourist transport and other investments, to "prevent the

21 Connor and Vickers, "Crisis, Citizenship, and Cosmopolitanism," 160 and 167–69.

22 On Friend's "ethnographical conscience," see Barry Pearce, "Donald Friend and Bali," in *Donald Friend's Bali: An Exhibition Arranged in Conjunction with the Donald Friend Retrospective, 9 February – 25 March 1990*, ed. J. Menzies (Sydney: Art Gallery of New South Wales, 1990), 39–44.

23 For examples, see Pearce, "Donald Friend and Bali"; and Friend, *Diaries*, 59, 60, 67, 82 and 94.

24 Friend, *Diaries*, 296 and 301.

25 See Friend and Bawa, *Batujimbar Bali*, 3–5; and Donald Friend, *Donald Friend in Bali: A Picaresque Novel* (London: Collins, 1972).

26 Jayawardene, *Geoffrey Manning Bawa*, 78, 81–82 and 121–22.

27 On the capacity of tourism, as a form of leisure and cultural industry, to be the basis of organizing social action, see MacCannell, *A New Theory of the Leisure Class*, 6.

28 See Michael Picard, *Bali: Cultural Tourism and Touristic Culture* (Singapore: Archipelago Press, 1996), 74; and Darling, *Tandjung Sari*, 34.

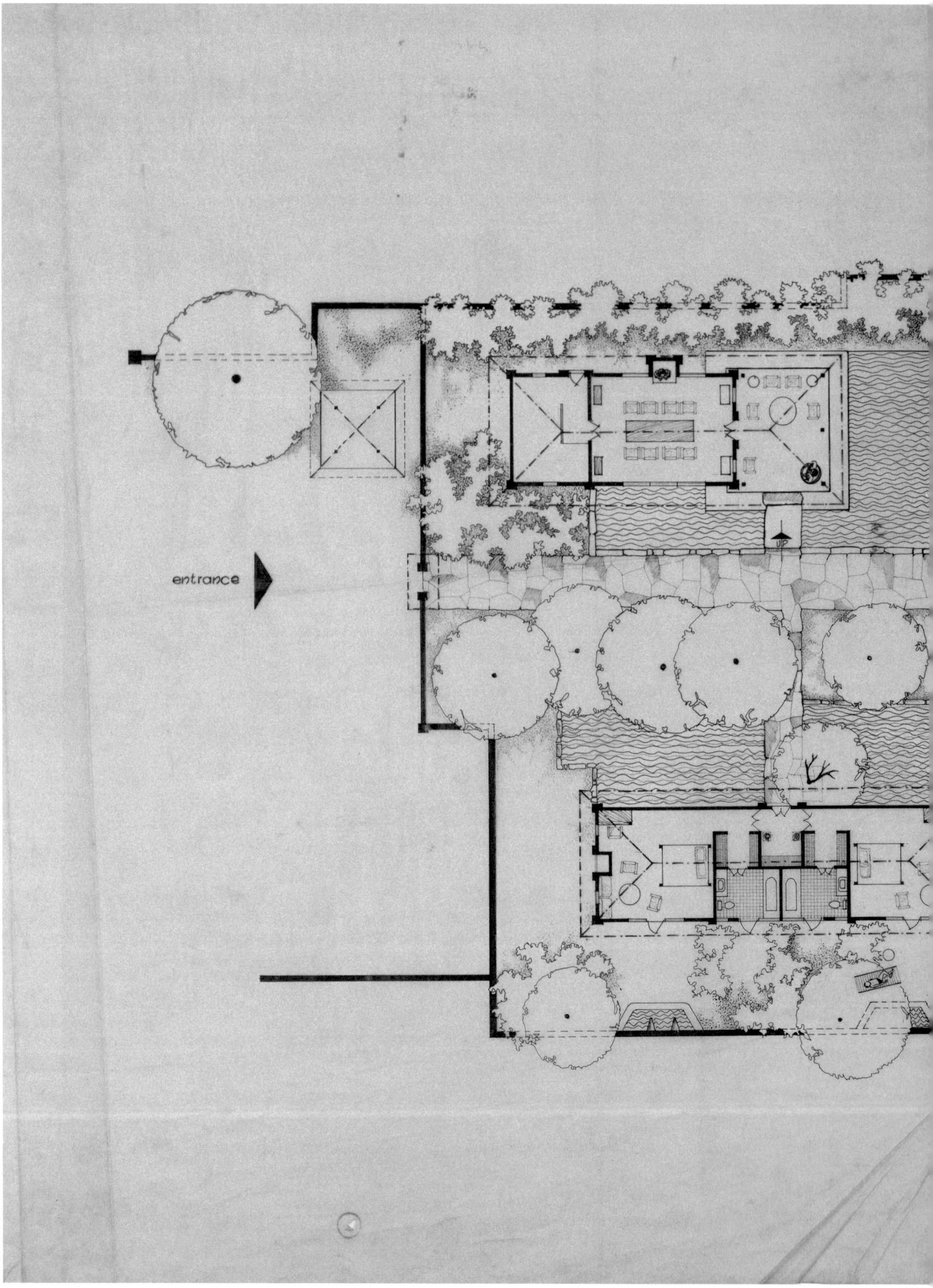

Batujimbar Estate, Bali, plan of house "A"
on plot 06, ink on tracing paper

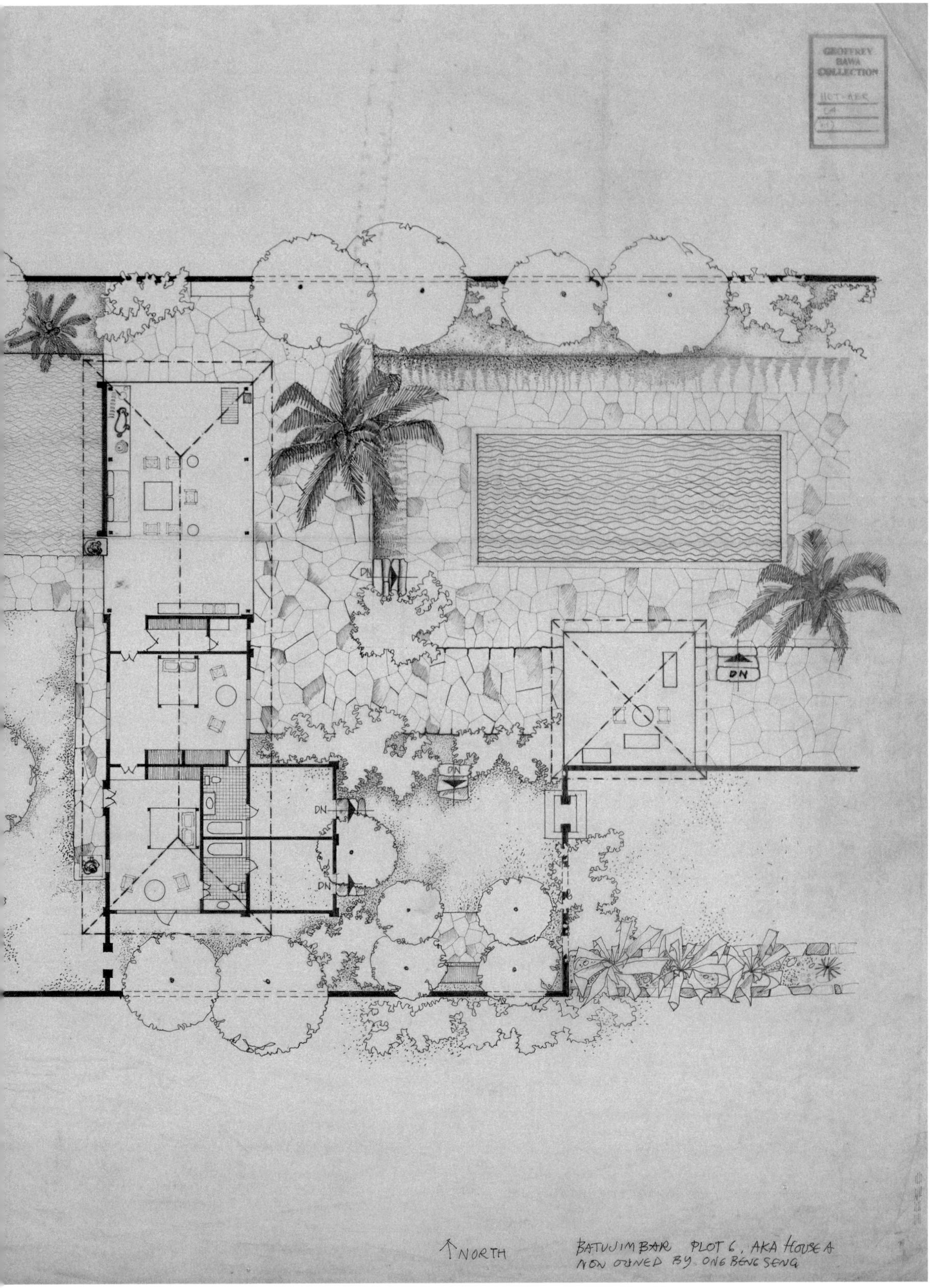
GEOFFREY BAWA COLLECTION
DN
DN
DN
DN
DN
NORTH
BATUJIMBAR PLOT 6, AKA HOUSE A
NON OWNED BY ONG BENG SENG

island [from] degenerating into a tourist hell."[29] Apart from Batujimbar Estate, Waworuntu and Friend's investment in another hotel development called Matahari – designed by Australian architect Peter Muller – similarly impacted the design development of hotels in Bali. While the project failed, its design in the form of a Balinese village-like collection of walled compounds, built using local materials and building methods, caught the imagination of Texan Wynncor Development Ltd, which was developing the Bali Hyatt after the Hiltons in Malta and Hong Kong. Designed by Hong Kong–based Palmer and Turner, Bali Hyatt was not only completed in two years to host the important Pacific Asia Travel Association (PATA) Conference, it changed the face of high-end hotels with its successful infusion of locality, its open-air lobby under a vast *alang-alang* roof and its restaurants and corridors opening to the gardens and beach.[30] At the PATA Conference in 1974, the government announced the development of the Nusa Dua resort complex, which sought to be a vanguard of modern tourism by protecting local culture and benefitting Bali's infrastructural development. Robi Sularto of Indonesian architectural firm Atelier Six – executive architect for the Batujimbar Estate – led the design of the Nusa Dua Beach Hotel.[31] It was thus not an overstatement when Friend expressed pride over the effect of their architectural ideas – in the form of projects like the Matahari and the Batujimbar Estate – on southeast Bali and its impact on local entities.[32] As a collective enterprise and transnational production across Colombo and Bali, Batujimbar Estate provided another compelling model of developing luxury tourism without losing a sense of place through careful consideration of scale, materiality, craft, labor and typology.

Place and Transformation

The place of Batujimbar Estate within a web of multiple sites, actors and socioeconomic-cultural forces shows that the design's appropriation of vernacular architecture was not a reaction against Western modernism but rather an affirmation of local culture.[33] It entailed varying degrees of a "willingness to accept things as they are" and a "desire to transform."[34] The process and outcome of the project reveal a belief in architecture's role in weaving disparate periods, geographies and programs into a fabric of modern existence.[35] Here, tradition was not inherently static, but a source to form new knowledge, through its engagement with present needs, pleasures of inhabitation and a more porous globalized modernity.

Bawa once wrote that to build well, one must hold "in true respect" how "each civilisation promotes its own philosophies and ways of life." While the sentence continues with how a building in Sri Lanka must be designed "in accord and sympathy with [the] ambience" of the island's beauty, climate and land, his premise was to design based on understanding the conditions wherever one

29 Friend, *Diaries*, 106.
30 Darling, *Tandjung Sari*, 33–34.
31 On Robi Sularto's role as executive architect for Batujimbar Estate and main architect behind design of Nusa Dua Beach Hotel – Bali's first major modern resort hotel designed by Indonesian architects, see Friend, *Diaries*, 315; and Nadia Purwestri and M. Nanda Widyarta, "Mencari Lokalitas: Atelier 6, Y. B. Mangunwijaya, dan Gedung Pusat Administrasi Universitas Indonesia," in *Tegang Bentang: Seratus Tahun Perspektif Arsitektur di Indonesia* (Jakarta: Gramedia Pustaka Utama, 2012), 122–24.
32 Friend, *Diaries*, 332 (May 24, 1974).
33 On how the architecture of Latin America was not about a resistance to the West but an affirmation of local culture, see Eggener, "Placing Resistance," 233.
34 MacCannell, *A New Theory of the Leisure Class*, 3.
35 MacCannell, *A New Theory of the Leisure Class*, 8 and 13.

builds, whether in Sri Lanka or elsewhere.[36] Indeed, Bawa applied these principles to his first overseas project, a staff club in Madurai, South India, by using locally sourced stone, antique columns and doors.[37] Bawa's goal during his first work trip to Bali was thus to visit as many sites as possible to "take architectural notes."[38] Photographs of palatial and rural pavilions and stepped entrances with carved stone figures and wooden posts reveal the extent of Bawa's study of buildings and spaces, from which he would grasp their tectonic qualities, materiality, proportions and layouts to utilize them as key elements and principles in his design.[39] In *Batujimbar Bali*, Bawa stated that "it was not difficult to imagine or establish the principles to govern the planning and design of the buildings," namely the use of Bali's time-tested material culture and craftsmanship, and for the Estate to be woven into the island's landscape and built environment.[40] His introduction also highlights integrating Balinese antiques and crafts, as well as the presence of water, which he observed as "essential to any Balinese house." However, Bawa did not reference vernacular building residential types, despite their clear affinity with his design. Instead, he focused on other principles related to allowing the "greatest range of visual pleasure" in spatial experience and ease of living by including modern amenities "without visual distraction."[41] While these various principles may seem disjunctive, they signify the seeming paradox and potential of the touristic approach of simultaneous veneration and transformation of the vernacular.

The materiality of Batujimbar Estate demonstrates most strongly its Balinese origins. Each house is flanked by an elaborately carved entrance gate in coral and *paras* (porous volcanic sandstone) and an antique door opening to a "guardian demon," with a compound of pavilions enveloped by *alang alang* surrounded by red coral walls. It reflects Bawa's priority of applying the Balinese way of building and local materials which "all Balinese architecture had used for centuries," in particular "brick, coral, timber and thatch."[42] Bawa's text was accompanied by a composite drawing of elevations and cross sections of windows, bases of stone sculptures and roofs of a *wantilan* (traditional open-air pavilion) with notations of materials such as *bambu* (bamboo) and *batu karang bukit* (coral stone), and other structural features like *trasram* (water-resistant) and *grantang bambu* (bamboo tube posts and beams). Just as Bawa had highlighted the roof as the "unchanging element of all buildings" in Sri Lanka, "governing the aesthetic" across time and place, the *alang-alang* (of grass and woven coconut leaves) thatched hip roof contributed the Estate's "strongest visual factor."[43] An early drawing indicating the use of a clay tile roof for the two-story pavilion on Plot 11 reveals a later notation on the appropriateness of using *alang alang* as the final choice of material. Indeed, the *alang alang* roof was important not only for its protective function against the sun and rain in a monsoonal climate, but also its shape,

36 Geoffrey Bawa, "A Way of Building," *Times of Ceylon Annual* (1968): 1–17.
37 Taylor, *Geoffrey Bawa*, 156–61; David Robson, *Bawa: Genius of the Place: An Architect of Sri Lanka* (Frankfurt: Deutsches Architektur Museum, 2004), 137.
38 Friend, *Diaries*, 301 (June 27, 1973).
39 Jayawardene, *Geoffrey Manning Bawa*, 139–41.
40 Friend and Bawa, *Batujimbar Bali*, 6.
41 Friend and Bawa, *Batujimbar Bali*, 6.
42 Friend and Bawa, *Batujimbar Bali*, 6.
43 Taylor, *Geoffrey Bawa*, 16–18.

Batujimbar Estate, Bali
Bale kambang (floating pavilion), Kerta Gosa (Halls of Justice), Klungkung Royal Palace, gelatin silver print, Geoffrey Bawa

Study of a traditional Balinese storage pavilion, gelatin silver print, Geoffrey Bawa scale, texture, proportion and neatly woven patterns were of "first decorative importance," especially when seen from underneath in the bedrooms and living rooms.[44] It was a feat to construct, especially when its durability and beauty rely on the uniformity of long, fringed panels laid onto bamboo rafters erected at a precise angle and interval to create the right visual rhythm.[45] Yet despite Bawa's deliberate application of materials and construction methods of vernacular buildings, there remained an exercise of restraint in their use. Apart from the expressive and textured presence of the entrance gate and timber-and-thatch roof structures, white masonry walls and severe lines austerely render many of the pavilions' facades, carving out an emptiness and simplicity that highlight the presence of the antique, ornate and decorative, like the carved gilded doors, timber trellis window boxes, frangipani trees in the courtyard and coconut wood-lamp hood – with a pointillist effect. The use of white walls and ceilings to blur spatial boundaries, creating an illusion of infinite space in interiors within a limited space, is evident in the passageway of the two-story pavilion on Plot 11. Its white-painted walls and tight-weave textured ceiling, reflected on the polished floor tiles, emanate a brightness and expansiveness that lures the viewer from the courtyard, through the pavilion, to the village temple and beach.

Bawa's expressed intent to weave the houses of Batujimbar into the natural and built landscape is evident in the master plan design: not only is each plot laid out to integrate with the surroundings, but also the layout is reminiscent of a Balinese housing compound, with its asymmetrical cluster of thatch-roofed *bales* (single-story pavilions) organized around courtyards within enclosed walls. Bawa, however, did not mention the latter feature in the project's description. This may be due to his awareness that the arrangement and proportions of a traditional housing compound would have to align with the Hindu conception of cosmic structure and organization.[46] He instead highlighted the presence of water in each plot in the form of shallow reflecting pools in the courtyard, a moat surrounding the museum structure, and swimming pools.[47] However, water bodies are mostly found in Balinese temple or palatial grounds – like the reflecting pools or water-filled moats around *bale kambang* (floating pavilions) in Taman Ayun or Klungkung palace – not at everyday homes. Bawa's selective application of the local was therefore clearly negotiated with his goals of creating a seamless landscape and "greatest range of visual pleasure" in the interior and exterior. Bawa's placement of buildings in the landscape extended beyond a single compound, as various plots on the master plan are stitched such that "each is part of the other's landscape."[48] Spatial delineation between buildings – using water bodies and stone or concrete paving – is as important as the built structure in weaving various plots, as well as multiple pavilions on each plot. Drawings of pavilions, like the Dining Pavilion

44 Friend, *Diaries*, 70 and 301.
45 Darling, *Tandjung Sari*, 94.
46 Eiseman, *Bali: Sekala & Niskala*, 192.
47 Friend and Bawa, *Batujimbar Bali*, 8.
48 On the possible influence of the picturesque on Bawa's practice, see Jayawardene, *Geoffrey Manning Bawa*, 35.

Verandah and Living Pavilion in Plot 6, and the open living room of the two-story *bale* in Plot 11, show they are designed to be open on all sides. Similar to the drawings of Bawa's projects in Sri Lanka – in particular those of Laki Senanayake – the sectional drawings in the Estate's brochure reveal an exacting choice of tropical plants, from frangipani to palm trees, whose specific heights in relation to the buildings capture an interconnectedness between the built and natural environments on a single plane.[49] The rendering of each house with a floor plan and unfolded elevations from four sides presents the spatial relationships between rooms, courtyards and reflecting pools and deliberately placed sculptures, furnishing, hand-painted cloth, antique doors and trees, creating the desired axial views that "give the best possible view from every vantage point in every room."[50] Like his residential designs in Sri Lanka, Bawa's scenographic preoccupation with dramatic views trumps any strict adherence to local traditions. While a traditional sleeping pavilion is designed as an individual, enclosed cell with no other functions, bedrooms – such as those in Plot 11 – connect in one long pavilion to create expansive internal vistas within a confined space and are equipped with indoor and outdoor bathrooms. Indeed, it was the focus on creating an integrated landscape and enhancing the inhabitant's spatial experience – coupled with a selective appropriation of the vernacular – that made each of the houses Bawa designed distinct in its arrangement and atmosphere.

The most significant transformation in terms of scale and proportion of the *bale* would be in the form of the two-story semi-outdoor-and-indoor pavilion structures in Plot 5 and Plot 11. This is especially true considering no buildings within a Balinese housing compound rose to a second story; there is no tradition of domestic staircase construction.[51] While Bawa's design could be considered as reinterpreting the traditional part of a domestic *bale* in terms of height and use, photographs of Bawa's visits around Bali reveal his choice to work with the nondomestic *bale* structure as the basis of designing the two-level museum and living-room structures on Plots 5 and 11, respectively. A *bale* is typically a long pavilion whose framework consists of stout wooden posts set on a raised stone or concrete foundation, which supports a bamboo and/or coconut-wood frame tied to a hip-style roof of thatch.[52] The structure of Bawa's two-story pavilions is similar to a domestic *bale*, though their scale is closer to a *bale* for ceremonial use, especially with its many more carved and gilded timber posts.[53] Yet Bawa was able to identify different types of ceremonial *bale* and to appropriate them into a more public-facing, nonresidential gallery structure to house Friend's art collection, and one that is a more intimate and understated house for multiple occasions and seasons. The museum structure surrounded by a lily-filled moat directly referenced the *bale kambang* (floating pavilion) in the former Klungkung royal palace. Bawa "made a thorough examination

49 Friend and Bawa, *Batujimbar Bali*, 23. The drawings of tropical plants in the brochure were credited to Laki Senanayake.
50 Friend and Bawa, *Batujimbar Bali*, 6.
51 Robson, *Beyond Bawa*, 76.
52 Eiseman, *Bali: Sekala & Niskala*, 93.
53 Darling, *Tandjung Sari*, 82.

of the judging pavilions" of Kerta Gosa (Halls of Justice) at Klungkung and extracted its proportions and structural details for the design of the museum pavilion.[54] The stairwell from the edge of the reflecting moat toward the upper story – similar to the access across a causeway at Klungkung – presents a grand ascension. While its base is similarly hollowed out for the gallery space like the pavilion in Plot 11, it is characterized by a heavy red brick base with window openings of "severe and classic" proportions, framed in cut *paras* stone carving, with a centralized entrance.[55] Inside, Friend described its lofty windows as "deeply embrasured, conveying the illusion of being protected by walls six feet thick"; its interiors as being of "classically elegant proportions" emanating "aesthetic indulgence."[56] The two-story pavilion on Plot 11, on the other hand, is more akin to the *bale bengong* (royal pavilion) for ceremonial use on the outer wall of palaces such as the Puri Gede Karangasem or – as another of Bawa's study photographs seems to show – one for the humble use of gathering or storage. Characterized by white masonry walls at its base, entry to the pavilion's succession of spaces – living room, dining room and kitchen on the ground floor and living room on the mezzanine – is more intimately accessed through a tunnel-like pathway that bisects its solid base, linking the main courtyard to the village temple beyond. The stairway takes one through a half-enclosed mezzanine with built-in seats and alcoves before reaching the fully open upper story. Among these calibrated variations, the two-story pavilions in Plots 5 and 11 reflect the overarching goal of transmuting both private and public vernacular building types to be characterized with domestic grandeur as well as intimacy and connectedness to its surroundings. They reflect the Estate's goal: preserving and reviving Bali's traditional architecture for contemporary living.[57] The pavilions also boast *alang alang* roofs much loftier than those in the interiors, complemented by a forest of timber posts and beams on concrete bases, intricately carved and gilded just as they may be found in temples and palaces like Klungkung.[58] Just as the dense visual rhythm of the *alang alang* panels was of "first decorative importance," ornate wooden sculptures as apex pieces on main beam-post intersections display the virtuosity of local woodcarvers. Lastly, building the two-story *bale* led to the workers' combined use of new construction methods and materials – namely cement mixers and temporary scaffolding stairs constructed with very basic tools in order to pour cement to form the upper floor.[59]

Almost fifty years since the design of Batujimbar Estate, the Balinese housing compound, *wantilan*, *bale* and *alang-alang* roofs have been overly used in the proliferation of the "Bali resort style" in homes, residences and hotels from Bali's beachfronts to the residences of urbanites in tropical cities. Yet, its existence alongside developments characterized by a similar ethos of venerating local

54 Friend, *Diaries*, 301 (June 27, 1973).
55 Friend, *Diaries*, 337 (July 5, 1974).
56 Donald Friend, *The Cosmic Turtle: Batujimbar Bali* (Perth: Carroll's, 1976).
57 Friend and Bawa, *Batujimbar Bali*, 23.
58 Eiseman, *Bali: Sekala & Niskala*, 201.
59 Friend, *Diaries*, 331 (May 21, 1974).

Batujimbar Estate, Bali
Entrance to living and dining pavilion on plot 11, digital photograph, color, Shirley Surya, 2019

Interior view from mezzanine level to upper story of pavilion on plot 11, digital photograph, color, Shirley Surya, 2019

materials, craftsmanship and building types, which stood in contrast to the 1970s Miami-Modern style high-rise Bali Beach Hotel, was a microcosmic contribution to a regionalism that confidently intersects with a more porous globalized modernity. While some may consider its mixed idioms as revival pastiche or cheap nostalgia, Batujimbar Estate represented Bawa's and his collaborators' rethinking of both indigenous and European architectural precedents as equally valid and interdependent cultural resources. As a project that preceded the mainstream postmodern architectural discourse and production, it provided a significant model in engaging with history and refiguring the past and the vernacular as part of the rubric of contemporaneity. Unlike the sign-obsessed historicism of Postmodernism, Bawa's explicit engagement with the vernacular constituted an abstract translation and pragmatic exploration of the essence and logic of centuries-old solutions to the tropical monsoonal climatic conditions. It put forward a regeneration of regionality beyond mere extraction of tradition, such that the architecture of the past, or of a region, could contribute to the vicissitudes of contemporary architectural production and consumption while addressing the issue of placeless homogeneity.

Polontalawa Estate Bungalow, Nikaweratiya

1963–67

Exterior view, gelatin silver print, Geoffrey Bawa, ca. 1965 GB/DOC/143/004

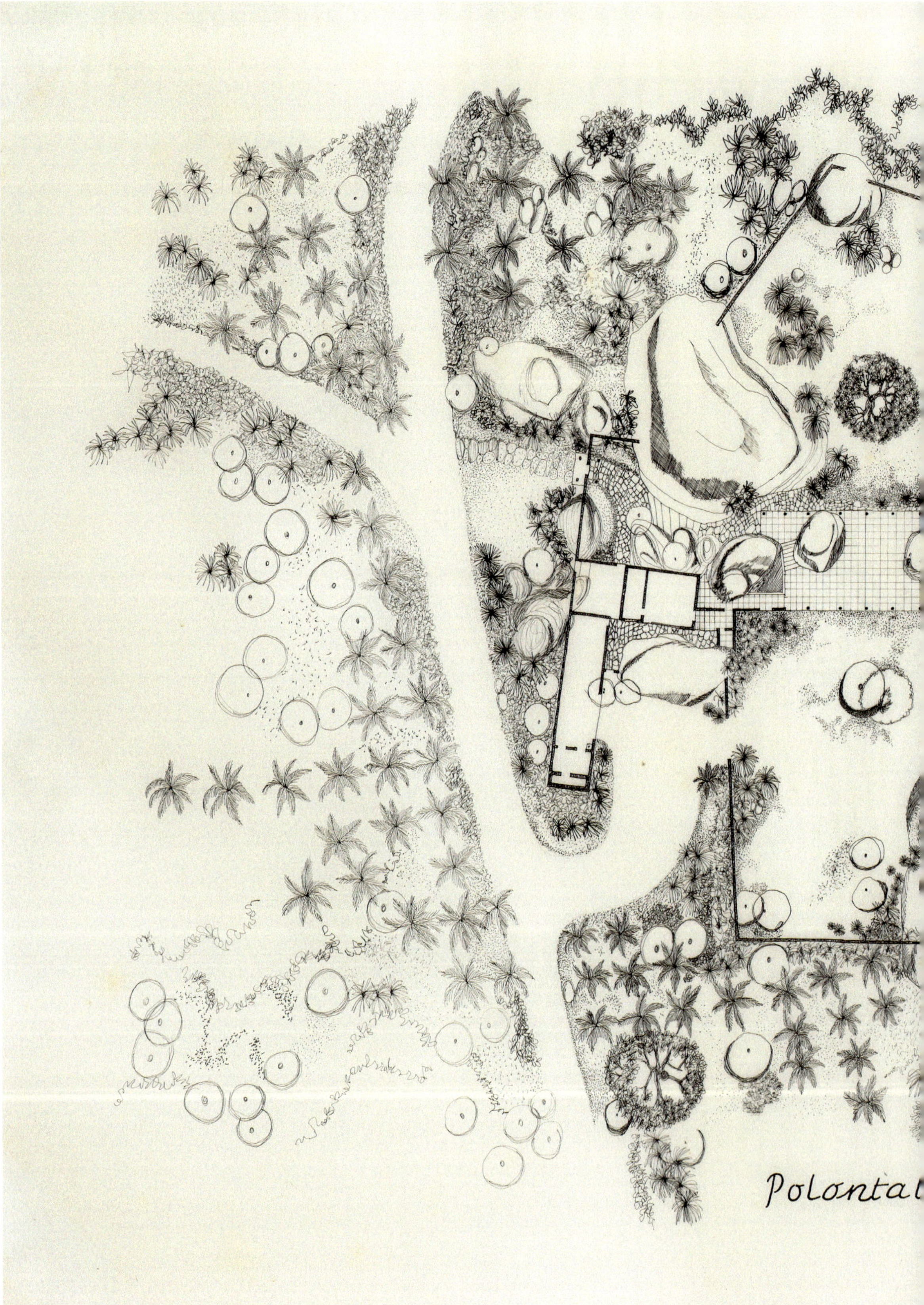

Site plan, ink on vellum, ca. 1967
GB/DA/074/001

5 4 3 2 1 0 5 10 15
METRES
estate bungalow.

Interior view of boulder on site used as structural column, gelatin silver print, Geoffrey Bawa, ca. 1965 GB/DOC/143/003

Exterior view and interior view of open living room (top), site view (bottom), gelatin silver print, Geoffrey Bawa, ca. 1965
GB/DOC/143/005, 001, 002

Yahapath Endera Farm School, Hanwella

1965–71

Water tower at Yahapath Endera Farm School, Hanwella, gelatin silver print, Geoffrey Bawa, ca. 1965–71 GB/DOC/144/001

Site plan, ink on tracing paper, Ismeth Raheem, ca. 1965–71 GB/DA/050/001

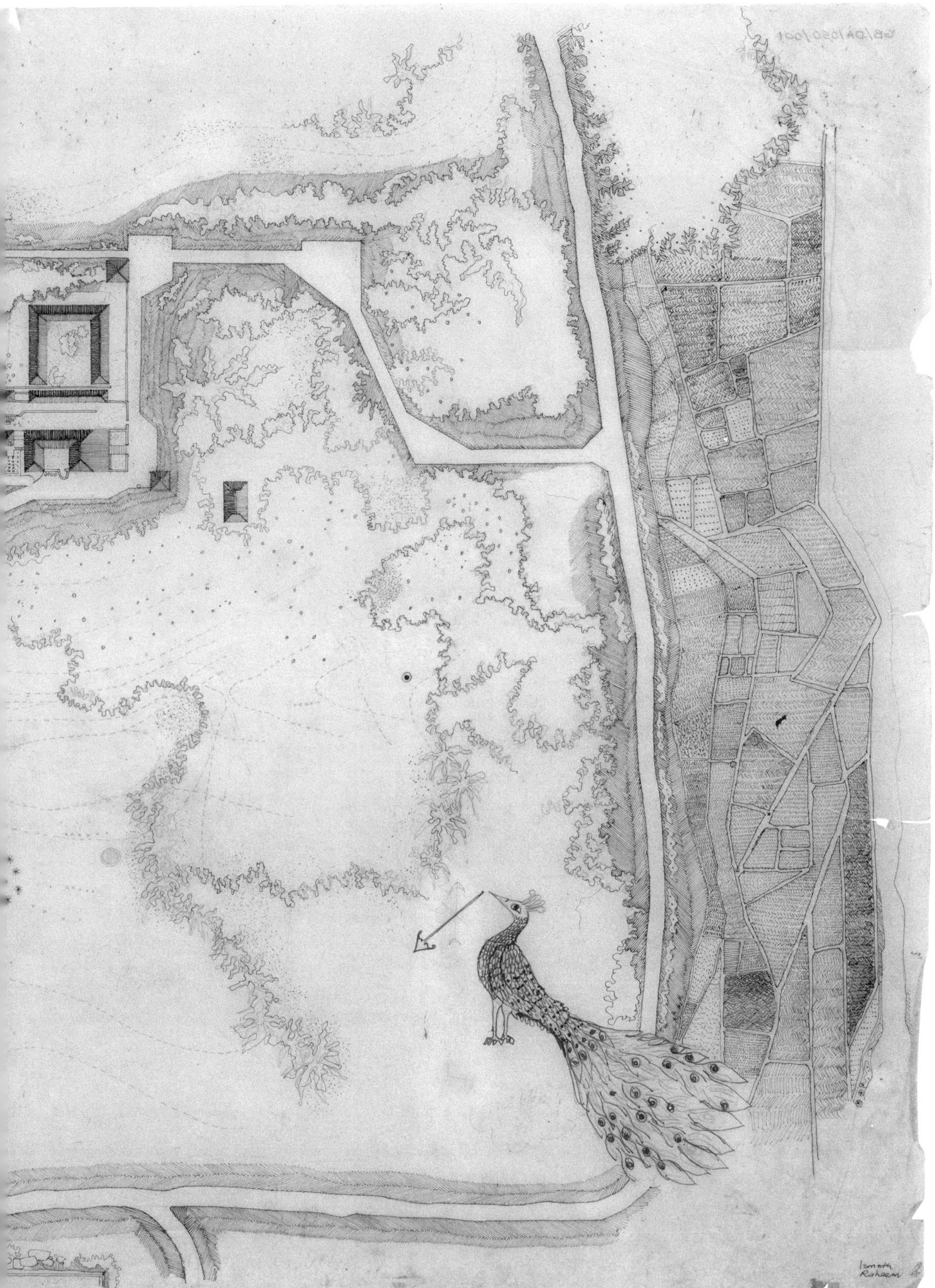

Entrance to the Girls' Center, chromogenic color print, Geoffrey Bawa, ca. 1986 GB/DOC/119/002

Convent building as viewed from main approach, chromogenic color print, Geoffrey Bawa, ca. 1986 GB/DOC/119/003

Kitchen and dining area of Girls' Center, chromogenic color print, Geoffrey Bawa, ca. 1986 GB/DOC/119/003

Exterior view of laundry block, gelatin silver print, Geoffrey Bawa, ca. 1965–71 GB/DOC/144/003

Interior view of mosaics at Yahapath Endera Farm School, Hanwella, gelatin silver print, Geoffrey Bawa, ca. 1965–71 GB/DOC/144/002

Site elevation, ink on vellum, 1966
GB/DA/050/002

77

Exterior view of central courtyard with chicken house in the foreground, gelatin silver print, **Geoffrey Bawa, ca. 1965–71** GB/DOC/144/006

Geoffrey Bawa, Jean Chamberlin and Christoph Bon at Yahapath Endera Farm School, Hanwella, gelatin silver print, **Geoffrey Bawa, ca. 1965–71** GB/DOC/144/005

Interior view of dormitories, gelatin silver print,
Geoffrey Bawa, ca. 1965–71 GB/DOC/144/004

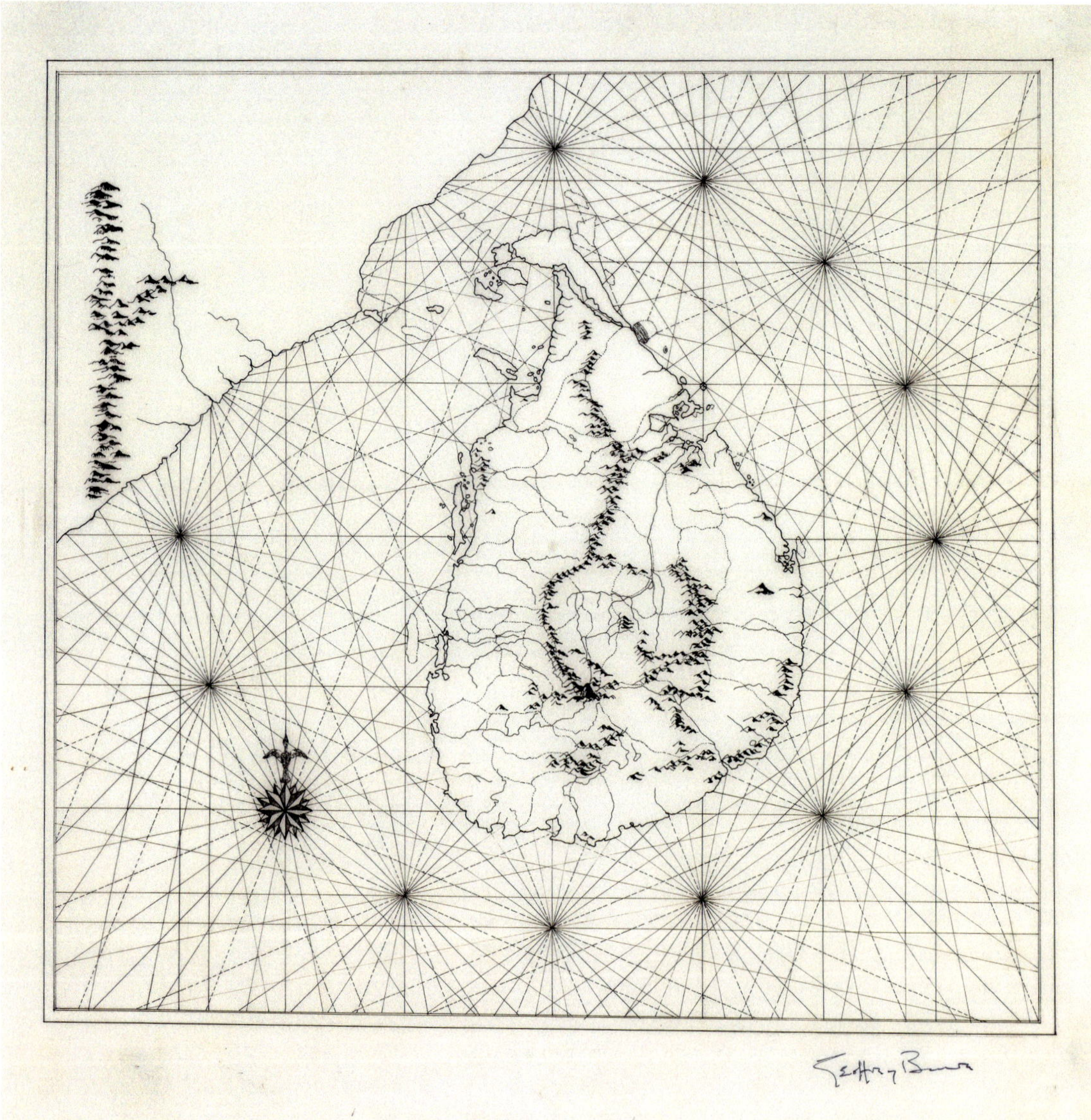

Map of Sri Lanka, ink on vellum, ca. 1985

Vanishing Points

Sean Anderson

If we leave out the modernistic, individualistic philosophies of today and consider the greatest traditions of magnanimous philosophers, it will be found that distinctions of East and West are comparable only to differences of dialect while the essential spiritual language remains the same.

Ananda K. Coomaraswamy

From the invention of tracing paper, which catalyzed the first flight of the hot-air balloon, to cybernetic footfalls within an Internet that presaged structures composed by coding and drones, acts of making continue to affect how we experience the built and natural environments. Coupled with each technological advancement, however, the sometimes invisible lines that organize the world have been used to circumscribe spaces with our own kinetics among its dimensions. Intersected by transnational migrations of capital and ideas, the island nation of Sri Lanka (formerly Ceylon) is a nexus through which new spatial forms emerged and were redefined through graphic and spatial boundaries. To inscribe, define and offer lines – for a map, in a drawing – demands certain political trajectories from which to view and organize the self. The drawing, in turn, invents visual and spatial languages while also constructing newfound graphic ecologies that simultaneously confer bodily experience.

Throughout the early and mid-twentieth century, prototypes for seeing were engaged by architects, artists and designers to inscribe critiques within shifting terrains. Apart from eschewing the binaries embedded within Sri Lanka's centuries-old colonial legacies, modern architecture on the island was a mechanism for asserting difference by articulating a convergence of diverse viewpoints while also registering their limits. Throughout Geoffrey

Bawa's storied oeuvre, drawings were used to depict an unearthing of built and unbuilt boundaries among the multitude of projects executed by his office. Not necessarily beholden to the finality (or banality) of construction documentation, Bawa's use of drawings instrumentalized bodily perception. Drawings of his works were suspended at the intersection of multiple thresholds: positioning landscape and structure, reason and knowledge. It is this limen of enframed ocularity and physicality among multiple worlds and geographies that provokes contrasting readings. By observing a selection of drawn representations produced over decades by dedicated colleagues and associates, this essay attempts to detect an awareness of continuities among aesthetic domains across architectural and landscape drawings produced by Bawa's office that rescripted approaches to the manifestation of post-colonial spaces.

Surfaces

The emergence of a modern architecture in Ceylon and more broadly, in South and Southeast Asia, conferred the potential of spaces and their material manifestations as a dynamic in meaning and scale. Following the nation's independence from colonial rule in 1948 and its name change to Sri Lanka in 1972, its geography continued to inform the containment of movements and peripheries. While the introduction of concrete traversed the region at the beginning of the twentieth century and emboldened the rise of industrialized techniques and associated systemic forms, Ceylon ostensibly did not embrace the material and its processes immediately. Rather, as evidenced by the work of British-owned architecture-engineering offices such as Edwards, Reid and Begg, of which Geoffrey Bawa was a partner, a noticeable reliance first toward the ground, and not necessarily to international appropriations, allowed a particular tonality for buildings in Ceylon to be engaged as local emblems of modernity. In other sectors of the subcontinent, the emergence of concrete and steel production rendered the late-colonial industrial and increasingly mechanized landscape, as seen, for example, among the photographs of Sunil Janah in the 1940s, as significant indicators toward a coalescing of nation-building drives vis-à-vis industry.

For Ceylon, by contrast, the appearance of these elements did not immediately find resolution in architecture's conventional approaches toward hegemonic visual and spatial hierarchies. Due to austerity measures brought forth as part of the nation's convergence with the Non-Aligned Movement, self-sufficiency in both material and as appropriative manners of form was paramount. The modern, rather, while transnational in scope yet divergent and local in formation, was demonstrated through the island's long-standing sociocultural connectivities. Among anti-colonial art practices of the period – including those of the Colombo-based

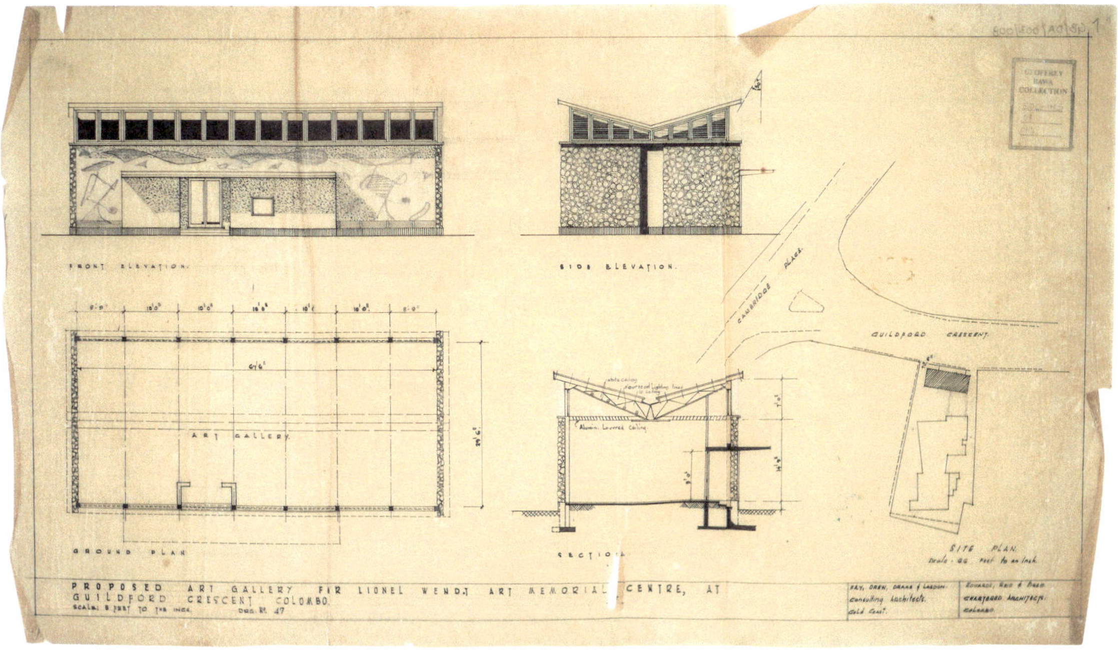

Lionel Wendt Memorial Art Center, Colombo, elevations, section, plan and site layout, ink on tracing paper

Adventure in Space, composite photograph, Lionel Wendt Memorial Fund Collection, Colombo, ca. 1940

Lunuganga, Bentota, north elevation,
ink on tracing paper, Sumangala Jayatillaka,
1988

SUMANGALA '88
0 5 10 FT

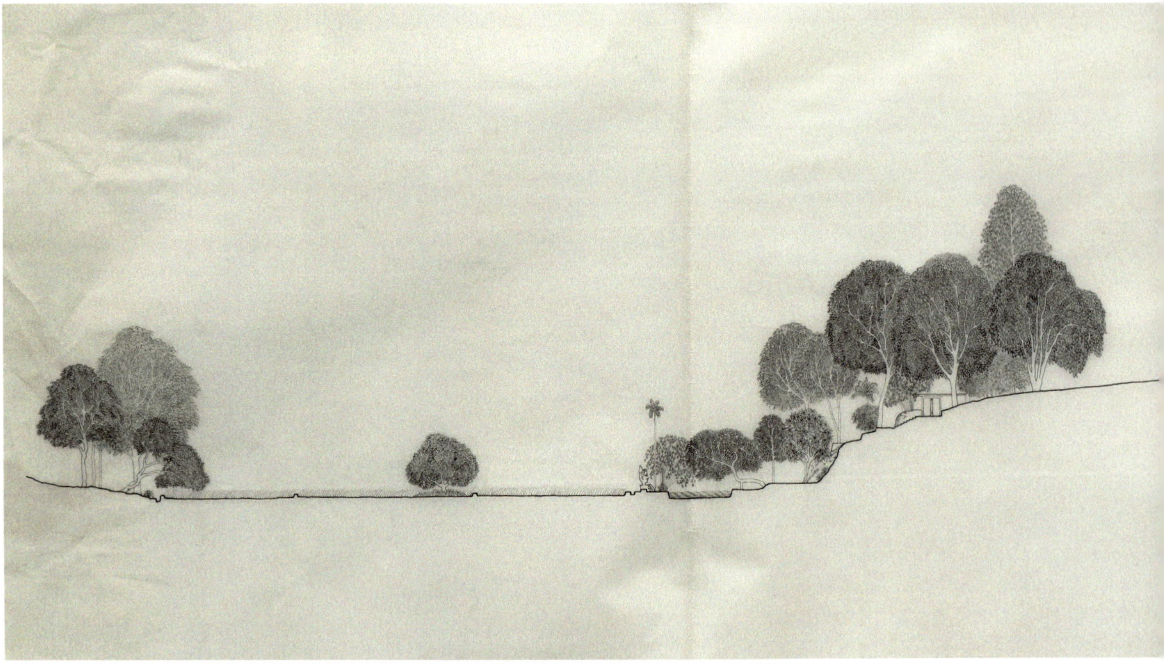

'43 Group, whose embrace of the natural landscape and reductive forms, especially those found among the photographs of Lionel Wendt – the Ceylonese modern countered Orientalizing gestures. Ceylon became a locus for an assertion of new approaches to building, to histories in and out of time, as well as a multivalent context for acknowledging that nature remained an essential companion to an architecture that transcended scales and temporalities.

In one of the earliest descriptions of a syncretic paradigm for a modern architecture on the island, architect Minnette de Silva writes that the Karunaratne House in Kandy (1946–50), her first project in Ceylon, was "an attempt [...] to synthesize indigenous traditions with an architecture designed for a contemporary Buddhist Sinhalese family and its way of living – using whatever materials and means were suitable – both modern and traditional," including those building materials that were found nearby.[1] While such a reclaiming of locality within the domain of cultural specificity furthered Geoffrey Bawa's initial architectural forays following his studies in London and personal travels in Italy and Western Europe, his drawings and built projects are invested in tectonics that reconfigured how surfaces might be understood both as symbol and method. Registered at opposing scales, the reflective surface, seen in numerous drawings and executed materially among built spaces, became both a conceptual and material hallmark of Bawa's synthetic architecture.

Among the earliest drawings associated with Bawa's nascent practice, and indeed those of completed projects, articulated surfaces recode nature as a space of disappearance within and

1 Minnette de Silva, "A House at Kandy, Ceylon," *MARG* 6, no. 3 (1953).

Lunuganga, Bentota, west elevation showing Upper Gallery, Henhouse and Yellow Courtyard, ink on tracing paper, Sumangala Jayatillaka, 1988

among landscapes framed by a Ceylonese architecture. Unlike eighteenth-century notions of placing the body at both the visual and spatial center of a Western analytic perspective – the vanishing point – Bawa assembled in drawing and building contrasting (im)materialities among precise configurations of settings. To construct a vanishing point for Bawa was, in part, to enmesh long views toward the horizon that held the island and its people more so than the edge of land that defined it. To vanish among Bawa's drawings is to glimpse past and future simultaneously as if from an unbound ocean.

A series of sections and elevational perspectives created for Bawa's magnum opus, the Lunuganga Estate (1949–2003) provides entry into and potential occupation of pavilion-like edifices in tandem with the cultivated yet undeterred landscape. These drawings decenter the eye inasmuch as one's projection into singular volumetric realms. They are conceived instead as private spaces that one may inhabit alone. Comparatively, the sectional elevations for a midcareer project, the University of Ruhuna (1978–84) gather the landscape and its topographic contours as the hinge between a public institution and that of the national endeavor toward a renewed educational system. The line – as varied indications of ground seen in both drawings – becomes the denomination of (colonial) histories now subsumed. Both sets of drawings reveal how convergences found among the interplay of visual signifiers centered on the manipulation of the ground might also serve as agents in the spatial ordering for an independent Sri Lanka.

Ruhuna University, Matara
Elevation, ink on paper, ca. 1984

Section, ink on tracing paper, ca. 1984

113

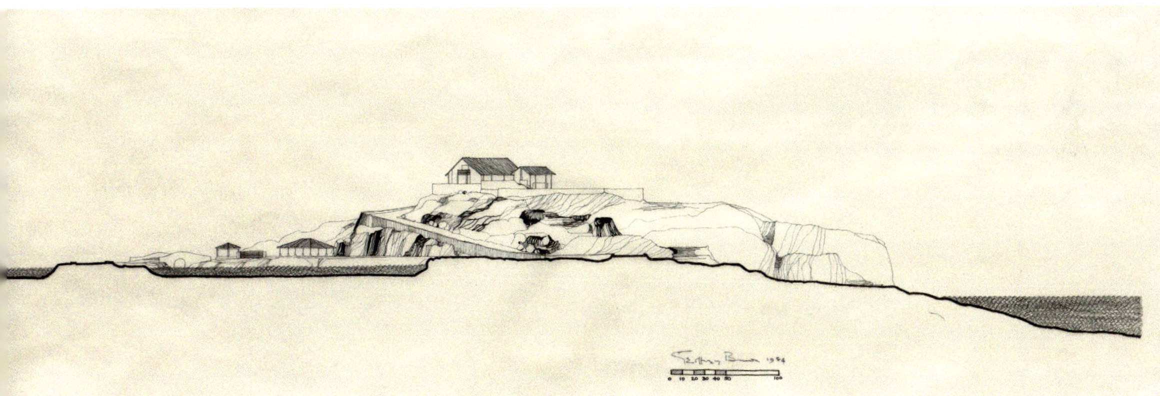

Bentota Beach Hotel, Bentota
Perspectival drawing, ink on tracing paper

View of internal corridor, Geoffrey Bawa,
gelatin silver print, ca. 1973

Transparencies

Phenomenological and social deployments of transparency are a hallmark of global manifestations of modern architecture.[2] Throughout the first decades of the twentieth century, the use of glass, as both a tool and medium, provided surfaces of contextual reflexivity and historical inscription outside of South Asia. While gravity absorbs building and its temporalities are informed by an interpolation of function, transparency too may be understood not only as a material condition but also as being embedded within the formation of a body-politic. Among Bawa's drawings, where glass is absent, and thus substituted by light and air, as found among much of early building in Ceylon, the threshold for bodily flows is amplified.

Drawings, too, perform like glass. As a lens that transgresses worlds while also hinting at compositional dialectics, those drawings assembled in Bawa's studio illuminate a reading of philosopher Henri Bergson's definition of "the image." In his 1896 volume, *Matter and Memory*, Bergson writes that the image shares in "a certain existence which is more than that which the idealist calls a *representation*, but less than that which the idealist calls a *thing* – an existence placed halfway between the 'thing' and its 'representation.'"[3] Drawings produced by Bawa's associates instill the "thingness" of furnishings, of walls, of scaled objects in space. At the same time, these things discovered in Bawa's drawings are imbued by ineffable registers of liminality – the contours of architectural space, an individual's preoccupations, a foreshortening of the spectra of distances that occur from one's movement outside to inside and back again. And yet Bawa's drawings do not craft images per se, but rather insinuate spatial experiences created for and by the imagining eye.

As the calculation of architectural spaces within the late nineteenth and early twentieth centuries in South Asia was arguably one of fixity, the drawings and built works of Bawa's office depict a composition of mobilities, of methodic transience, in which the collapse of foreground and background accentuates individual and collective bodies in motion. In others, the far and middle distances are also focused, precise. Such ocular effects are preserved throughout Bawa's built and unbuilt works. From a survey of drawings in the Geoffrey Bawa Archives, most drawings for the studio's projects begin and end with the use of an extended ground plan. The plan, for Bawa, is a fundamental strategy for one to visually access a haptic choreography of moments, textures and other sensorial elements expanding what, for some critics, reveals a horizontal cross section. Such registers are prominent, for the ground of Ceylon and Sri Lanka was one of unlimited but muted signification following the colonial periods.

If the activation of likeness is a condensation of dissimilar elements and spaces assembled over time, then among Bawa's

2 See Colin Rowe and Robert Slutzky, "Transparency: Literal and Phenomenal," *Perspecta* 8 (January 1963): 45–54. Tracing the lineage of transparency in Western architectural theory, Rowe and Slutzky's key 1963 text observes the ideas of Sigfried Giedion, Walter Gropius, György Kepes and László Moholy-Nagy as essential to the transmission of its properties within modernism.

3 Henri Bergson, *Matter and Memory* (London: Allen and Unwin, 1962), ix. See also Zahid Chaudhary, *Afterimage of Empire: Photography in Nineteenth-Century India* (Minneapolis: University of Minnesota Press, 2012).

Triton Hotel, Ahungalla, sketch,
graphite on tracing paper, Geoffrey Bawa

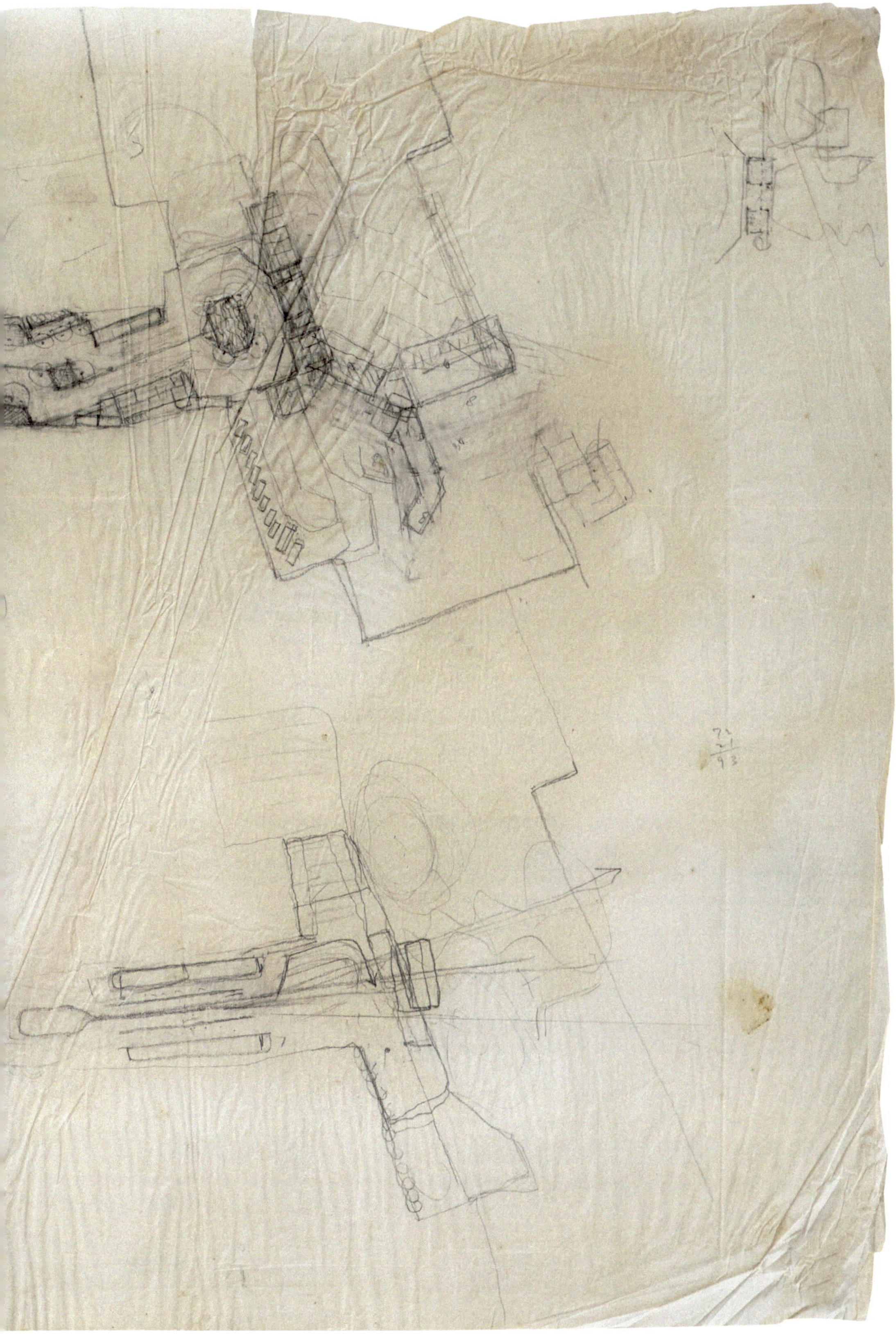

drawings of his own house in Colombo (1960–69), the Batujimbar Estate in Bali (1972–75) and a number of his earliest hotel projects such as the Bentota Beach Hotel (1967–69) and the Triton Hotel in Ahungalla (1979–81) coincide with a fashioning of Sri Lanka's outward image following independence. Among these drawings, there is the simultaneous revelation of old and new, an interface of the now and the yet to come. In the instance of Batujimbar, for example, artist Donald Friend's interest in the overlay of depth and surface in his own paintings no doubt had an influence in the spatial embroidery of proposed building sites within Bawa's drawings and disparate buildings set within groves of palms, water-courses and meandering pathways toward the beach. It is this productive tension between a physical and social transparency that is interrogated, if not redrawn, by Bawa's binding of quotidian architecture to the new nature(s) of a modern, independent Sri Lanka and beyond.

A presence of the past, whether as a hybrid State or landscape-body, within Bawa's drawings oscillates at the intersection of the visible and invisible. The spaces that the drawings depict – their grounding, their organization – are in constant motion; they bespeak the island nation's imagining undergoing change. With such internal transformations materializing scale and structure, form and formality, the articulation of structures in Bawa's image-drawings further intimates that modern architecture in South Asia is at once an index of temporalities serving to redefine the subcontinent as both free from and perhaps still embodying the afterlives of Empire.

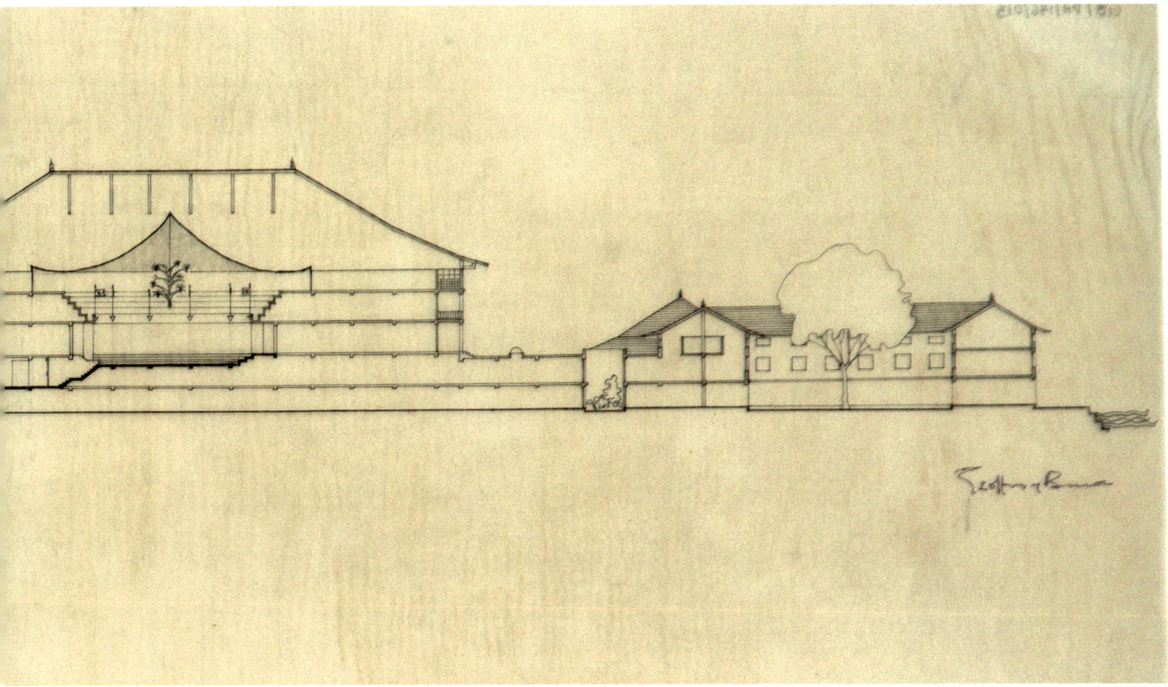

Bawa's translations through drawing of Sri Lanka's simultaneous political and economic apertures disassemble scene from scenery. The ground is never neutral. Much like French philosopher Maurice Merleau-Ponty's delimiting of the haptic vis-à-vis those objects that structure our consciousness, Bawa's drawings are manifold worlds that are rarely fixed and remain unsettled even after their composition, if not construction. With their assembly, in a transference from an imagined to a speculative "real," drawings remain as semiautonomous realms that may prove antithetical to the steadfast positioning maintained by monumental building. In his own few sketches and presentation drawings for the new Parliamentary Complex in Kotte (1979–82), Bawa emblematizes how a "national" image is unmasked by a return to architectural forms that contain such conflicting associations as those made visible with its dominant roof profile and the internal ordering of a design and craft-laden central parliamentary chamber. These drawings offer an optical infrastructure pressing upon the making of an architecture that extends the State's body. Bawa's drawings, buildings and landscapes are thus vision machines that capture and blur their inhabitants, holding them in suspension. Merleau-Ponty writes, "The untouchable is not a touchable that happens to be inaccessible; the unconscious is not a representation that happens to be inaccessible. The negative here is not a positive that is elsewhere (something transcendent). It is a true negative."[4] Bawa's drawings inform a kind of sublimated nation-building that function as an arbiter of reification and instill a multiplicity of enchantments, consistently disclosing meaning.

New Sri Lankan Parliament, Sri Jayawardenepura Kotte, section, ink on tracing paper

4 Maurice Merleau-Ponty and Claude Lefort, *The Visible and the Invisible* (Chicago: Northwestern University Press, 1968), 254. The original quotation is as follows: "L'intouchable, ce n'est pas un touchable en fait inaccessible, – l'inconscient, ce n'est pas une representation en fait inaccessible. Le négatif n'est pas un positif qui est ailleurs (un transcendant) – C'est un vrai négatif."

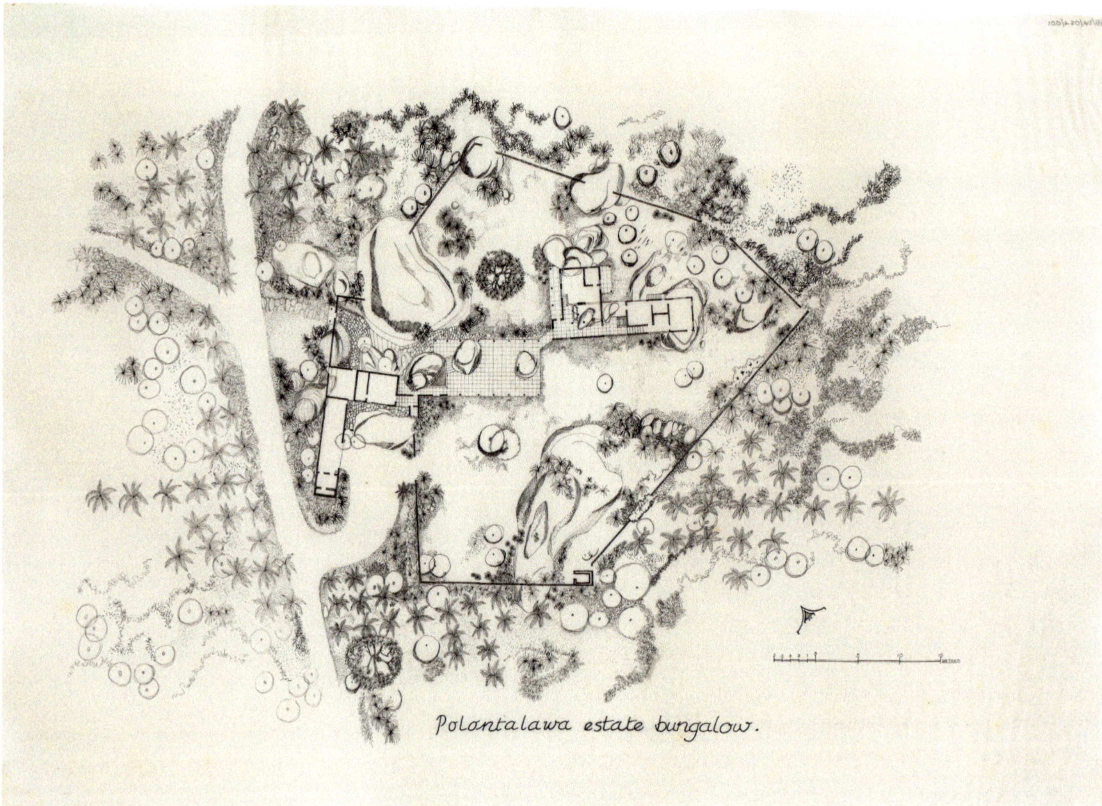

Polontalawa Estate Bungalow, Nikaweratiya, site plan, ink on vellum, ca. 1967

Deviations

Drawings are artifactual. They speak across time. Embedded within the dimensions of their making as well as forging formerly indeterminate sites for proposed execution, the drawings by Bawa's studio adopted and amplified conventional architectural techniques such as the elevation, plan and perspective to speak of their own revision as diachronic narratives of architectural and artistic contrivance. For each project anticipated in drawing, a scaling of boundaries and their unmasking is underscored. Conjunctions of movement, of interdependent bodies in space, expand the surface of drawing as well as those spaces marked by their actioning. Compound transparencies are evidenced from Bawa's less-documented projects, such as the Polontalawa Estate Bungalow (1963) near Nikaweratiya. Here, catalytic degrees of openness display not only organizational delineations that mirror the working agricultural estate but also allude to the negotiable capacity of architecture to be both "in" the landscape and of it. A circuit of grounds enfolding the building's open structure is evidenced by this and other Bawa studio drawings including those of the later Kandalama Hotel (1991–95). Discourses that point to an overarching "tropical architecture" are diminished when observing the drawn and built translations of both the conceptual as well as emotional realities for Bawa's ever-changing work.

A paradox is found within the reception of modern architecture and its emergent representations in Sri Lanka and in South Asia. Where does one find the slow imminence of the island when responding to Bawa's projects? By upending linear historical narratives, Bawa's drawings and buildings, like nations, remain outside of simple definitions that govern thresholds. Informing our visual and haptic faculties, drawings collapse the negotiable, the in-between, presenting the viewer with opportunities to be present while neither here nor there. Bawa's drawings are encapsulated within the eye yet speak to diverse bodies and senses. There is agency found within them; their limits extend beyond the page, the frame, the horizon. Concomitant with Bawa's architecture, we too continuously unravel among surfaces that may have been "designed" or "chosen" while also subject to entropy, to the passage of time. To find ourselves among Bawa's drawings is to be there or nowhere. Do drawings possess time? Or do they erase it?

The collaborative nature for how Bawa's built works transpired during his decades-long practice allows for a questioning of labor, of the who in architecture and its drawn fabulation. Even with a drawing's insistence to portray an aspect of the real, it is that which is not seen where one locates strategies to expand architecture's definitions and making. Not everyone is able to "read" a drawing. If drawings are objects of a private visual-spatial language, then their grammar – their evolving dialect – is one of momentum, change that transcends arbitrary limits. Intention, similarly, as found in the discreteness of point and line, links processes that broaden one's understanding of affect. At the horizon of the known, or perhaps at the edges of any building's foundational edge, the drawing likewise catalyzes a way forward, guiding us toward a precarious yet more complete mapping of our own being.

Bawa's drawings oscillate as the imaging of material and the material of image. The drawings locate newfound manifestations of transparency across histories of the island's evolving landscapes. Among such imperfect yet cultivated grounds, from which a deeply ingrained dialectical armature upon which architecture was founded and now moves past, the drawing offered Bawa and his associates revelatory modes by which to challenge the intersection of visual and temporal experiences. Even as Bawa's architecture today continues to redefine the capaciousness of Sri Lankan and Asian spaces, the drawings produced by his atelier counter the hypervisibility of buildings as media, accelerate narratives of becoming and embody, as ever, the complex truths of their materialization. In their trapped air and light, we can disappear.

Bentota Beach Hotel, Bentota

1966–69

Exterior rear view across swimming pool,
Geoffrey Bawa, gelatin silver print, ca. 1973
GB/DOC/145/002

Lower ground-level entrance (top) and cochère (bottom), Geoffrey Bawa, gelatin silver print, ca. 1973 GB/DOC/145/002, 006

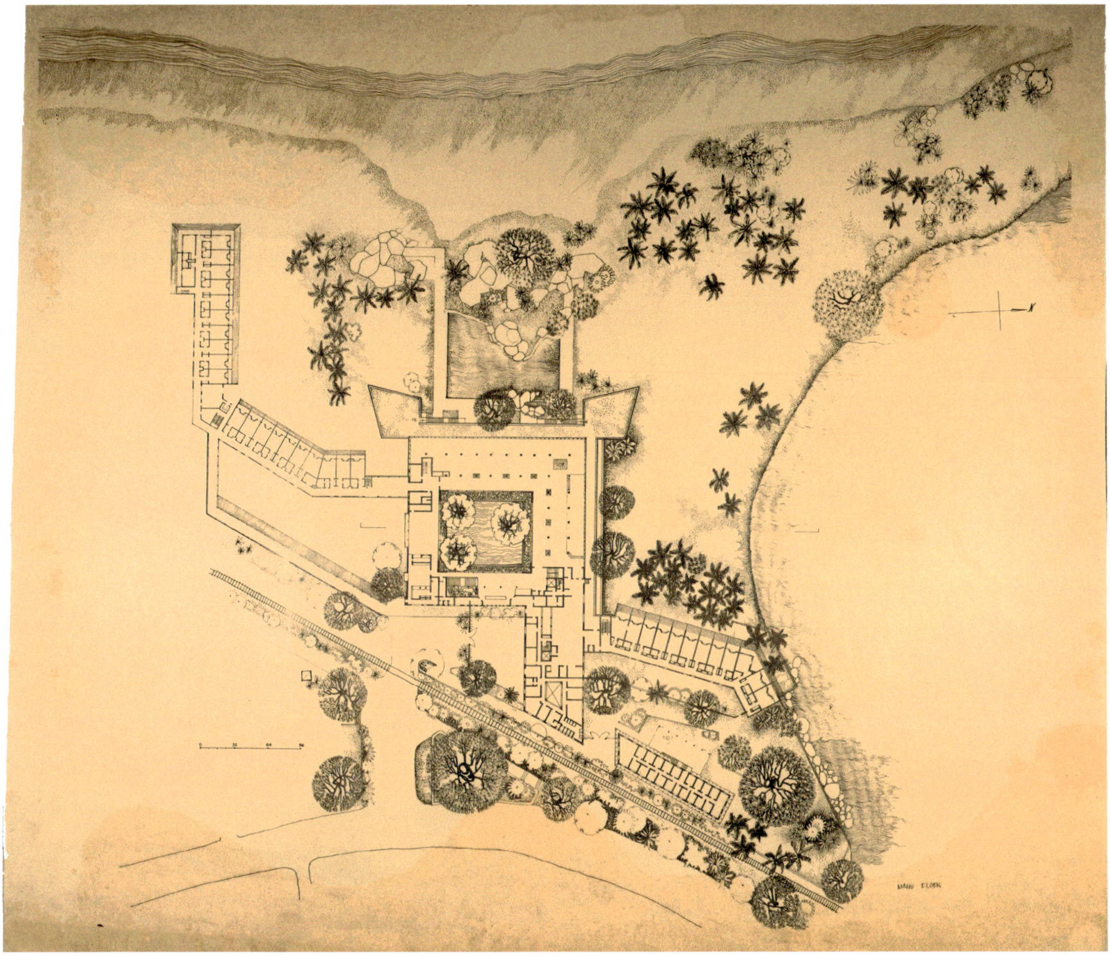

Site plan, bromide print, ca. 1969
GB/DA/068/032

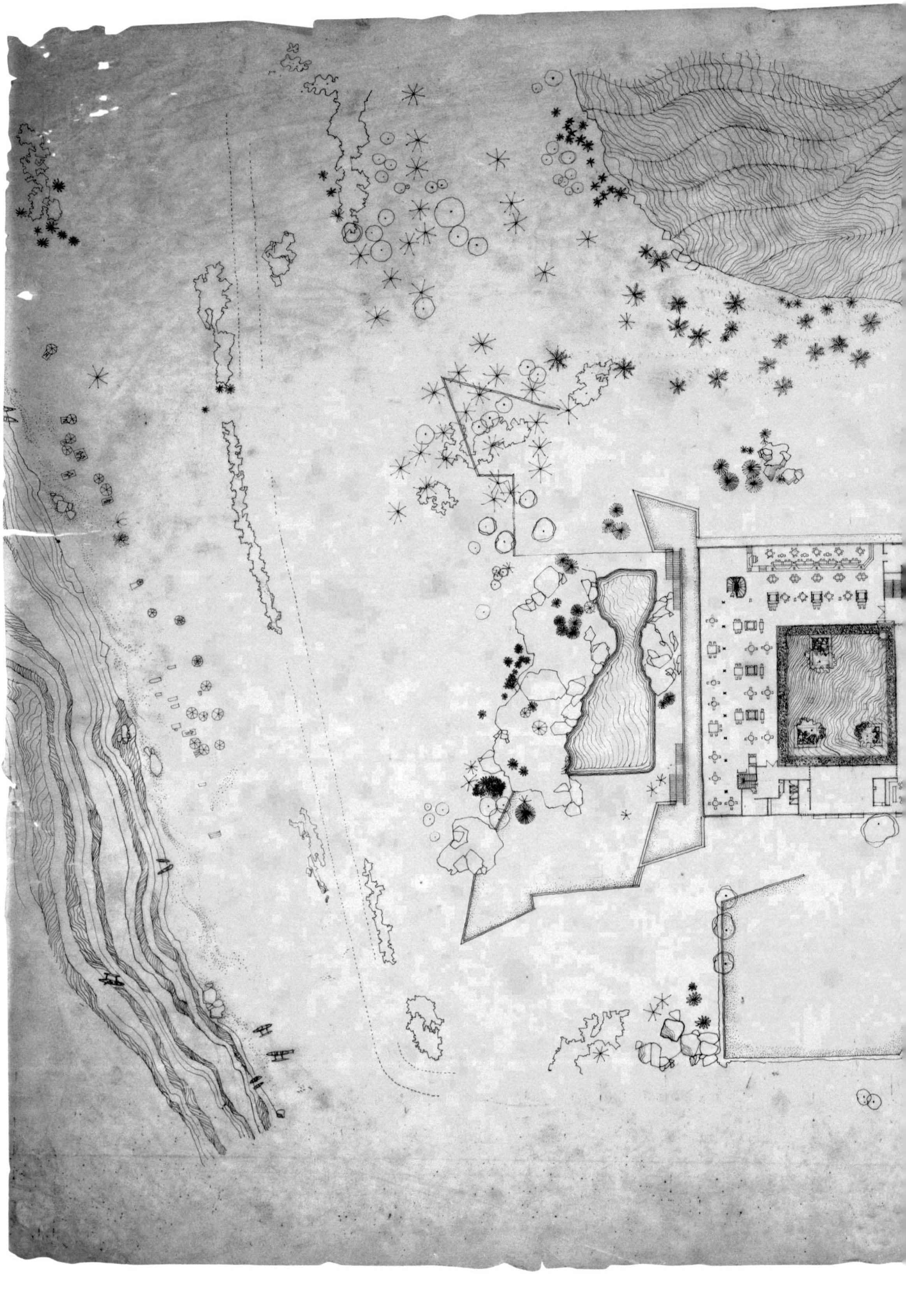

Site plan at ground-floor level, ink on tracing paper, ca. 1969 GB/DA/068/002

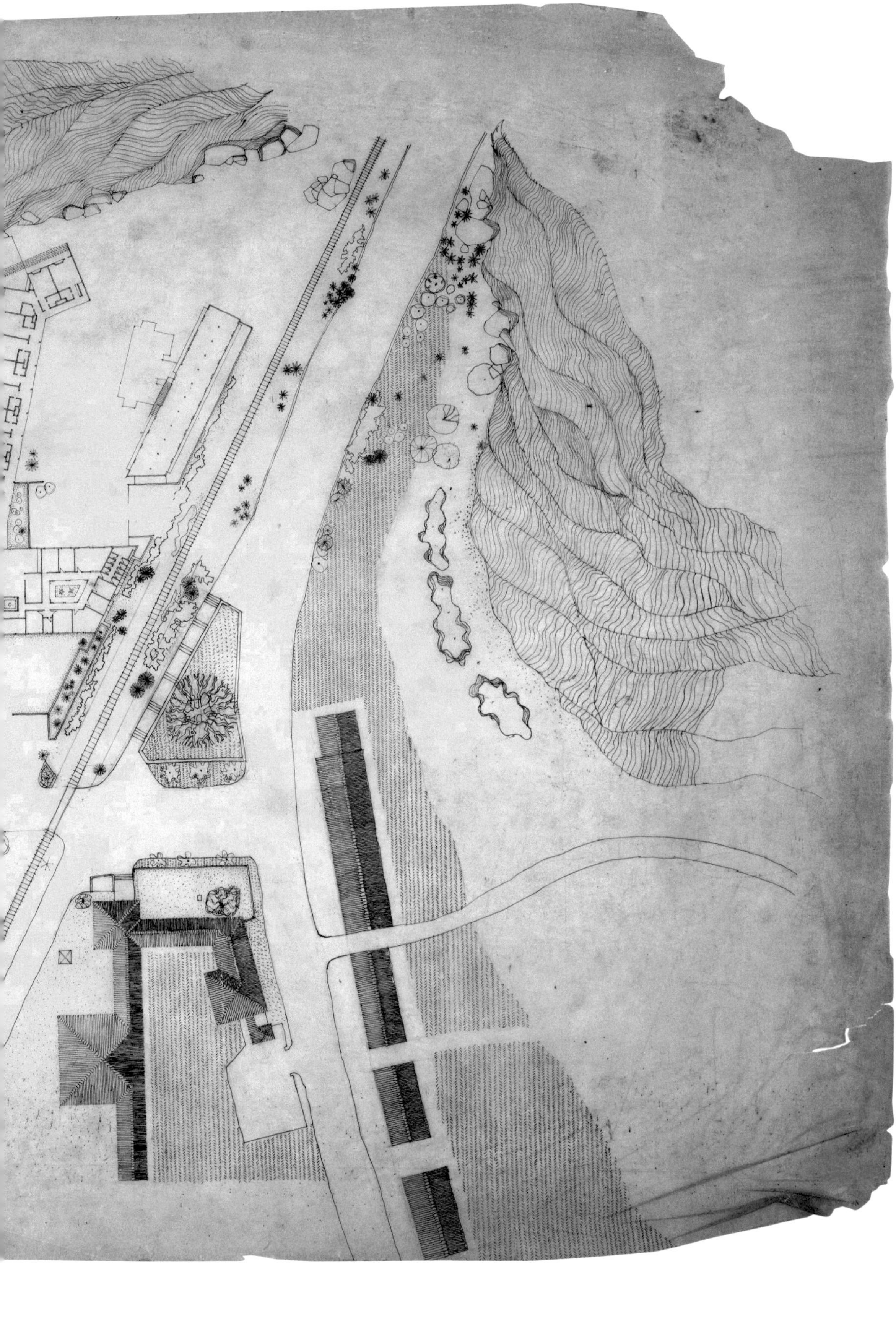

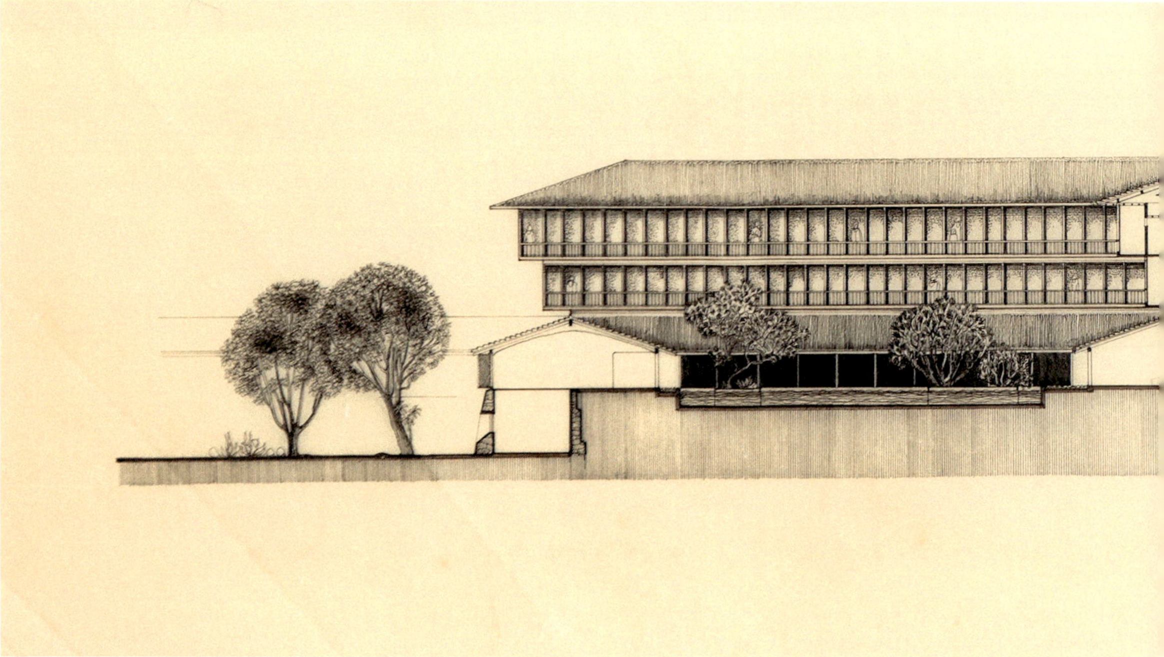

Section, ink on tracing paper, ca. 1969
GB/DA/068/0028

Hotel entrance, Geoffrey Bawa,
gelatin silver print, ca. 1973 GB/DOC/145/001

Exterior view, Geoffrey Bawa,
gelatin silver print, ca. 1973 GB/DOC/145/002

Corridor leading to hotel rooms as viewed from upper-floor level, Geoffrey Bawa, gelatin silver print, ca. 1973 GB/DOC/145/004

Roof overhang on upper levels,
Geoffrey Bawa, gelatin silver print, ca. 1973
GB/DOC/145/003

Ceylon Pavilion at Expo '70, Osaka

1969–70

Gelatin silver print, Geoffrey Bawa (attributed), 1970
GB/DOC/141/001/E

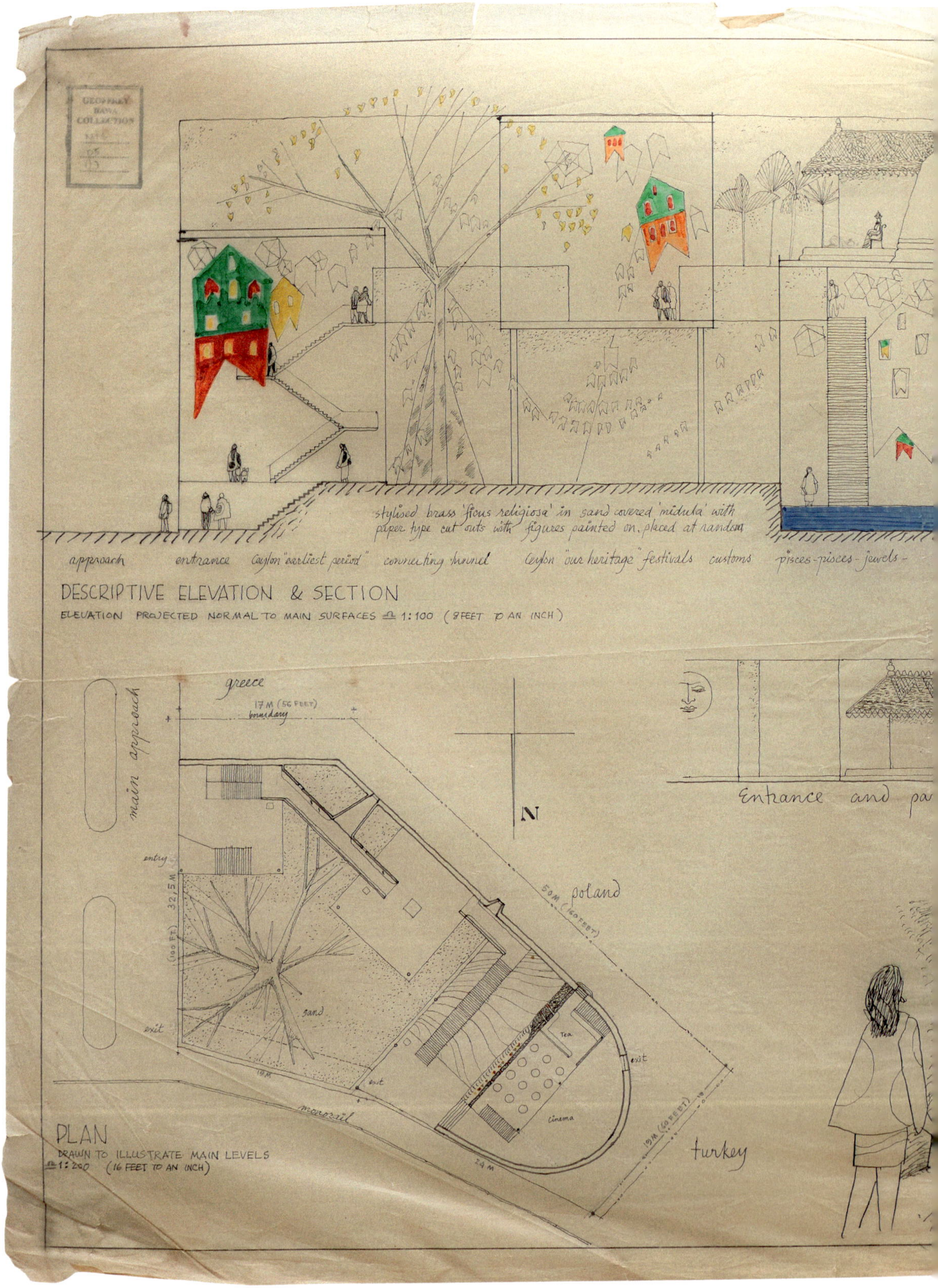

Plan, elevation, section and perspectival drawing through tunnel, ink on tracing paper, Anura Rathnavibushana, 1969 GB/DA/076/001

Ceylon name display
gilded statuettes
simultaneous multiple cinema projection
Industrial progress
agricultural progress
ancient and modern engineering
Ceylon Tea Lounge and cinema
levation ≏ 1:50 (4 FEET TO AN INCH)
paper cut-figures on side walls
perspective through tunnel
ceylon pavilion
at expo 70
osaka japan
approximated scale
scale 1:50 1:100 : 1:200
date 25 march 1969
edwards reid & begg
architects & engineers
2 alfred house road
colombo 3 Ceylon
drawing no.

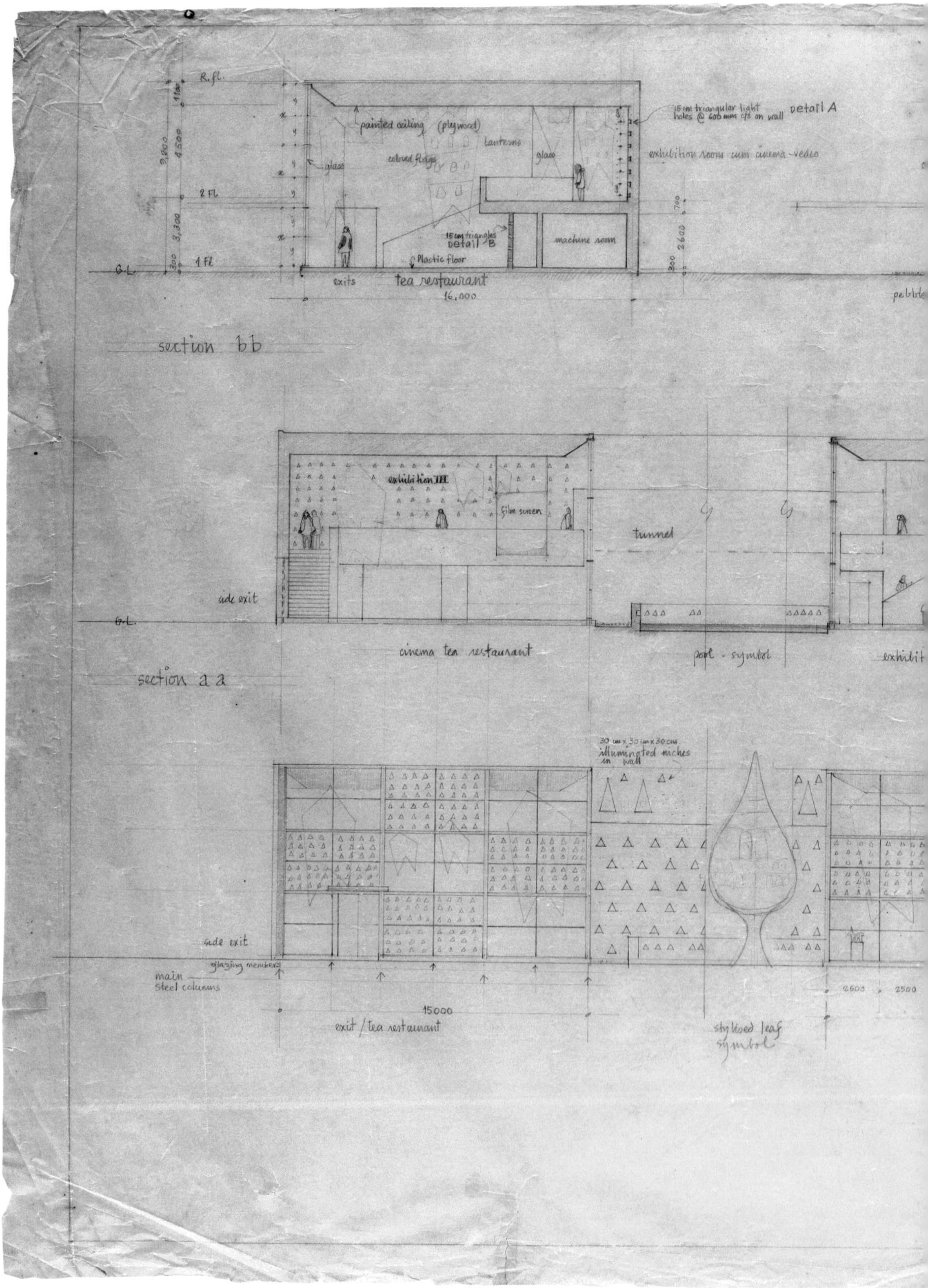

Elevation and sections, graphite on tracing paper, Anura Rathnavibushana, 1969
GB/DA/076/042

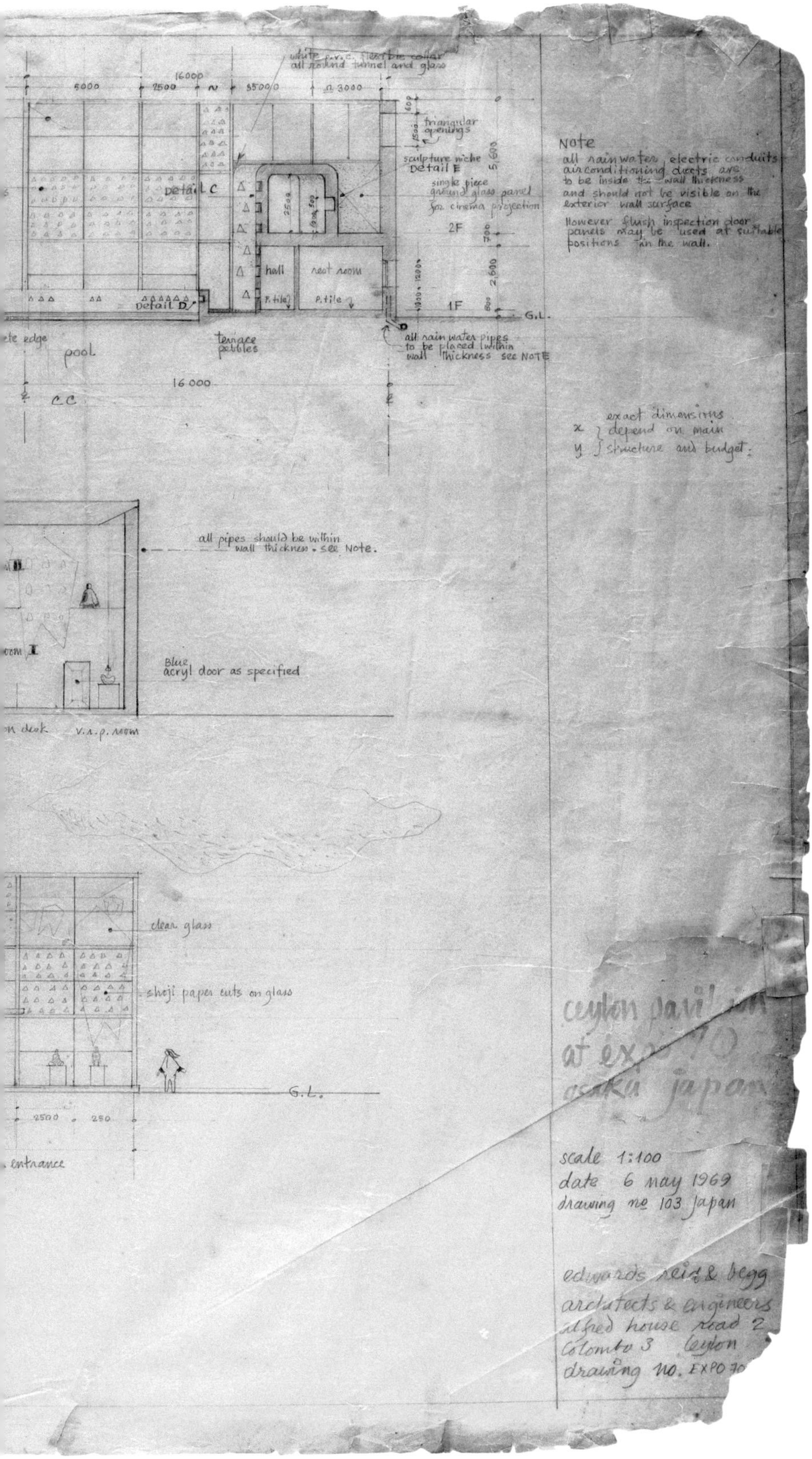
Note
all rainwater, electric conduits
airconditioning ducts are
to be inside the wall thickness
and should not be visible on the
exterior wall surface
However flush inspection door
panels may be used at suitable
positions in the wall.
triangular openings
sculpture niche
Detail E
single piece
ground glass panel
for cinema projection
Detail C
Detail D
hall
rest room
P. tile
2F
1F
G.L.
all rain water pipes
to be placed within
wall thickness see NOTE
terrace pebbles
pool
16.000
exact dimensions
x depend on main
y structure and budget.
all pipes should be within
wall thickness. see Note.
Blue
acryl door as specified
clear glass
shoji paper cuts on glass
G.L.
entrance
ceylon pavilion
at expo 70
osaka japan
scale 1:100
date 6 may 1969
drawing no 103 Japan
edwards reid & begg
architects & engineers
alfred house road 2
Colombo 3 ceylon
drawing no. EXPO 70

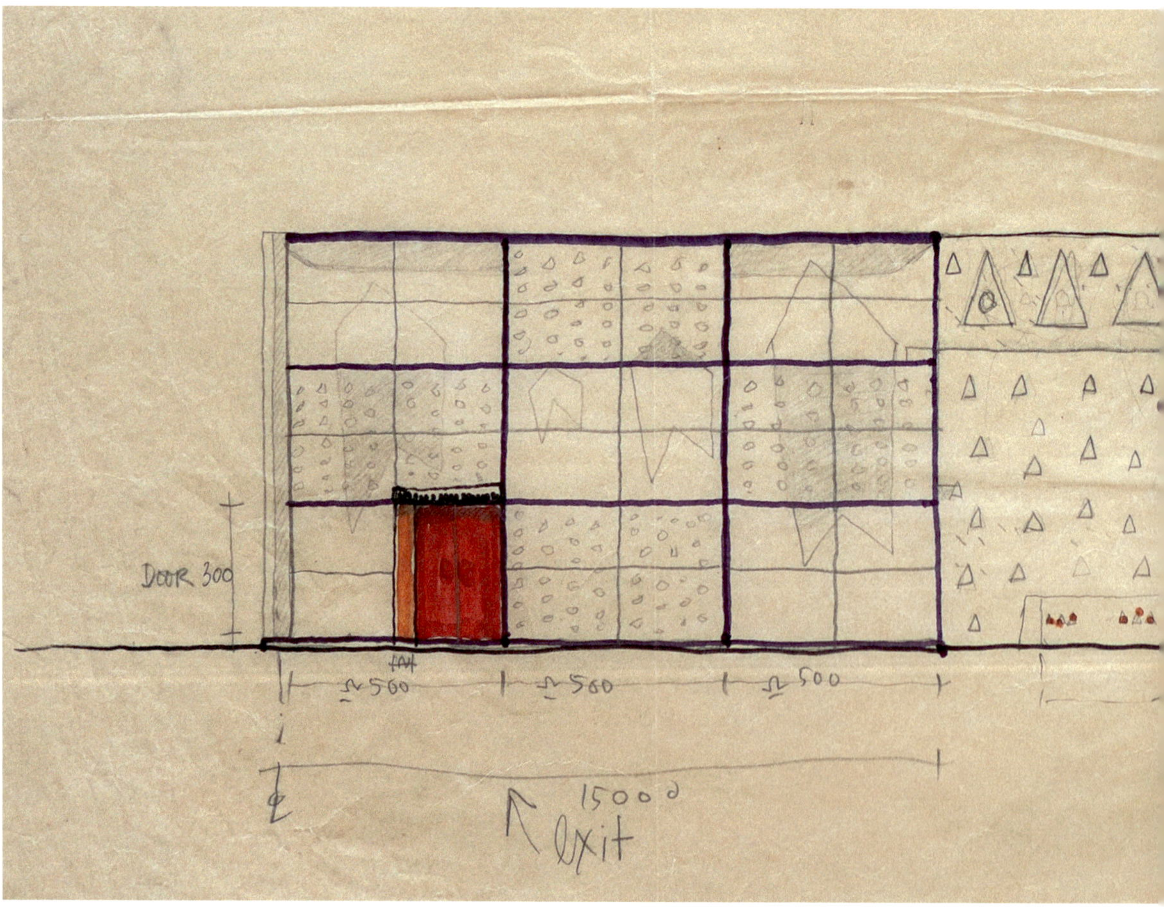

Exterior view of the two connected steel and glass cuboidal pavilions with Laki Senanayake – designed 30'-high Bo Leaf sculpture in foreground, chromogenic color print, Geoffrey Bawa (attributed), 1970 GB/DOC/141/001/A

Interior view of double-height tea room with batik banners and table-tops designed by Ena de Silva, chromogenic color print, Geoffrey Bawa (attributed), 1970 GB/DOC/141/001/B

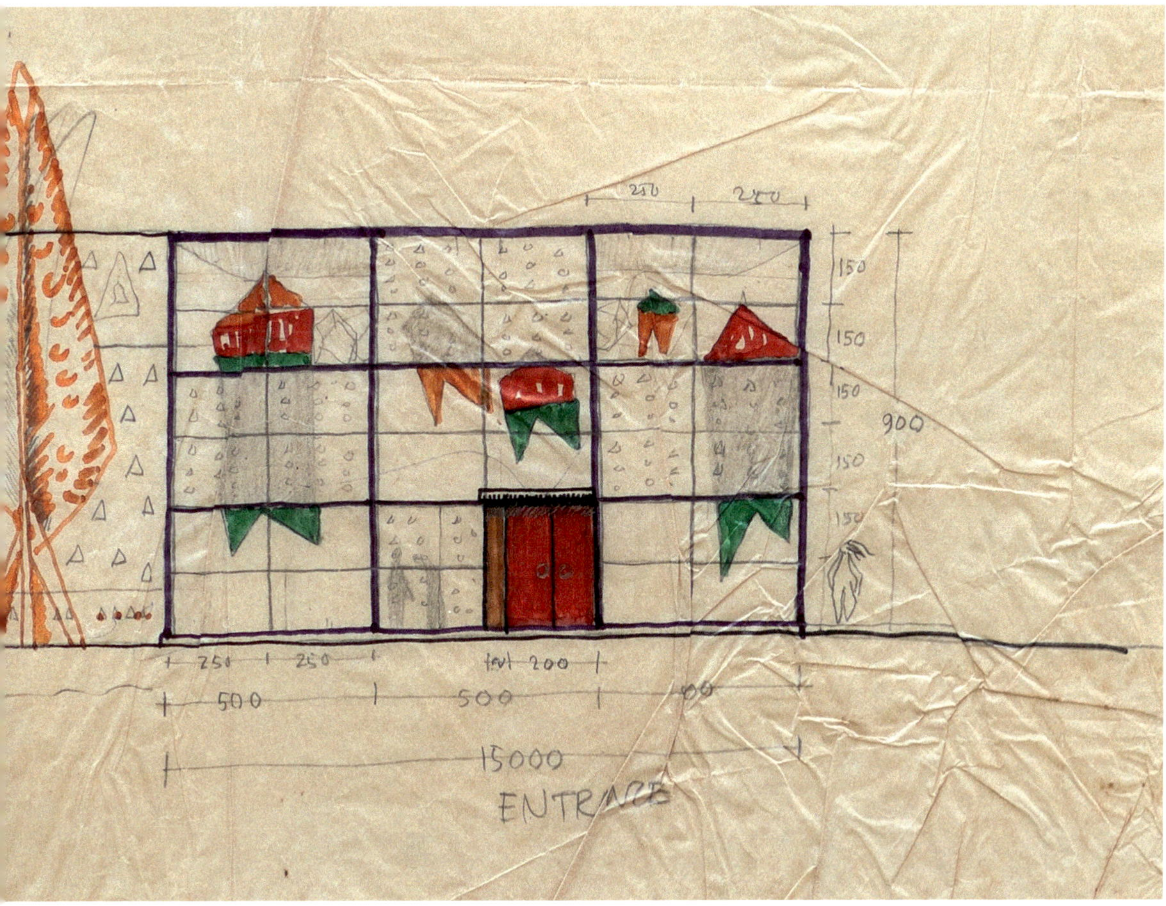

Elevation, graphite and colored ink on tracing paper, Anura Rathnavibushana, 1968
GB/DA/076/003

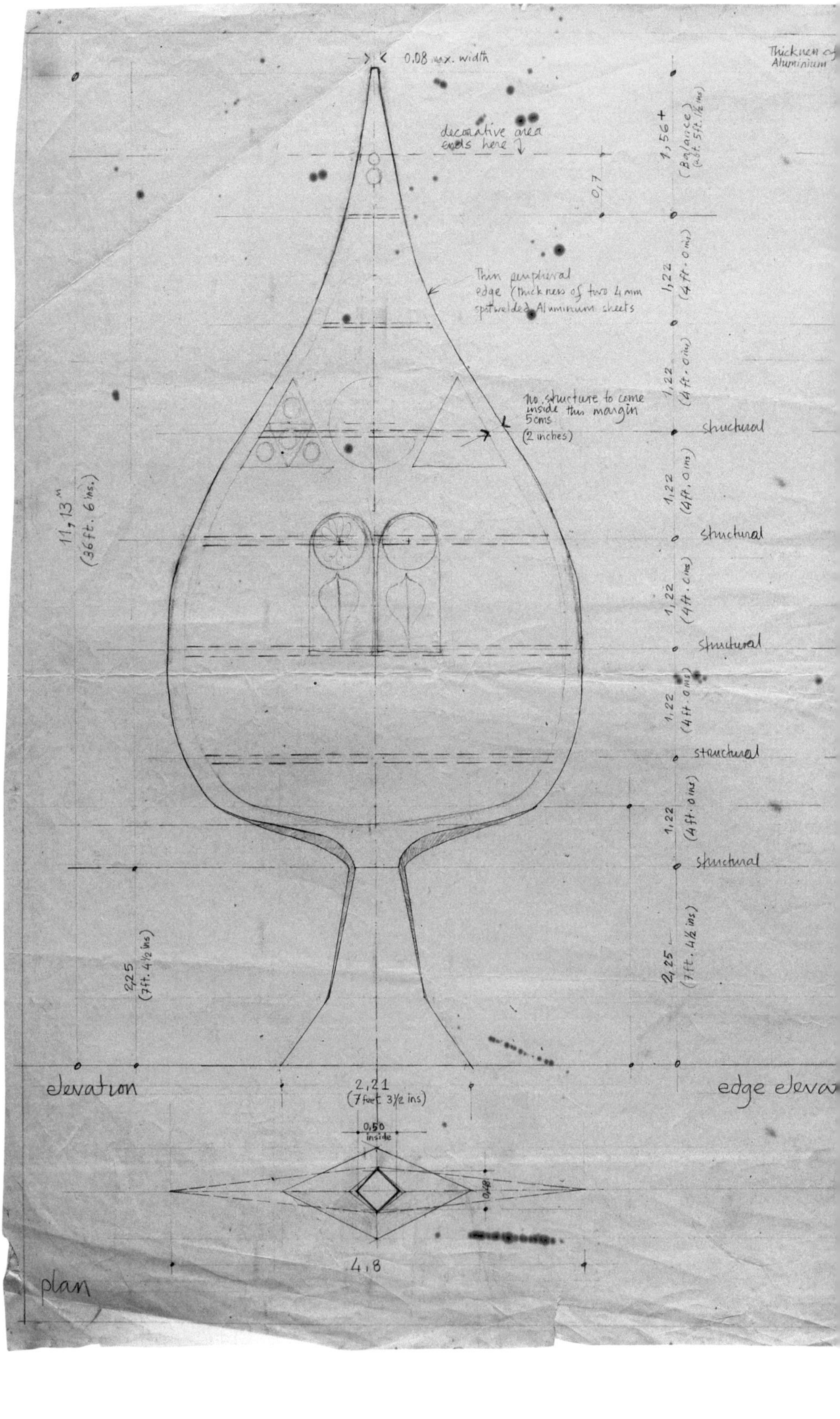

Section and elevation of Bo Leaf sculpture,
diazotype with annotations in ink,
Anura Rathnavibushana, 1969 GB/DA/076/011

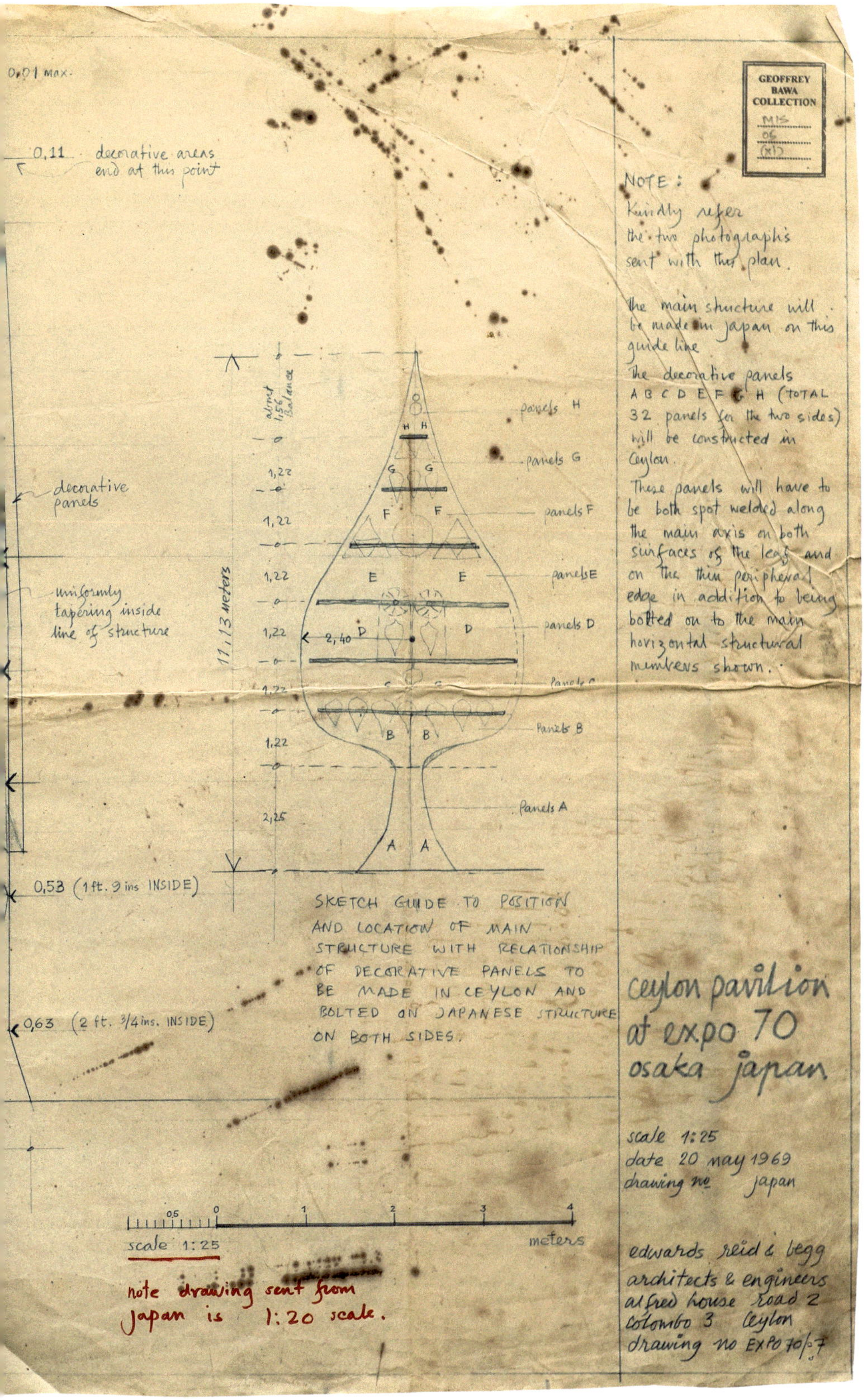
GEOFFREY BAWA COLLECTION
NOTE: Kindly refer the two photographs sent with the plan.
The main structure will be made in Japan on this guide line
The decorative panels A B C D E F G H (TOTAL 32 panels for the two sides) will be constructed in Ceylon.
These panels will have to be both spot welded along the main axis on both surfaces of the leaf and on the thin peripheral edge in addition to being bolted on to the main horizontal structural members shown.
SKETCH GUIDE TO POSITION AND LOCATION OF MAIN STRUCTURE WITH RELATIONSHIP OF DECORATIVE PANELS TO BE MADE IN CEYLON AND BOLTED ON JAPANESE STRUCTURE ON BOTH SIDES.
ceylon pavilion at expo 70 osaka japan
scale 1:25
date 20 may 1969
drawing no japan
edwards reid & begg architects & engineers alfred house road 2 colombo 3 ceylon
drawing no EXPO 70/p7
scale 1:25
note drawing sent from Japan is 1:20 scale.
0,11 decorative areas end at this point
decorative panels
uniformly tapering inside line of structure
0,53 (1 ft. 9 ins INSIDE)
0,63 (2 ft. 3/4 ins. INSIDE)
11,13 meters
meters

Ceylon

This elegant small pavilion consists of two glass-walled steel-framed cubes, 30 and 31, set at an obtuse angle and connected at balcony level. The glass is partly obscured by cut-out paper to prevent glare. Exhibits—in the entrance cube, 32, and on the balcony—are temple sculptures and gems. In the exit cube visitors can buy and consume Ceylon tea. Paintwork, pedestals and balcony-fronts are white, but both interiors are enriched by the strong colours of banners of modern Ceylonese batik-work hung from the ceiling. The dark silhouette seen in both the exterior views is a bronze-surfaced sculpture based on the leaf of the sacred bo-tree. Architect, Geoffrey Bawa (of Edwards, Reid and Begg).

30

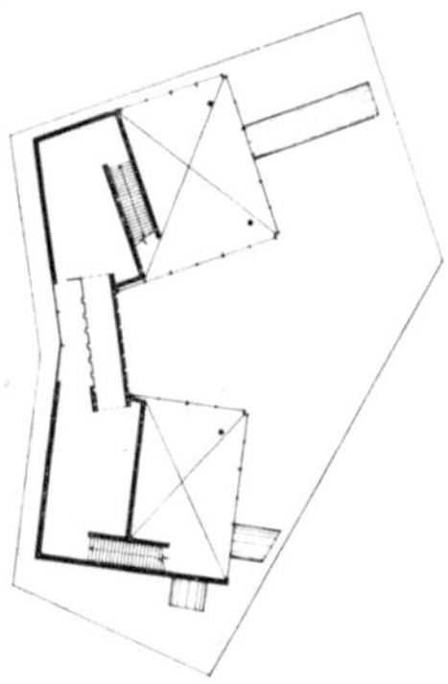

plan of Ceylon pavilion at balcony level

Page from *Architectural Review – The Osaka Expo* issue, London; feature on Ceylon Pavilion, printed ink on coated paper, edited by Kenzo Tange, Jim Richards and Nikolaus Pevsner, August 1970 GB/DOC/141/004

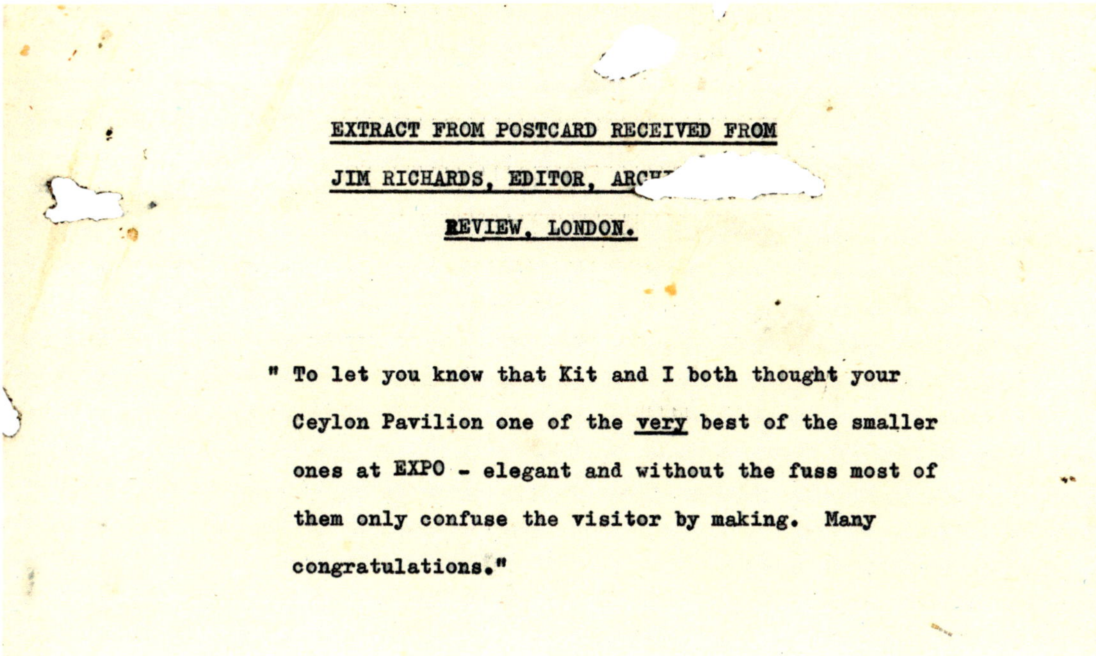

EXTRACT FROM POSTCARD RECEIVED FROM
JIM RICHARDS, EDITOR, ARC[illegible]
REVIEW, LONDON.

" To let you know that Kit and I both thought your Ceylon Pavilion one of the very best of the smaller ones at EXPO - elegant and without the fuss most of them only confuse the visitor by making. Many congratulations."

Typewritten note from Jim Richards, editor, *Architectural Review*, London, 1970
GB/DOC/141/003

Interior view at upper level entrance to tunnel connecting two pavilion cubes, gelatin silver print, Geoffrey Bawa (attributed), 1970
GB/DOC/141/001/D

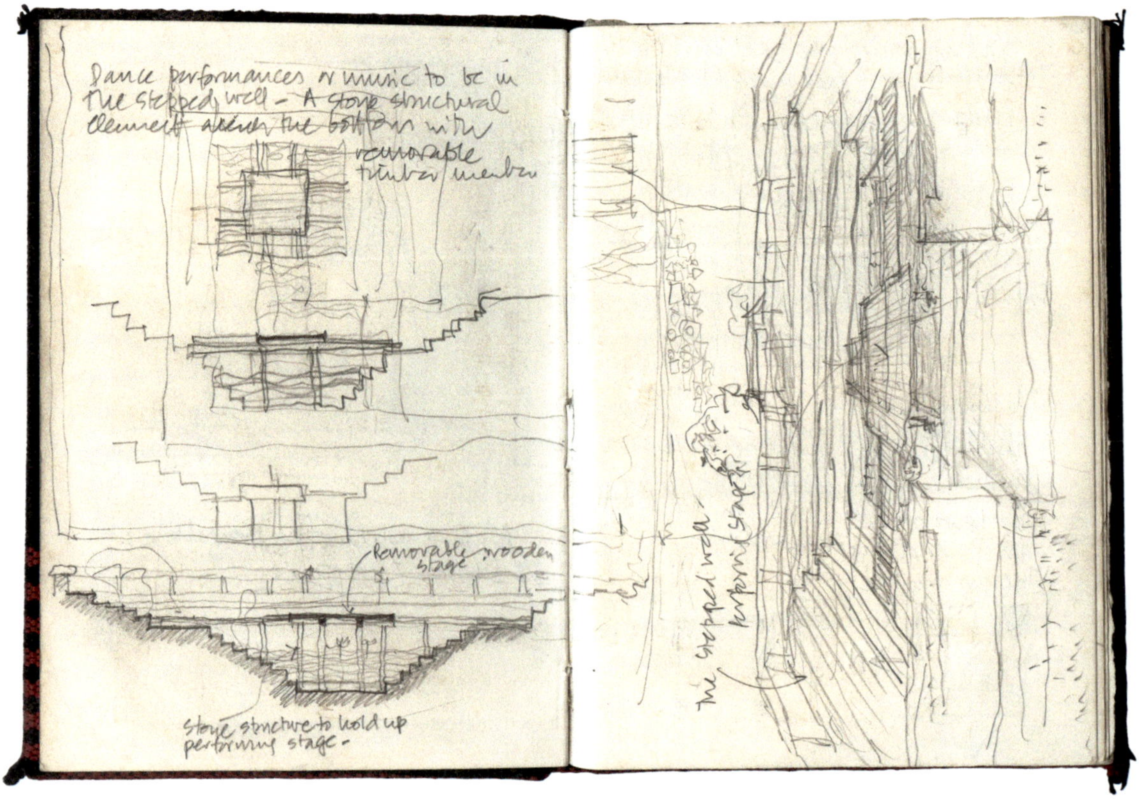

House for Bimal Poddar (unbuilt), Chikajalla, spread from sketch book, graphite on uncoated paper, Channa Daswatte, 1996

Epilogue: Drawing Stories

Channa Daswatte

A drawing in the Geoffrey Bawa office was two things: an intention and a record. The drawing, as far as those of us who worked with Bawa in his office were concerned, was never a final object or instruction simply to be followed but always allowed for accommodating the views of those who implemented the instructions on site. The drawing was a tool to think with when reflecting on the site and eventually, as a measured drawing, it became a log of what was put on the site, the record of a built reality. Until the project was completed and the final drawing finished, the drawing was a process and incomplete. Bawa once reacted to my irritation at being asked to make the same drawing for the umpteenth time, which in the days of ink on paper was no mean task, by explaining that if he could convey his intention, as a final idea, directly to the mind of the builder, he wouldn't need a drawing or architectural assistants!

Bawa said that once he spent some time and stood on a site, he knew how it should be changed to suit the intended purpose. A clear objective formed in his mind, and this was initially expressed as a drawing on square-ruled paper, which was then translated into a more conventional form by his team of associate designers. Each change to the drawing or redrawing was a process of clarifying this original thought. This utilization of the eye, the mind and the hand exemplified the idea of "the thinking hand" described by Juhani Pallasmaa in the book of the same name.

Technical drawings comprise a language that can be read by others trained to do so, who will then carry out the coded instructions to make a physical object. The medium of the drawing may have changed from parchment to vellum, to paper and now to a digital screen, but the language describing the elements that constitute the eventual object has not. This makes architectural drawings repositories of ideas and technologies for physical structures, by which the history of a period and the lifestyle that it enjoyed can be studied. While many drawings may not have ended up as instructions for any kind of reality, ending up as unbuilt work or simply as tools that were used to think about physicality, they will contain the thinking behind the intended structure. This is why the archiving and care of architectural drawings is important to a culture.

Measured drawings made by architects have also played an important role in the dissemination of ideas. Those done of the classical buildings of Rome played a significant role in spreading the aesthetics and technical knowledge contained in those monuments. Sebastiano Serlio's *Tutte l'opere d'architettura et prospetiva,* published in the mid–sixteenth century, is one of the first folios to contain extensive architectural drawings. Subsequent publications played a significant role in disseminating knowledge about classical Western architecture that possibly led to the beginning of the Neoclassical style in Europe and its colonies from the sixteenth century. Serlio was not content with simply recording the existing architecture of a lost culture but also offered variations on the theme of each of these so it might be adapted to contemporary use at the time. This suggests that the act of drawing is not simply a matter of conveying information, which it is, but that it also sparks a process of creativity. The act of drawing often reveals another layer of potential that might exist in the initial ideas that are put to paper. The drawing, in the case of those done by hand, is often the first time the ideas in the imagination are seen as a physical manifestation. It becomes a record of thought, and as a single drawing or a series of drawings develops, it could be compared to a story being told. After all, the drawing could also be an end in itself, since architectural

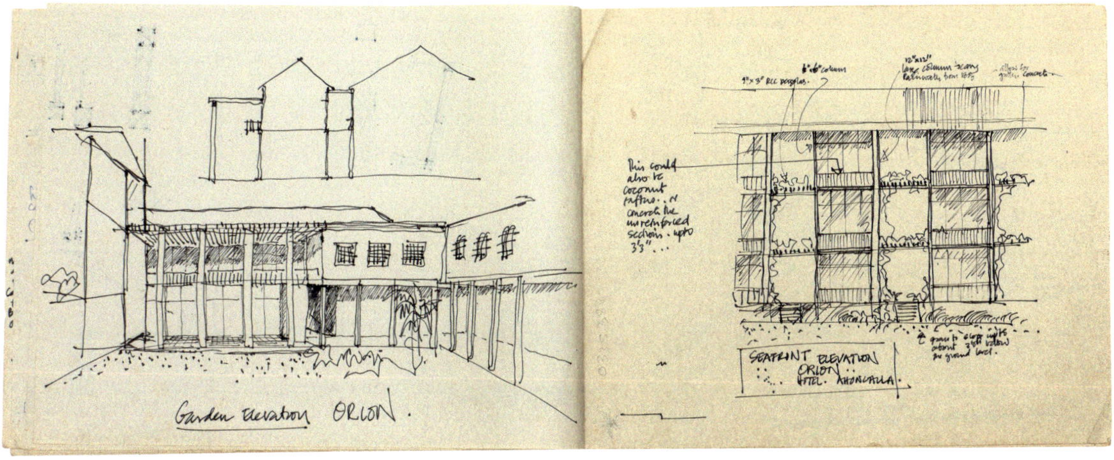

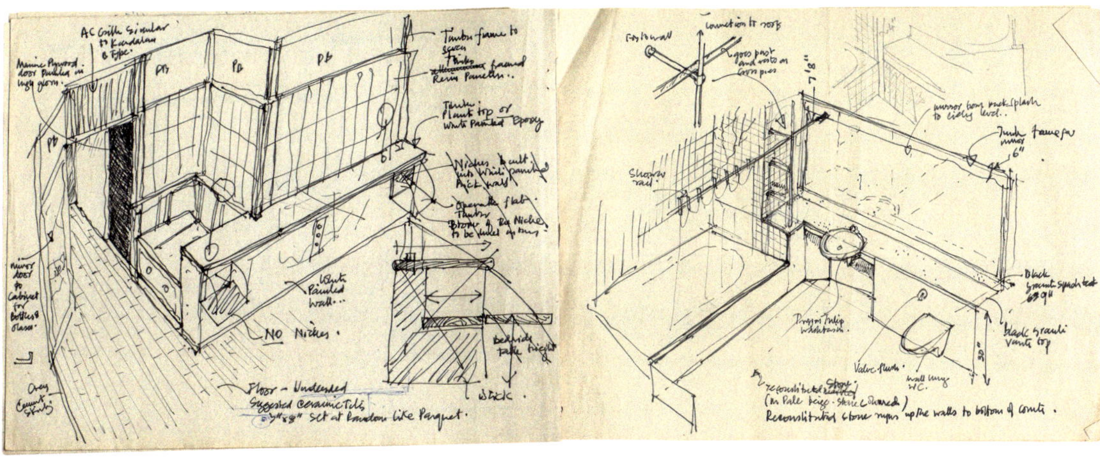

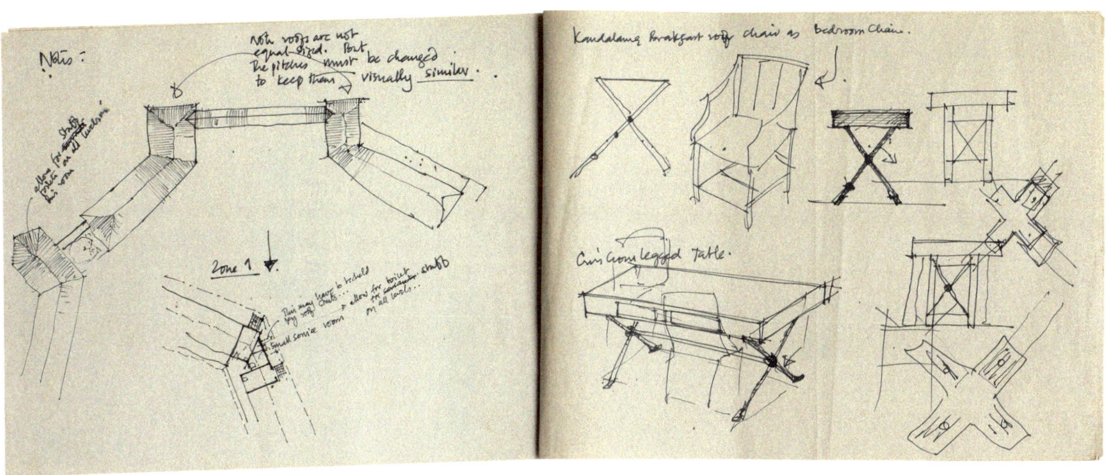

Orion Hotel (unbuilt), Ahungalla, spreads from sketch book, ink on paper, Channa Daswatte, 1992

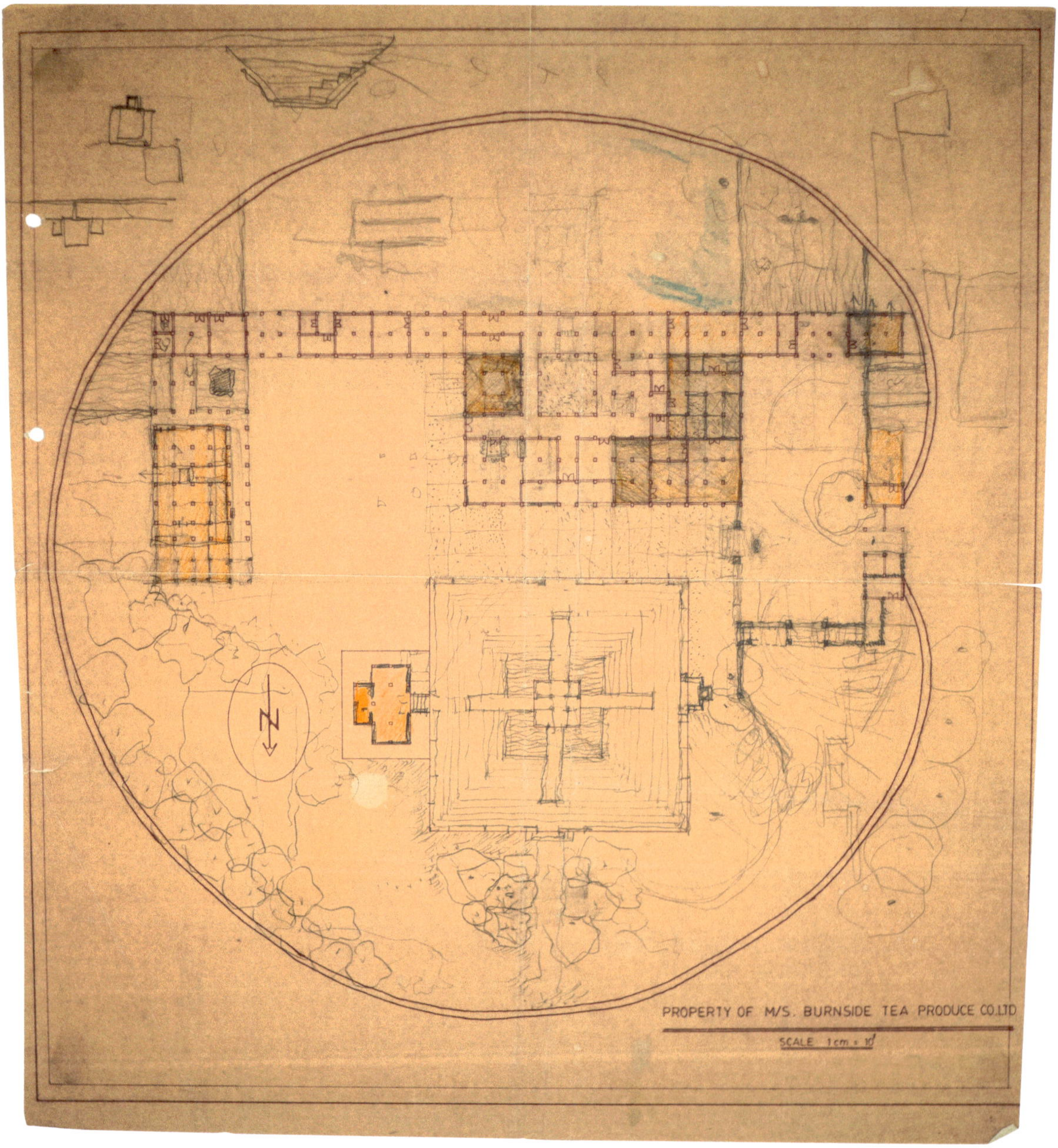

House for Bimal Poddar (unbuilt), Chikajalla
Floor plan of stepwell, graphite and colored pencil over diazotype, Channa Daswatte

Section through stepwell, ink on vellum, Neelanga Weerasekera, 1996

drawings often represent intention and not an existing structure. The intention might even be fictional, as in the case of Piranesi's *Vedute di Roma* drawings, which appear to represent a reality that did not exist.

It was not uncommon for Bawa to draw up a fictional story of life or a lifestyle as it might happen in a place, on a site. The spaces he drew on paper would be those that allowed for that story to enact itself. The rest of the process was usually a conversation over these drawings, in which the scheme was explained to others who took on the conversion of these scribbles on square-ruled paper into more conventionally recognizable architectural drawings. These would contain much more than was technically required, as the context that the building was set in or even the landscape that would be generated in the future helped the people using the drawings to interpret them better. Hence a tree seen on the site would be drawn in exactitude to highlight the technical requirements that may be required in relation to something that was to continue living on the site.

In 1993 Bawa worked on a plan for a client he had never met and a site he had not seen, based on qualities of the client he discerned over a conversation on the phone and an imagined topography of the city in which the site was located. The spaces were organized around a narrative of how he himself would visit the client and the sequences of spaces he would come across, imagining the spaces beyond his actual vision but that would exist to back up the event. Of course, all this changed or was adjusted to suit what he saw once he arrived at the site, reaffirming his maxim "it is essential to be there."

In another project where an existing structure was to be converted to a weekend home, he literally walked and talked his way through a series of events that would happen between endless rows of columns and recorded it on a site survey. Works of art were placed to mark pivotal points along the space, and furniture was devised to make best use of the existing structure and spaces. Dining tables and beds were suspended from columns, and an ancient temple to Hanuman was rethought of as an amphitheater for traditional dance performances. The conversations were carefully recorded on paper as sketches with notes and then made into drawings for presentation to the owners.

Even at a time when his mobility was compromised, Bawa walked through the stone ruins on this site in rural Bangalore to visualize the potential life that would be led on it. He went to great lengths to be there, once being carried on a cane chair fixed with bamboo to reach the top of a hill on the site of the Kandalama Hotel despite his age and illnesses at the time.

While he was on a site, he was also able to draw from his prodigious memory of places he had visited that were directly relevant to the building he was involved in at a particular moment. Thinking about the organization of the Sinbad Garden Hotel, now the Anantara Kalutara, he invoked the endless walls and corridors of Hadrian's Villa in Tivoli within which servitors moved to appear almost magically wherever they were needed. The hotel was designed around great three-story walled service corridors which served spaces that were sheltered by soaring roofs that either floated over or leaned on these walls.

Many of these process drawings are now unfortunately lost, but where they are extant, it is exciting to see how a design changes through drawing, by the marks made on the paper. Often the clues to the reason for an outcome are to be found on the margins of a drawing, representing a side conversation that would lead to significant changes to a scheme.

In the case of Bawa, who wrote sparsely, the drawings also become a repository of his own thinking about architecture in general and the buildings he made. He once suggested that if people see the point of the building, that is its theory. He was a firm believer in making buildings that were understood by the people using them. His belief that the theory was the building is perhaps the reason that most of the drawings in the archive are records of built forms rather than of the process or even the intention. However, where there are surviving associated

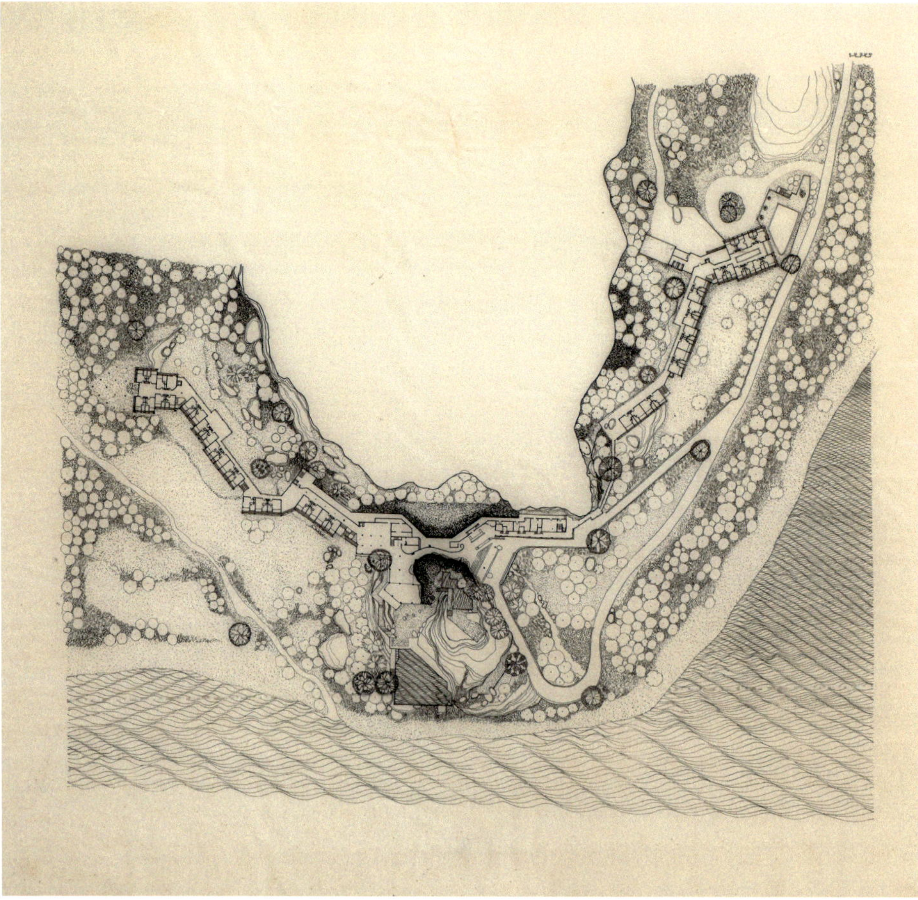

Kandalama Hotel, Dambulla
Ground-floor plan, ink on tracing paper,
Tim Beacher, 1994

View through corridor to reception, black-and-white film negative, Channa Daswatte, 1995 drawings, his thinking is often revealed through a careful examination of the spaces and materials suggested. By recording the final built object, he was recording his resolution.

Perhaps this suggests why he had little interest in preserving the piles of drawings stored in the attic over the entrance to his old office at Number 2, Alfred Place, in Colombo. Hundreds of drawings were lost by Bawa's own order in a bonfire at the entry court of Alfred Place or thrown into a suburban well. It took much convincing on the part of people around him to stop that destruction. He believed, perhaps, that the process was just that; a process to be lost with time. The surviving drawings comprise the bulk of the archive. These were joined in 2018 by a set of more carefully curated records of buildings that had resided in the UK with his friend Christoph Bon and later with David Robson.

When visiting the Kandalama Hotel many years after it had been completed and after he had been affected by a devastating stroke that left him speechless and wheelchair-bound, rounding a corner he suddenly put his feet down and looked out at the building with tears in his eyes. The creepers he had instructed to be planted were slowly covering the minimal structure, and the shrubs on its roof had begun to cascade over the edges. He saw what he expected to see, a process initiated by his thoughts and actions through drawings and instructions. There never was a drawing of that corner of the hotel, but here it was, as he intended it to be. He once said to me that Kandalama would only finally be complete when the leopards roamed its corridors and the bears took shelter in its rooms, concluding a process that began with a mark of a pen on a sheet of square-ruled paper.

In Bawa's mind, drawings were only a small part of a process, and it was the final outcome, be it a fixed one or an ongoing one, that mattered. Hence the obsessively beautiful drawings made postconstruction.

Arguably, preserving the archive was not something Bawa particularly wanted. In fact, preserving anything was perhaps not a part of his

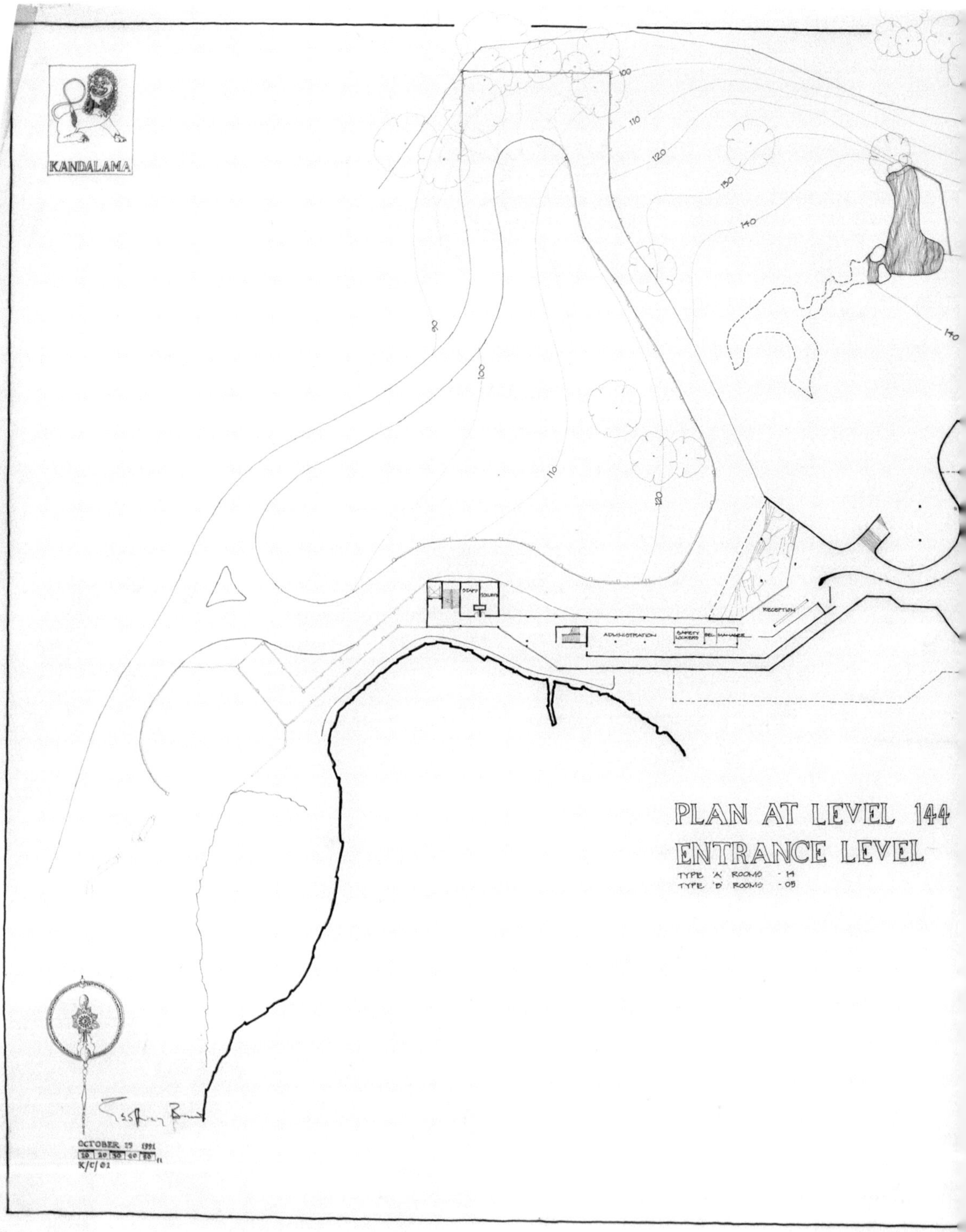

Kandalama Hotel, Dambulla, plan at level 144',
ink on tracing paper, 1991

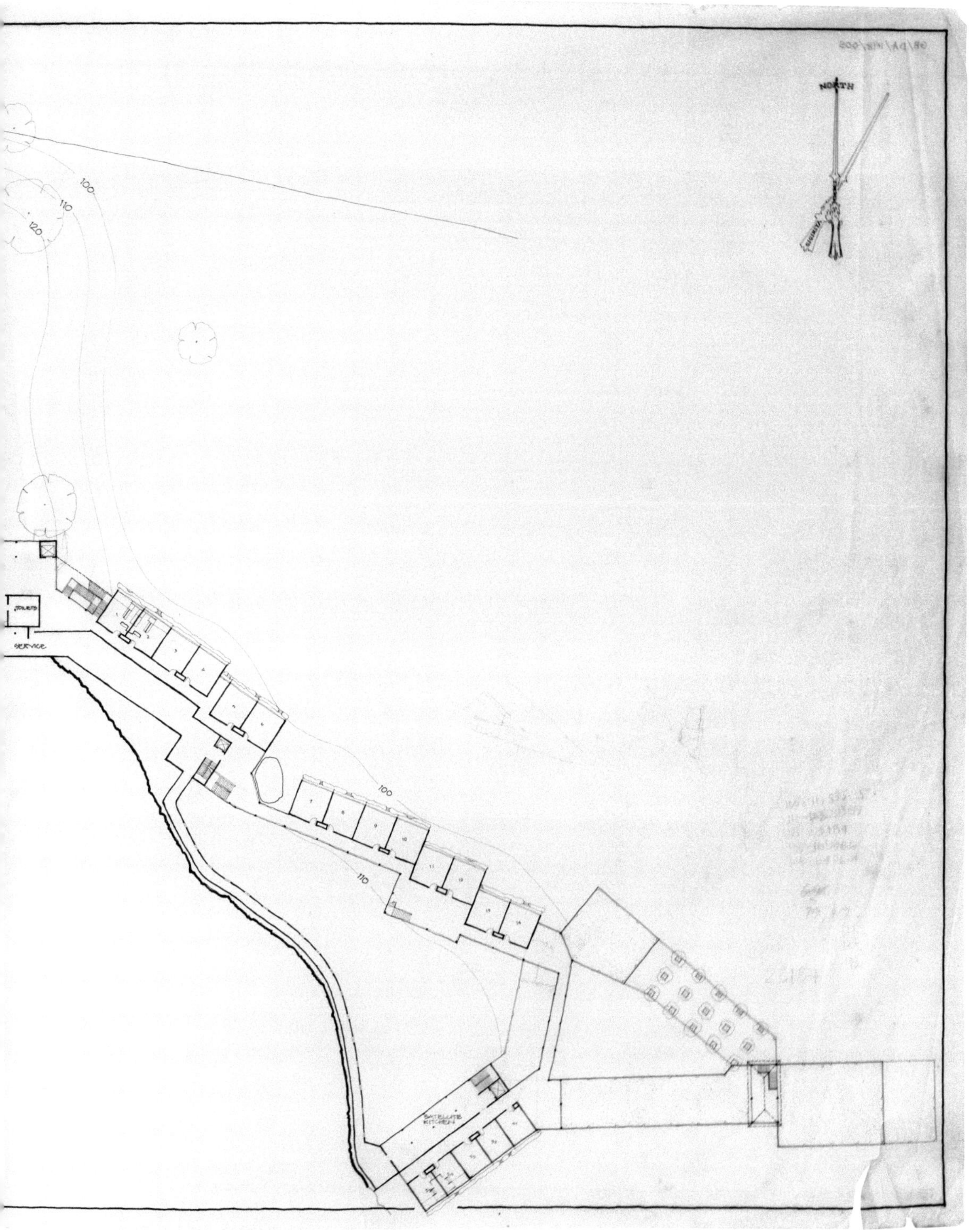
NORTH
100
110
120
TOILETS
SERVICE
SATELLITE KITCHEN

Geoffrey Bawa with Channa Daswatte and Pradeep Jayawardena at Jayawardena House, Mirissa, black-and-white film negative, Dominic Sansoni, 1996

being. Sitting on a terrace at Lunuganga on the last evening on which he was able to exchange words, there seems to have been a premonition of things to come. Should he be struck down by another stroke like the first one he had just recovered from, his desire was, if nothing else could be preserved as instructed in his trust deed, to keep the lawns of the upper terraces in order, so he could reach their edges and watch the jungle take back his beloved garden. Would he have had the strength to do what he said? We will never know. The trustees of his estate and his friends ensured the garden survived as set out in his last will and trust deed, to be shared by the many visitors who now contemplate its peace and grace. Which makes the archive more important than ever. It was perhaps not supposed to survive. But by its very survival we now have an opportunity to contemplate the origins of the buildings that Bawa and his associates caused to be built and the cultural ethos, with its multiple inspirations, from which they arose.

In the years since Bawa's demise, his stature has grown, particularly internationally. His work is studied in architecture faculties in several countries, and professionals and students come to Sri Lanka to experience and study his buildings. Several substantial monographs have been published, including a complete works, and critical titles attest to his continuing influence. His public buildings, particularly hotels, remain drawing cards for domestic and visiting tourists. This examination of the archive, left by an architectural practice that worked in a changing world order to forge an identity for an ancient nation-state at the crossroads of history as it looked to its future, is not only revealing and engaging, it is simply important.

Kandalama Hotel, Dambulla

1991–95

Black-and-white film negative, Channa Daswatte, 1995 GB/DOC/009/A

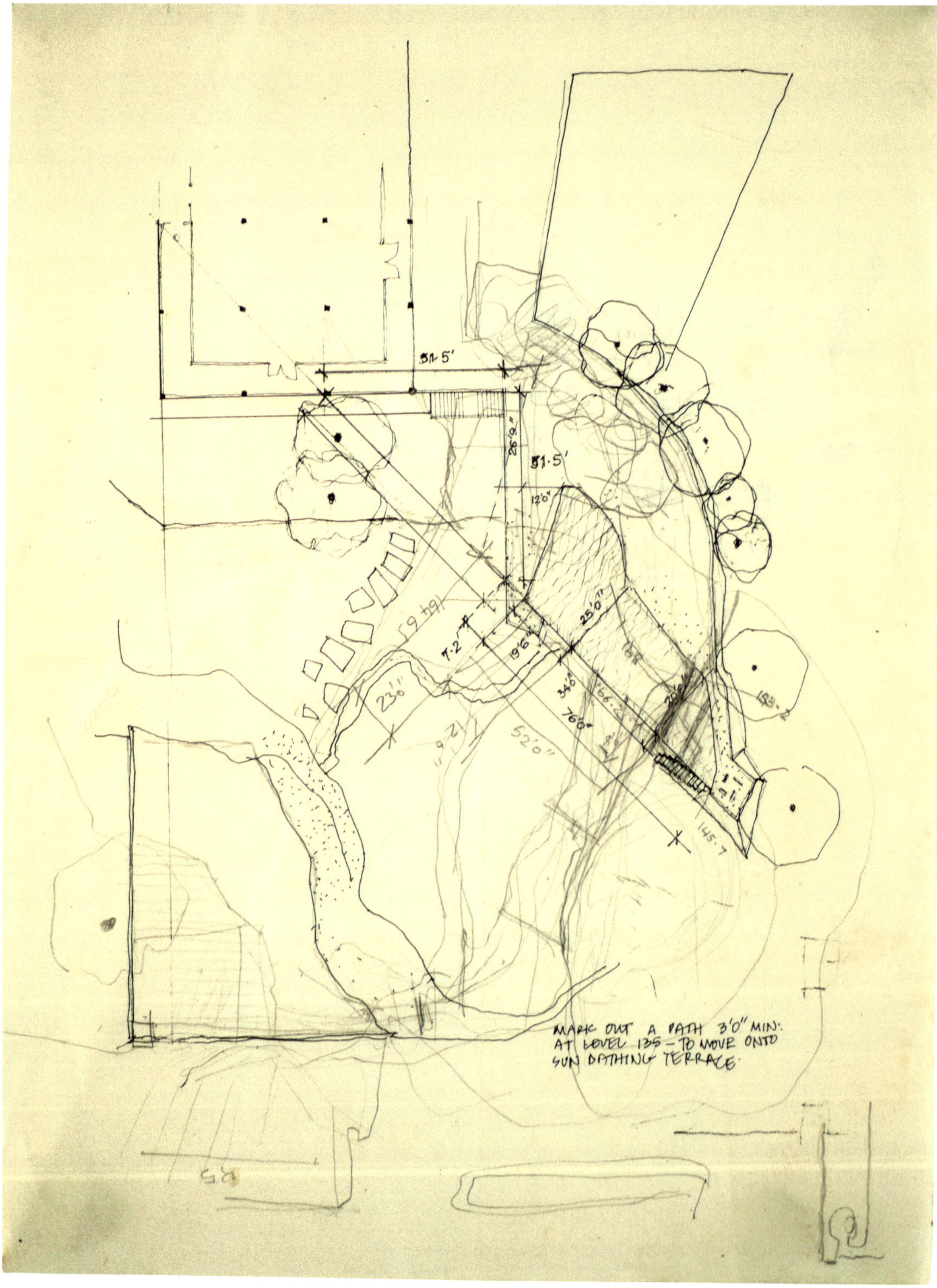

Sketch of path to pool, ink on paper, Channa Daswatte GB/DA/198/034

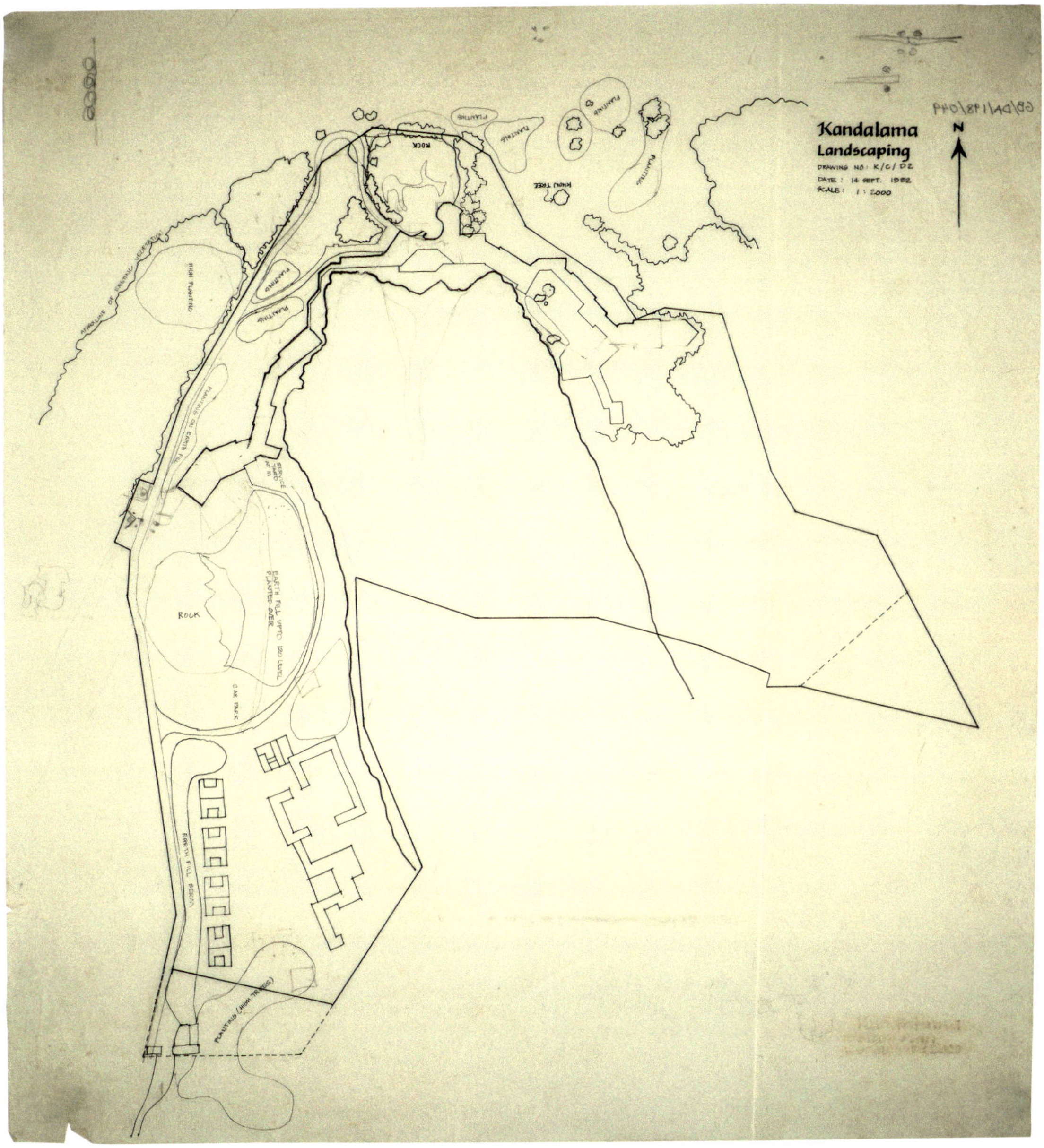

Site plan for landscaping, ink on tracing paper,
Channa Daswatte GB/DA/198/034

Perspectival drawing of earlier scheme, artist impression of hotel, ink on tracing paper, Dilshan Ferdinando GB/DA/198/042

Sectional elevation through the site, ink on tracing paper, Tim Beacher, 1994 GB/DA/198/176

Exterior view, black-and-white film negative,
Channa Daswatte, 1995 GB/DOC/009/B

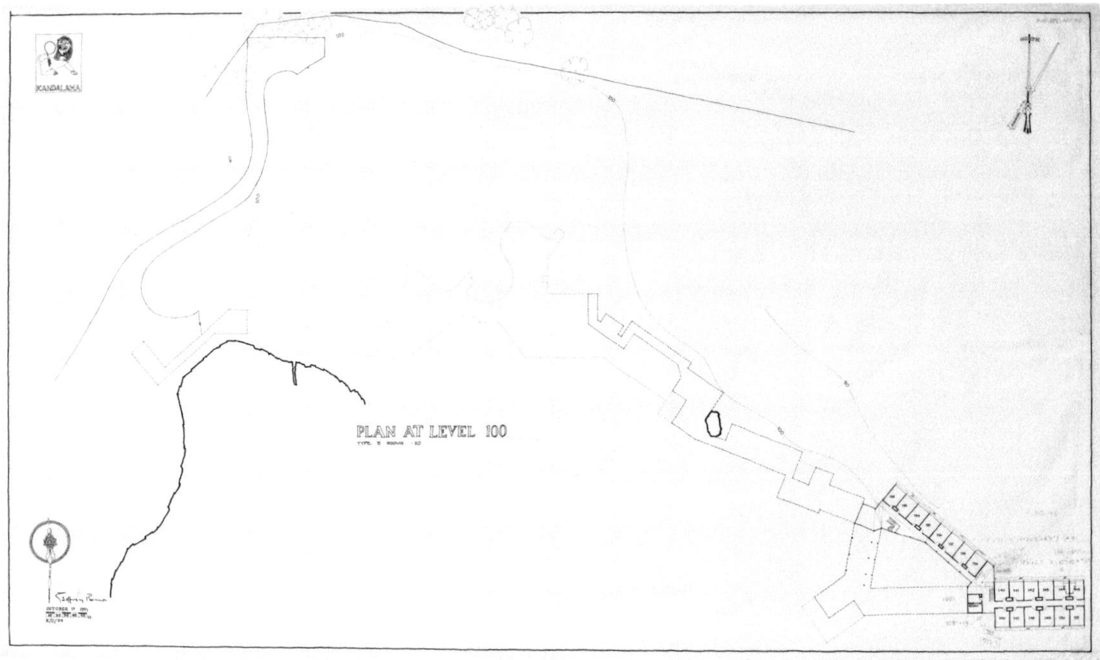

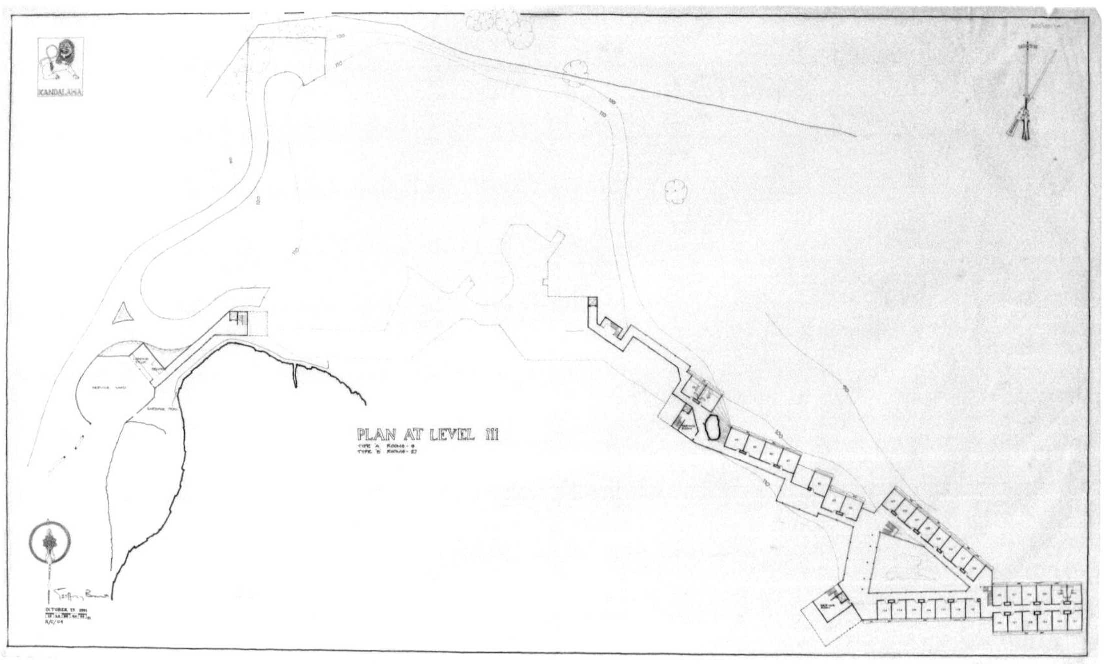

Plans at levels 100' and 111' (left), 122' and 133' (right), ink on tracing paper, 1991
GB/DA/198/009, 008, 007, 006

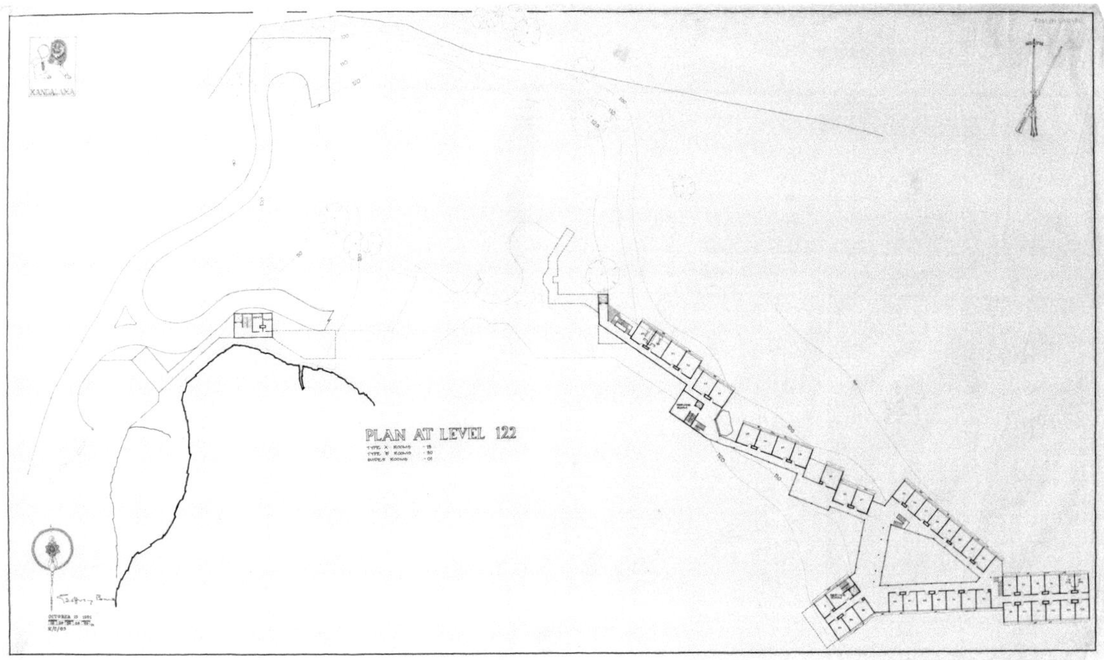
PLAN AT LEVEL 122

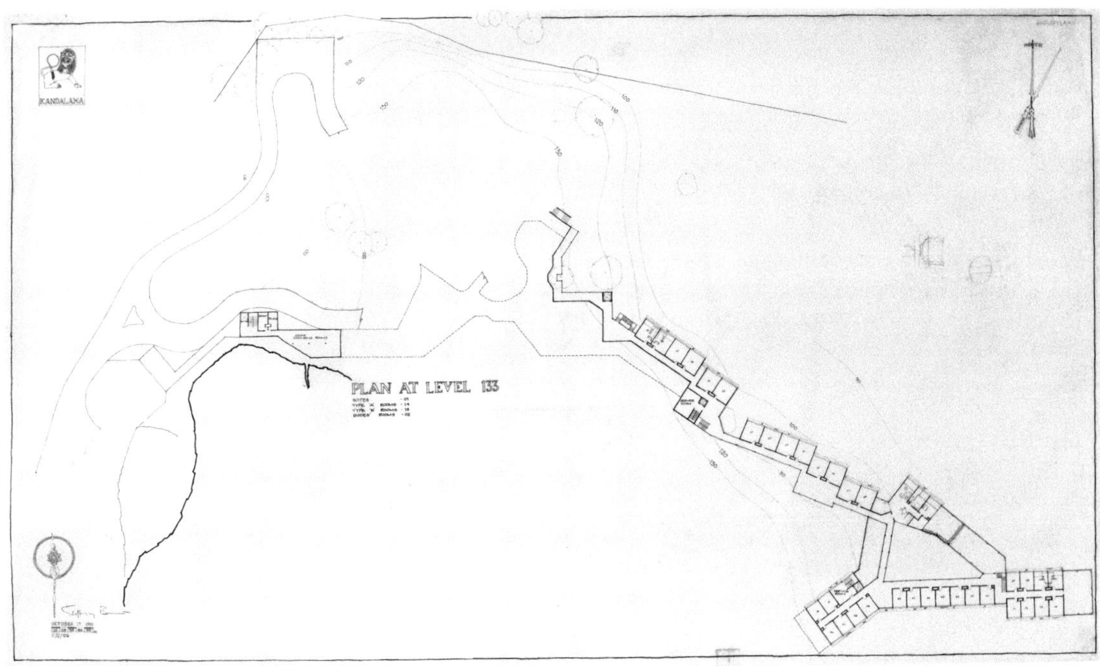
KANDALAMA
PLAN AT LEVEL 133

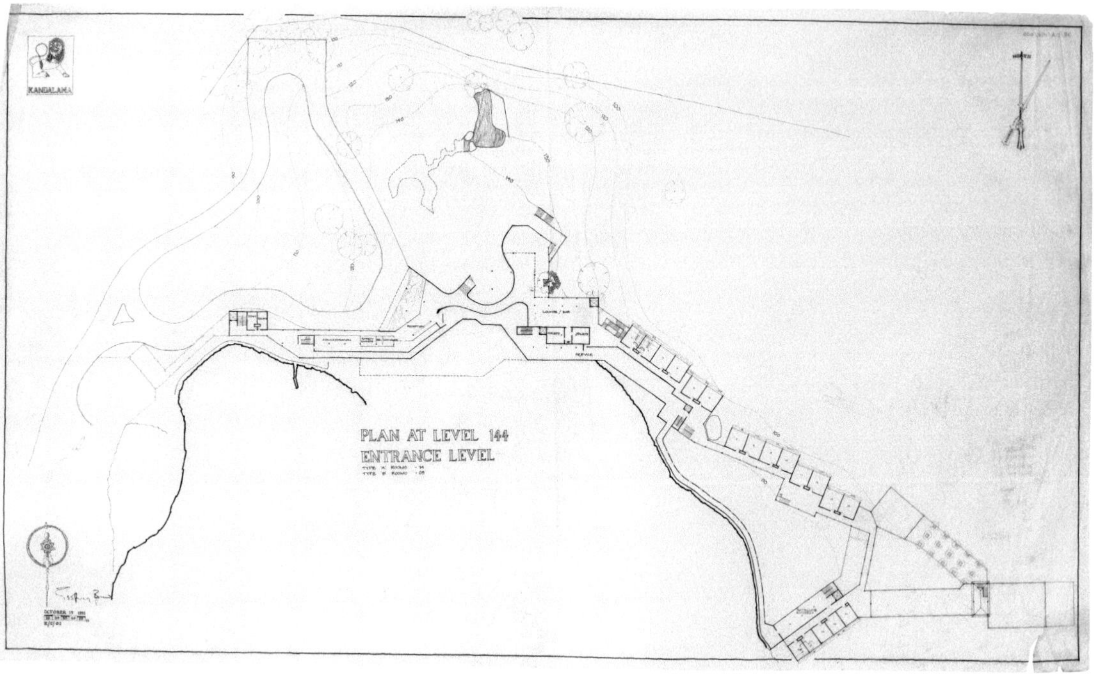

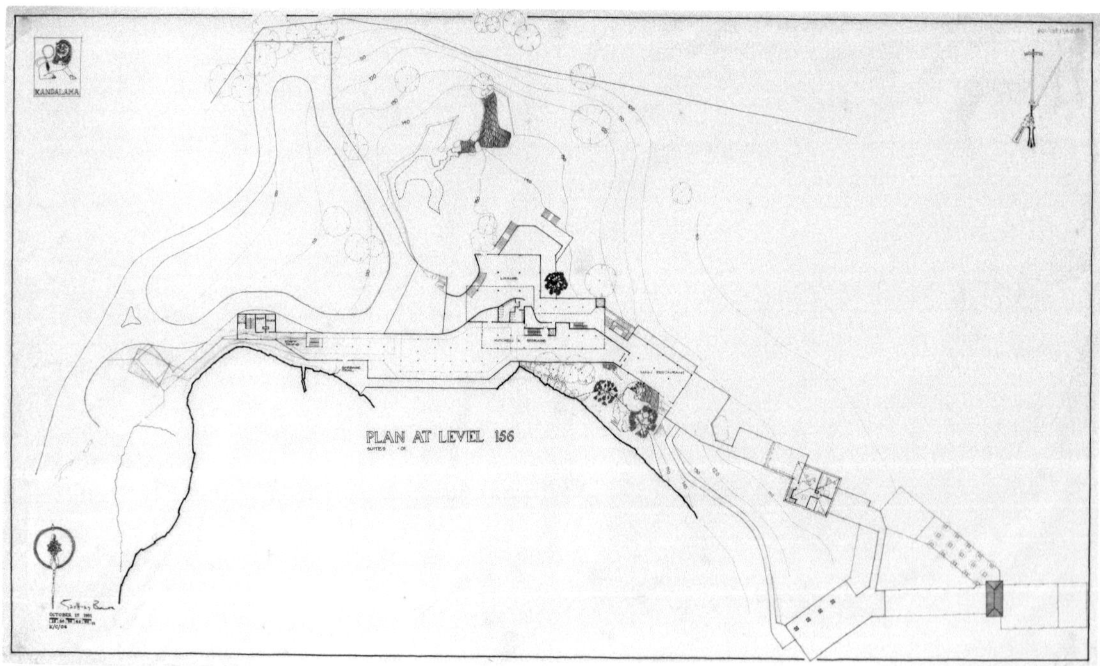

Plans at levels 144' and 156' (left), 170' and roof plan (right), ink on tracing paper, 1991
GB/DA/198/005, 004, 003, 002

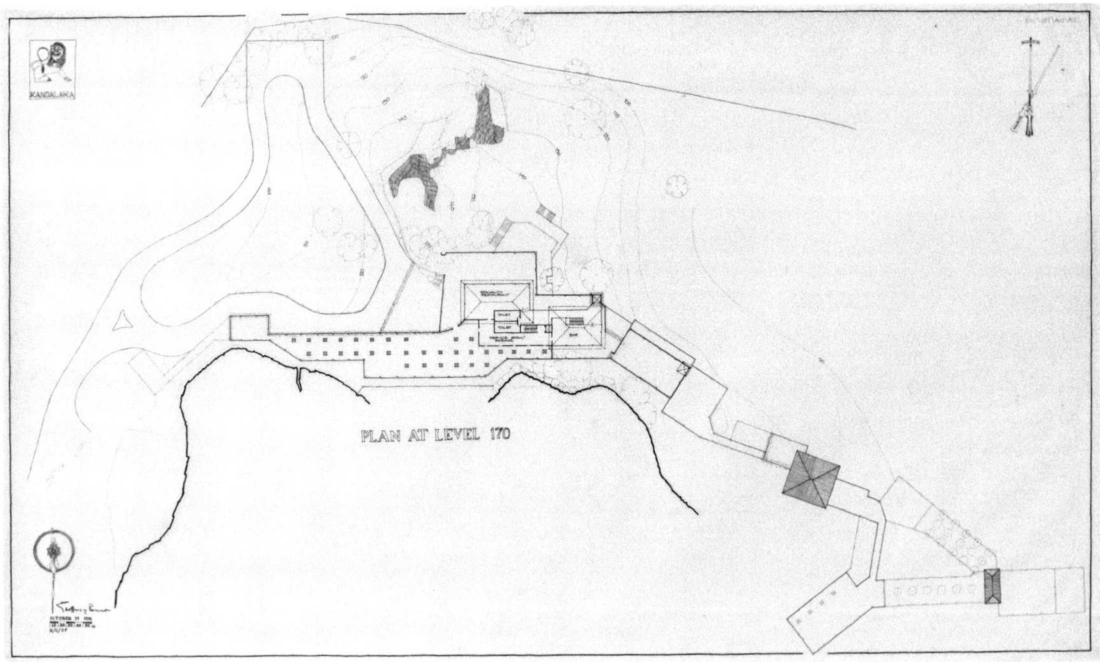
KANDALAMA
PLAN AT LEVEL 170

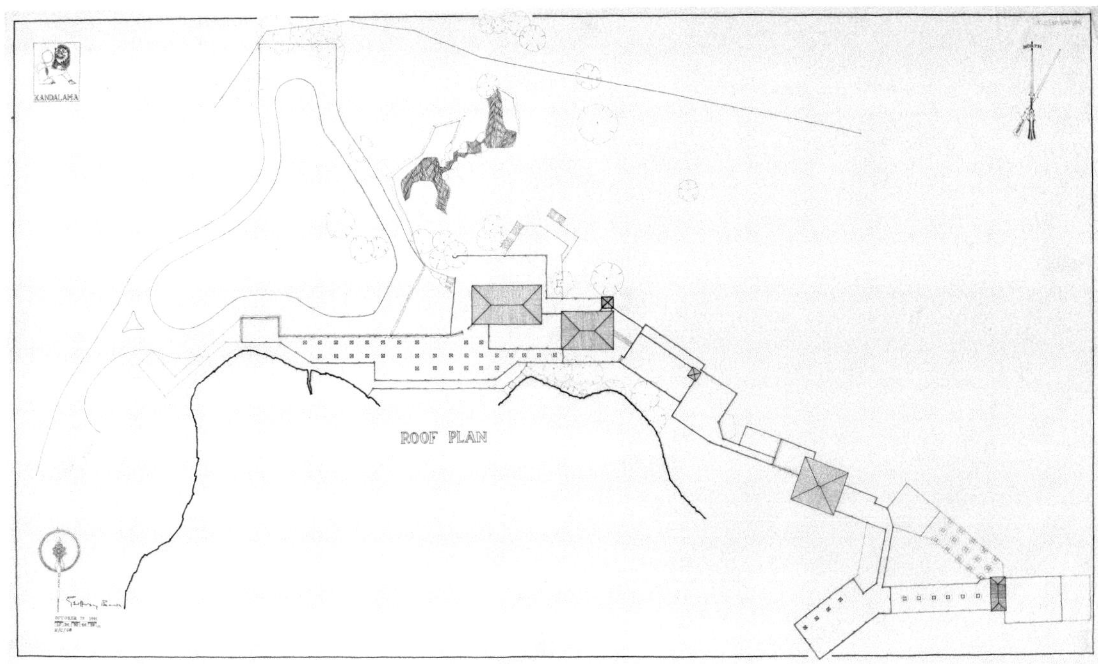
KANDALAMA
ROOF PLAN

View through corridor to reception, black-and-white film negative, Channa Daswatte, 1995
GB/DOC/100/009/B

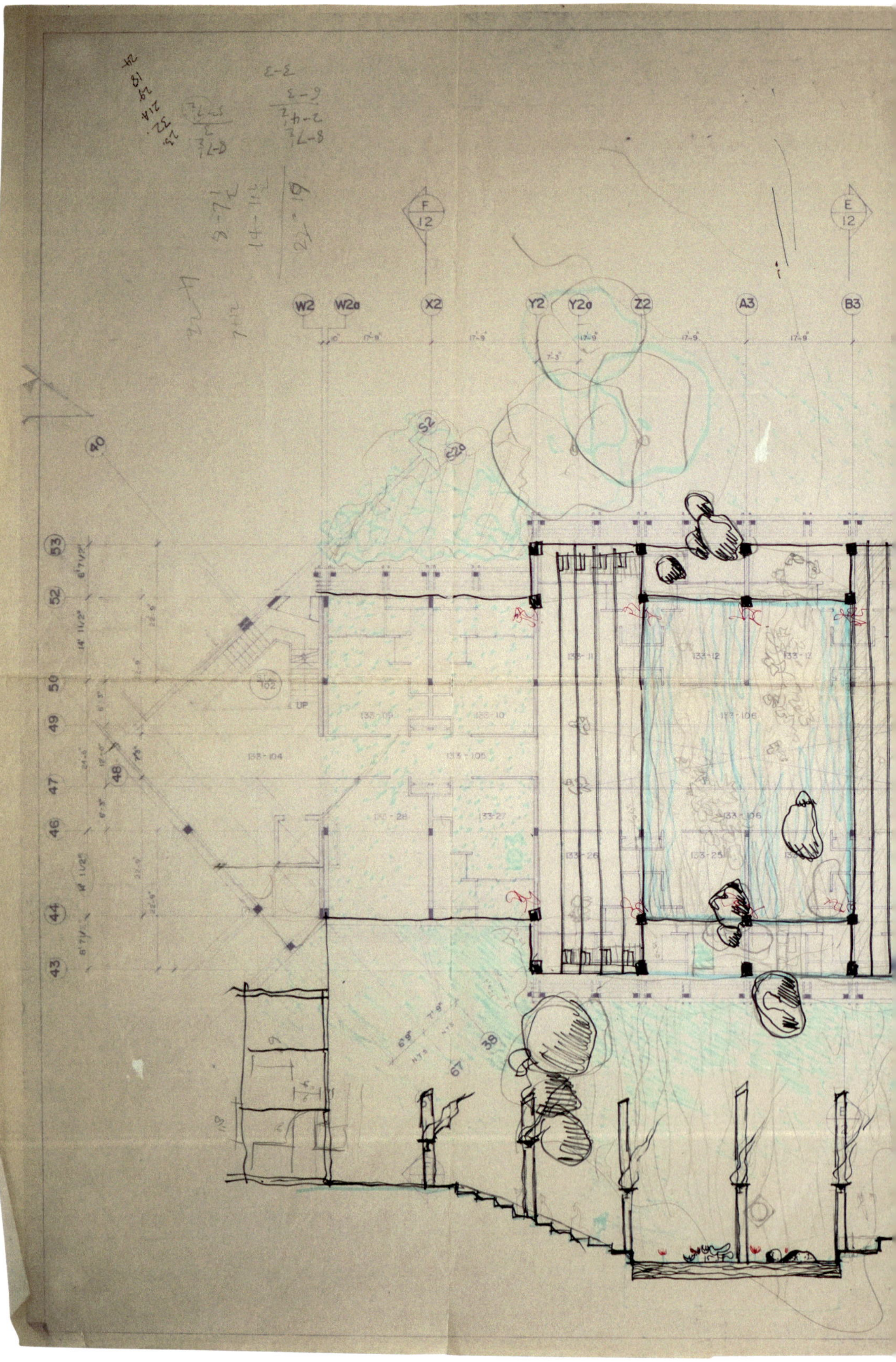

Part plan of first-floor level showing design for pool and pavilion over partially built, abandoned building foundations, graphite and colored pencil over diazotype, 1992
GB/DA/198/116

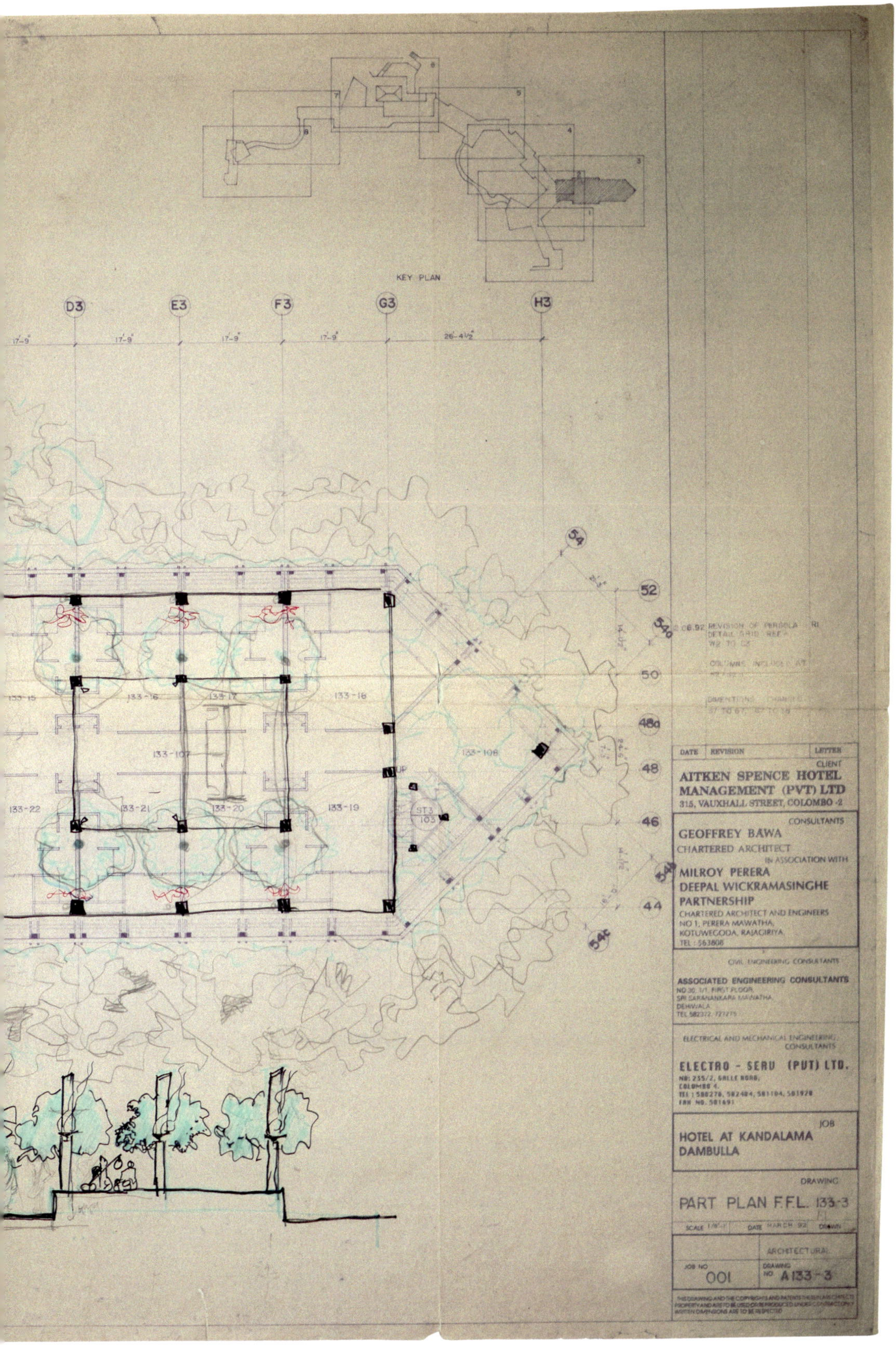
KEY PLAN
D3
E3
F3
G3
H3
52
50
48a
48
46
44
DATE
REVISION
LETTER
CLIENT
AITKEN SPENCE HOTEL MANAGEMENT (PVT) LTD
315, VAUXHALL STREET, COLOMBO -2
CONSULTANTS
GEOFFREY BAWA
CHARTERED ARCHITECT
IN ASSOCIATION WITH
MILROY PERERA
DEEPAL WICKRAMASINGHE
PARTNERSHIP
CHARTERED ARCHITECT AND ENGINEERS
NO 1, PERERA MAWATHA,
KOTUWEGODA, RAJAGIRIYA.
TEL : 563808
CIVIL ENGINEERING CONSULTANTS
ASSOCIATED ENGINEERING CONSULTANTS
ELECTRICAL AND MECHANICAL ENGINEERING CONSULTANTS
ELECTRO - SERU (PUT) LTD.
JOB
HOTEL AT KANDALAMA
DAMBULLA
DRAWING
PART PLAN F.F.L. 133-3
SCALE
DATE MARCH 92
DRAWN
ARCHITECTURAL
JOB NO
001
DRAWING NO A133-3

Gelatin silver print, Channa Daswatte
GB/DOC/100/008

Entrance, black-and-white film negative, Channa Daswatte GB/DOC/009/E

View through corridor to reception, black-and-white film negative, Channa Daswatte GB/DOC/100/009/D

Geoffrey Bawa at his private residence, Number 11, 33rd Lane, Colombo, black-and-white film negative, Dominic Sansoni

Biography

1919	Born in Colombo, July 23
1939	Matriculated at St. Catharine's College, Cambridge, to read English Literature
1942	Awarded Bachelor of Arts, Cambridge
1944	Called to the Bar, Middle Temple, London
1946	Worked in law office of Noel Gratiaen, Colombo Embarked on two years of travel
1948	Purchased abandoned rubber and cinnamon estate near Bentota; begins creating Lunuganga
1951	Apprenticed with Edwards, Reid and Begg in Fort, Colombo
1954	Enrolled at Architectural Association in London
1957	Qualified as an architect Became a partner at Edwards, Reid and Begg
1958	Classroom and assembly halls at St. Thomas' Preparatory School, Colombo, commissioned
1960	Ena de Silva House in Colombo, commissioned
1960	Became an associate of the Ceylon Institute of Architects
1963	St. Bridget's Montessori, commissioned Polontalawa Estate Bungalow, commissioned Yahapath Endera Farm School, commissioned
1968	Bentota Beach Hotel, commissioned
1969	Elected president of the Ceylon Institute of Architects
1970	Design of Ceylon Pavilion at Expo '70, Osaka
1979	Sri Lanka Parliament Building in Kotte, commissioned
1981	Ruhuna University campus, commissioned
1983	Elected Honorary Fellow of the American Institute of Architects
1986	Publication of the monograph *Geoffrey Bawa* by Mimar (with Concept Media) in Singapore
1989	Closes No. 2, Alfred House Road, office
1990	Publication of *Lunuganga* by Christoph Bon and Dominic Sansoni
1991	Kandalama Hotel near Dambulla, commissioned
1993	Honored as "Deshamanya" (Pride of the Nation) by the President of Sri Lanka
1998	Forced by illness to retire from practice
2001	Received the Aga Khan's Special Award for lifetime achievement
2002	Publication of *Geoffrey Bawa: The Complete Works* by David Robson, Thames and Hudson, London
2003	Died in Colombo, May 27

Authors

Sean Anderson is an associate professor in architecture and director of the B.Arch. Program at Cornell. Previously, he was was the associate curator in the Department of Architecture and Design at The Museum of Modern Art (MoMA). A Fellow of the American Academy in Rome with a Ph.D. in African art history, he has practiced as an architect and taught in Afghanistan, Australia, India, Italy, Morocco, Sri Lanka and the United Arab Emirates. He has authored books on South Asian ritual sculpture and modern architecture of colonial Eritrea, and coedited a volume dedicated to contemporary architecture and design in Sri Lanka. In 2020 he cocurated the exhibition *On Muzharul Islam: Surfacing Intention* at the Dhaka Art Summit in Dhaka, Bangladesh. At MoMA, he organized the exhibitions *Insecurities: Tracing Displacement and Shelter* (2016–17); *Thinking Machines: Art and Design in the Computer Age, 1959–89* (2017–18); and four iterations of the Young Architects Program at MoMA PS1. He has also been responsible for or collaborated on permanent collection galleries including the ongoing Building Citizens and 2019's Surrounds. He co-organized with Mabel O. Wilson *Reconstructions: Architecture and Blackness in America*, the first exhibition ever at MoMA to highlight the work of African American and African Diasporic architects (February 27–May 31, 2021).

Channa Daswatte joined Geoffrey Bawa's architecture practice in 1991 and was the last partner of the firm. In 1998 he established MICD Associates, where he is a principal, in partnership with Murad Ismail. Channa was the Chairperson of the Galle Heritage Foundation and has worked on a number of architectural, conservation and curatorial projects, including the *Corridors of Power* installation which was exhibited at the Dhaka Art Summit in 2018. Channa authored and edited *Sri Lanka Style* (2005), has written for and edited a number of publications including *A+U* and *Sri Lanka Institute of Architects' Journal*. Channa is the chairperson of the Geoffrey Bawa and Lunuganga Trusts.

Jyoti Dhar is an art writer and editor with a focus on contemporary art in South Asia. She is a contributing editor for *Art Asia Pacific* and regularly writes for *Artforum* and *The Sunday Times* in Sri Lanka. Her writing has appeared in monographs and magazines including *Aperture, Asian Art News, Even, Flash Art, Harper's Bazaar Art Arabia, Isskustvo Arts Journal, Modern Painters, Motherland, post at MoMA, Scroll Projects, Vogue India* and *WeAreOrlando.* Her editorial work includes being founding editor of ChinarTree.com (Dubai), reporter and editor of *City as Studio 02/03* (New Delhi) and assistant editor of *The Ceylon Chronicle* (Colombo). She has curated several workshops, exhibitions and residencies. In 2012 she was selected as a forum fellow at the Global Art Forum; in 2014 she won the Forbes India Emerging Art Writer of the Year award; and in 2017 she was awarded first prize at the International Award for Art Criticism. Dhar has essays in upcoming books on Lala Rukh, Muhanned Cader, Nasreen Mohamedi and Seher Shah. She currently heads editorial and content strategy at the Sharjah Art Foundation.

Tariq Jazeel is professor of human geography at University College London (UCL) and co-director of UCL's Sarah Parker Remond Centre for the Study of Racism and Racialization. He is author of *Sacred Modernity* (2013) and *Postcolonialism* (2019) and co-editor of *Spatialising Politics* (2009, with Cathrine Brun) and *Subaltern Geographies* (2019, with Stephen Legg). His research is positioned at the intersection of critical geography, postcolonial theory and South Asian studies, and his written work explores the politics of various forms of cultural production, including modern architecture, literature and contemporary art. He is also founding co-director of UCL's Centre for the Study of South Asia and the Indian Ocean World.

Meghal Perera is an interdisciplinary researcher with interests in the politics of public space, infrastructure and urban ecology. In 2020 she worked as an assistant curator for the Geoffrey Bawa Trust, conducting archival research on the transformation of the built environment in postcolonial Sri Lanka and supporting curatorial research for exhibitions. She currently works as a researcher for Colombo Urban Lab, an interdisciplinary think tank focusing on sustainable and equitable cities.

Suhanya Raffel joined M+ as executive director in 2016 and was appointed museum director in 2019. She has more than thirty years of experience as a museum curator and leader. Suhanya was formerly deputy director of the Art Gallery of New South Wales in Sydney from 2013 to 2016. She also held several positions, including deputy director of curatorial, at the Queensland Art Gallery / Gallery of Modern Art in Brisbane from 2002 to 2016. She is a trustee of the Geoffrey Bawa Trust and the Lunuganga Trust, and a board member of the International Committee for Museums and Collections of Modern Art (CIMAM). She was elected president of CIMAM in 2022 for the 2023–25 term and awarded the Chevalier in the Ordres des Arts et des Lettres by the French Government in 2020.

Shayari de Silva is trained as an architect and focuses on curatorial and editorial projects. She joined the Geoffrey Bawa Trust in 2018 as curator of Art and Archival Collections, and was appointed chief curator in 2022. Recent exhibitions include *The Gift;* five site-specific installations at Bawa's garden Lunuganga by Kengo Kuma, Lee Mingwei, Dominic Sansoni, Dayanita Singh and Chandragupta Thenuwara, part of the Bawa 100 Centennial Celebration, and *It Is Essential to Be There,* the first exhibition to draw from the Geoffrey Bawa Archives. Shayari co-edited *Perspecta 51: Medium,* the Yale architecture journal published by the MIT press in 2018. She has worked previously at the Yale Art Gallery and Yale Center for British Art, where she was a Bartels Scholar in Building Conservation.

Michael Snelling is an artist, writer, former CEO and artistic director, curator, project manager, teacher and consultant. He has been CEO and artistic director of organizations in the visual and performing arts as well as chair and board member of numerous government and not-for-profit entities. Most recently he was director and CEO of the National Art School, Sydney, Australia. He is currently a board member of Kaldor Public Art Projects and sits on the Hong Kong Arts Center School Advisory Committee. He lives in Hong Kong.

Shirley Surya is curator, Design and Architecture, at M+, museum for visual culture in Hong Kong. Since 2012, she has contributed to shaping the M+ Collections through her research of design and architectural production that engage with plural modernities and transnational knowledge networks in greater China and Southeast Asia. At M+, she co-curated *Building M+: The Museum & Architecture Collection* (2014), *NEONSIGNS.HK* (2014), *In Search of Southeast Asia through the M+ Collections* (2018), and opening exhibitions *Things, Spaces, Interactions* (2021) and *Hong Kong: Here and Beyond* (2021). Outside M+, she made curatorial contributions to *Incomplete Urbanism: Attempts of Critical Spatial Practice* (2016) and *Yung Ho Chang & FCJZ: Material-ism* (2012). Her writings have been published in *EXPANSIONS: How will we live together?* (2020), *The Museum Is Not Enough* (2019), *Encyclopedia of East Asian Design* (2019), *The Impossibility of Mapping (Urban Asia)* (2018), as well as *ARCH+*, *e-flux Architecture*, *Journal of the Society of Architectural Historians*, *Design and Culture*, and *Singapore Architect.* Shirley was a jury member of the Wheelwright Prize 2022 and Design Anthology Awards 2021.

Image Credits

Portrait of Geoffrey Bawa at Lunuganga, page 6: © Christoph Bon
Portraits of Geoffrey Bawa, pages 224 and 242: © Dominic Sansoni
Adventure in Space, page 175: © Lionel Wendt Memorial Fund Collection, Colombo
Ena de Silva House, pages 72 and 73: © Hélène Binet
Batujimbar Estate, pages 132, 133, 136, 137, 139, 142 and 146 are courtesy M+ Hong Kong, gift of the Geoffrey Bawa Trust 2022

Acknowledgments

Thanking the people involved in the making of a book is no small task; a book on archives makes it even harder and one on architectural archives becomes impossible. So, my attempt here, knowing that this is an incomplete and insufficient list, is in hope that all those named and unnamed who have helped make this possible know how grateful we are to them. To the authors of these essays – Channa, Jyoti, Meghal, Michael, Sean, Shirley, Suhanya and Tariq – who agreed to contribute when the book itself was a nebulous idea, I am immensely indebted – none of us would have imagined that a pandemic, an economic collapse and so much of life's best and worst would befall us in between the earliest conversations we had and this published book. Thank you so much for your generosity, insights and patience through it all.

Thilini Perera, designer extraordinaire, is an endlessly talented, patient and optimistic collaborator without whom this project would have been impossible. To Lars Müller, with whom it has been a dream to work, we are immensely grateful – we will so miss our weekly Tuesday morning meetings. Thank you for believing in this project, for taking the time to understand it and to both you and Thilini for making such a deeply considered and elegant book. Thanks also to Lars's stellar team, Esther Butterworth, Fanny Rakeseder, Maya Rüegg, Marius Wenger and Samuel Meier for all your assistance and to Keonaona Peterson for her careful copyediting and proofreading.

Channa, Michael and Suhanya: thank you for your unwavering support, notes and guidance, on this and all things GBT. The Trust's curatorial team, past and present, is a wellspring of inspiration and conviviality that makes even the wildest ideas seem possible and of whom I am always deeply appreciative. Aneesha Mustachi provided valuable research assistance and meticulous archiving support, Shanika Perera lent us her keen proofreading eyes, Christopher Silva assisted with photography, Larissa Guimaraes helped edit particularly challenging portions of text and Lara Wijesuriya, Arundhika Weerasekera and Indeera Lokuliyana, undertook various early parts of the process as interns.

Edine Weerawardane and Thirangie Jayatilake graciously offered additional eyes on the texts and my late father Anura de Silva was a scrutinous listener as I read aloud the texts several times over to him during the editing process. Manodha and my mother Dayaminie offer enduring support.

The Graham Foundation for Advanced Studies in the Fine Arts helped kickstart the funding for project, and James Pike patiently answered numerous questions from us on its behalf. Our Board of Trustees at the Geoffrey Bawa and Lunuganga Trusts: Channa Daswatte (chairperson), Chamika de Alwis, Nadija Tambiah, Sanjay Kulatunga, Suhanya Raffel, Sunethra Bandaranaike (emeritus chair) and Ward Beling as well as Jay Mehta, Phantom Hands, Edward Rothfarb (in memory of James S. Ackerman) and Susan Horowitz generously supported us in publishing this book – to each of you we are offer our sincerest thanks.

The research and publications of Shanti Jayawardena, Brian Brace Taylor and David Robson allowed a new generation to access and engage with the Geoffrey Bawa Archives. I am particularly indebted to Shanti's visionary book, *Geoffrey Manning Bawa: Decolonizing Architecture.* Hassan-Uddin Khan kindly permitted us to reprint Geoffrey Bawa's essay from the Mimar publication with Concept Media. The Lionel Wendt Memorial Fund, Dominic Sansoni and Hélène Binet generously shared photographs for use in this book; to them we are deeply grateful. The Bawa Archives exist due to the efforts of Christoph Bon and Jean Chamberlin, Amila de Mel, C. Anjalendran, Jeff Bourke, David Robson, the trustees past and present, fifteen (and counting) oral historians and several generations of interns – there would be no archive if not for them and of course one other key group: Geoffrey Bawa and his colleagues, to whom this book is dedicated.

Geoffrey Bawa
Drawing from the Archives

Editor: Shayari de Silva
Texts: Sean Anderson, Geoffrey Bawa, Channa Daswatte, Jyoti Dhar, Tariq Jazeel, Meghal Perera, Suhanya Raffel, Shayari de Silva, Michael Snelling, Shirley Surya
Research assistants: Aneesha Mustachi, Shanika Perera, Lara Wijesuriya
Copyediting and proofreading: Keonaona Peterson
Project coordination: Fanny Rakeseder, Maya Rüegg
Design: Thilini Perera with Lars Müller
Production, typographic editing: Esther Butterworth
Digitization: Thilini Perera, Aneesha Mustachi, Christopher Silva
Lithography: Gundula Seraphin, Bad Münstereifel, Germany
Printing and binding: DZA Druckerei zu Altenburg, Germany
Paper: Arctic Volume White 1.1, 130 g/qm

Lars Müller Publishers
Zurich, Switzerland
www.lars-mueller-publishers.com

ISBN 978-3-03778-705-2

Distributed in North America by ARTBOOK | D.A.P.
www.artbook.com

Printed in Germany

The Geoffrey Bawa Trust is grateful to the Graham Foundation for Advanced Studies in the Fine Arts, Jay Mehta, Phantom Hands, Edward Rothfarb and Susan Horowitz for their generous support in realizing this publication.

Graham Foundation

Phantom Hands